*Animal Spirits*

# Animal Spirits

## HOW HUMAN PSYCHOLOGY DRIVES
## THE ECONOMY, AND WHY IT MATTERS
## FOR GLOBAL CAPITALISM

*With a new preface by the authors*

### GEORGE A. AKERLOF
*AND*
### ROBERT J. SHILLER

*Princeton University Press* · PRINCETON AND OXFORD

*George Akerlof* is the Daniel E. Koshland Sr. Distinguished Professor of Economics at the University of California at Berkeley; co-director of the Program on Social Interactions, Identity and Well-Being of the Canadian Institute for Advanced Research; and a member of the board of directors of the National Bureau of Economic Research. *Robert Shiller* is the Arthur M. Okun Professor of Economics at the Cowles Foundation for Research in Economics and Professor of Finance at the International Center for Finance, Yale University; research associate at the National Bureau of Economic Research; and co-founder and principal of two U.S. firms that are in the business of issuing securities: MacroMarkets LLC and Macro Financial LLC. The views expressed herein are solely those of the authors and do not necessarily reflect the views of these institutions.

Published by Princeton University Press, 41 William Street, Princeton, New Jersey 08540
In the United Kingdom: Princeton University Press, 6 Oxford Street, Woodstock, Oxfordshire OX20 1TW
press.princeton.edu

Ninth printing, and first paperback printing, with a new preface by the authors, 2010
Paperback ISBN: 978-0-691-14592-1

*The Library of Congress has cataloged the cloth edition of this book as follows*

Akerlof, George A., 1940–
    Animal spirits : how human psychology drives the economy, and why it matters for global capitalism / George A. Akerlof and Robert J. Shiller.
        p.   cm.
    ISBN 978-0-691-14233-3 (hardcover : alk. paper)
    1. Economics—Psychological aspects.   2. Finance—Psychological aspects.
3. Capitalism.   4. Globalization.   I. Shiller, Robert J.   II. Title.
HB74.P8A494   2009
330.12′2019—dc22                                                         2008052649

British Library Cataloging-in-Publication Data is available

This book has been composed in Adobe Galliard and Formata by Princeton Editorial Associates, Inc., Scottsdale, Arizona

Printed on acid-free paper. ∞

Printed in the United States of America

10 9

# Contents

# Preface to the Paperback Edition

The worldwide recession that was raging just as the hardcover edition of this book was published in February 2009 seems to many observers, as of this writing in October 2009, to be coming to an abrupt end. There are definite signs of improvement. These observers could be right. Maybe this is just another recession that will eventually be forgotten among the annals of business-cycle history. But the theory that we lay out in this book gives us cause to worry that we may be in a sick economy over much of the world for years to come. Even the stirring success stories of the past decade or so in the developing world, notably China and India, may see their economic growth reduced to a disappointing level.

We think this because we have an unusual view of the economy, a view that *animal spirits*, as we define them in the Introduction, drive almost everything. Animal spirits are more than just confidence as measured by confidence indicators. We argue that declining animal spirits are the principal reason for the recent severe economic crisis. And, despite the recent positive economic indicators, we see no clear indication that these spirits are yet revived.

The news media are singularly lacking in any explanation for the recent resurgence of the world economy beyond the improvement in leading indicators, such as stock market prices and retail sales numbers. The reasons the leading indicators have improved remain mysterious. The stimulus packages put in place by most countries do not seem to have been big enough to be held responsible. By many popular accounts, the nascent recovery merely reflects a new willingness to spend all over the world, as if that is a primordial force of the economy that defies any further analysis.

There seems, to a reader of these accounts, to be an unseen force propelling the economy, driving it into its periodic booms and busts. But this perception is nothing new. In his 1873 book *Lombard Street,* Walter Bagehot said that it seems that in an economic recovery business "leaps forward as if by magic":

> Most people who begin to think of the subject are puzzled. . . . Why should there be any great tides of industry, with large diffused profit by way of flow, and large diffused want of profit by way of ebb? The

main answer is hardly given distinctly in our common books of political economy. These books do not tell you what is the fund out of which large general profits are paid in good times, nor do they explain why that fund is not available for the same purpose in bad times.[1]

Indeed, people are still puzzled today, in late 2009, by the sudden improvement in our world economy. Textbooks of economics, while vastly improved since Bagehot's day, still do not give much enlightenment about the ultimate drivers of the economy. They do not do so because the understanding of the drivers must lie somewhat outside the traditional boundaries of economic research, in the realm of psychology (as even Bagehot suggested), which is an intellectual tradition alien to most economists. Macroeconomists have found it difficult to formalize the concept of animal spirits on their own terms, and so they have largely neglected it.

The recovery we have been seeing of late certainly defies the analysis of many economists who build structural econometric models and see the sudden recovery as the result of "error terms" or "residuals" or "innovations" in their equations. It defies the analysis of those economists of the "real business cycle" persuasion, who are in the habit of thinking that all economic fluctuations are ultimately driven by exogenous changes in "technology" and "productivity," but cannot point to a description of the cause of such a change right now. And of course, it defies those who build purely statistical time-series models that quantify past patterns in the data and calculate an optimal extrapolation of recent wiggles in the same data.

Not only are we puzzled by the sudden turn toward recovery, we also do not clearly see the longer-term threat to the economy. The longer-term problem today remains that, after a terrible financial crash, the coherence of our animal spirits and our economic institutions is shattered. Humpty Dumpty is broken and cannot be put back together again. We need a new egg. We have to reinvent our capitalist economy, reestablish a genuine creative business spirit in people's minds, and support their attitudes via institutions that really work and satisfy their definition of justice. Instead, today we have, in their eyes, institutions "too big to fail," which are on life support from the government and our central banks, operating as money-printing machines, and a general feeling that business is corrupt and that the government support these institutions receive has been arranged by evil lobbyists. We are facing the same problem today that we faced in the later years of the Great Depression (described in Chapter 6)—business today is inhibited by uncertainty about the future, about the tolerance of an angry public, about a disaffected labor force, and about what further government actions may be coming.

The basic theme of this book is that *animal spirits* are the force that drives all of this, and that to understand animal spirits we have to use methodologies outside of traditional economics, leading us to other social sciences.

We identified five psychological factors, in Chapters 1 through 5 of this book, that we thought were of particular importance. They are confidence, fairness, corruption and bad faith, money illusion, and stories. Changes related to all of these factors are the ultimate reason for the boom that preceded the world economic crisis, for the crisis and recession in which we have been immersed, and for the apparent beginnings of recovery. These phenomena cannot be understood in terms of traditional economic theory alone.

The last item, stories, bears closer scrutiny. We argue in Chapter 5 that human-interest stories that give vitality and emotional resonance to economic views drive animal spirits. Since economic expansions and contractions in the modern world tend often to be worldwide phenomena, these are not stories confined to any one country. The stories spread amidst a growing world culture, from country to country, since the same salience that works for a certain kind of story in one country will generally work in another country as well. The names and places change, but the stories are similar.

For example, the U.S. television show *The Apprentice,* which first aired in 2004, near the height of the boom, features a real-world business tycoon who leads a competition among promising young would-be tycoons. The tycoon is a tough man who shouts belligerently "You're fired" at the losers, but who, in his own harsh and distant but ethical way, serves as a mentor to help them all. The story shows the challenges of a go-go business world, but it also affirms the quality of the people who inhabit it and of young people's ambitions to make it big there, if they can just take the heat. The U.S. version features the American real estate magnate Donald Trump, a colorful figure who was already famous even before *The Apprentice* ever aired.

This story spread rapidly all over the world through local remakes during a time of economic expansion. The only thing that producers needed to do to facilitate this spread was to substitute some locally famous tycoon or personality for Trump, to maximize the potential for word of mouth and gossip in each local culture. In the United Kingdom, there came a version featuring British billionaire Alan Sugar and an analogous program called *The Rebel Billionaire* with Richard Branson. In Germany they substituted Reiner Calmund and called their version *Big Boss*. In the Brazilian version, he was replaced by Roberto Justus. In Colombia it was Jean-Claude Bessudo. The Turkish version aired with Tuncay Özilhan. In Russia it was Arkadi Novikov. In Finland it was Jari Sarasvuo. In Denmark, Klaus Riskaer Pedersen. In Norway, Inger Ellen Nicolaisen. In Switzerland, Jürg Marquard. In India, Cyrus Sahukar. In South Africa, Tokyo Sexwale. In Dubai, Mohamed Ali Allabar. And in Indonesia, Peter Gontha.

With such contagion around the world, during the boom, of such a motivational television story, is there any reason to doubt that contagion of stories has economic significance, or that there could be worldwide fluctuations in animal spirits? What kind of new story will gain currency as we now go through the denouement of the financial crisis?

During the boom it was stories of people who were business and financial geniuses that had us most inspired, promoting overconfidence. After the bust, in 2008, it was stories about venerable financial institutions on the verge of collapse, of shady characters drawing huge salaries and bonuses at the expense of all of us. After the first signs of recovery, in 2009, partly due to governments' bailout and stimulus efforts, there was a relative dearth of collapse stories. But, so far, we have not seen a return of the confident stories, and sense of trust and opportunity in business dealings, that we saw during the boom. Reestablishing these stories is essential if we are to recover well from the severe economic contraction, whatever those leading indicators may imply. If the economy is to grow from here, we must see the story evolving in positive directions for economic cooperation and innovation.

The stories people tell are also stories about how the economy behaves. Indeed, it is in this last category, stories, where *Animal Spirits* itself fits in, because the goal of the book is to give its own story about how the economy behaves.

Its intent is to tell a more accurate story than the dominant one of the past thirty years or so, ever since the free market revolution that swept the world, under the leadership of Margaret Thatcher, Ronald Reagan, Deng Xiaoping, Manmohan Singh, Mikhail Gorbachev, Brian

Mulroney, Bertie Ahern, Carlos Salinas de Gotari, Fernando Henrique Cardoso, Carlos Menem, and others. These stories, embellished by oft-told vignettes of newly successful people, and in their mostly justi-fied enthusiasm for expanded free markets, led to too much economic tolerance.

Underlying this revolution is the powerful principle of the "invisible hand"—that market forces should be the fundamental framework of resource allocation. Recognition of this principle has produced the surge of economic growth that has defined our age. And yet, today, with the recent economic crisis, unregulated free markets are being questioned.

We believe that the unvarnished invisible hand story, although right in a fundamental way, is wrong at the level of detail and approximation that is necessary to explain what we need to know about macroeconomies.

The old story about capitalism is correct: it gives us what we think we want. But capitalism does not act as its own policeman if we fail to watch over it and give it proper directions. It actively, competitively, seeks the most profit-maximizing opportunities. Capitalism will follow such opportunities wherever they lead us.

That, of course, is relevant for the recent world financial crisis. The re-cession, deep as it has been, has been a tragedy for people around the world. They have been losing their jobs, their houses, and their dreams. But recessions do have at least one silver lining: the cut they take into economic life reveals how capitalist societies really work. To give one ex-ample, Keynes' *General Theory*, written in the heart of the Great De-pression, gave us for the first time an understanding of how macro-economies really behave. That is why it was so inspiring, prompting Paul Samuelson to say, in 1946, that the Keynesian revolution, which appeared during the Great Depression, has infected the thinking of virtually every economist. But as the memory of the Great Depression has faded, so too has an appreciation and understanding of Keynesian theory.

For the past year we have been seeing a great deal of excellent re-portage on how we got into the current mess. Economists and Wall Street financiers invented new ways to carve up debt obligations, such as mortgages. They would not only "securitize" the mortgages and pass them on, but they would securitize them into different "tranches." De-pending on the level of risk that people wanted to assume, tranches could be divided into senior, mezzanine, or junior. These could then be sold off, and different people would own different parts of the payments from the different mortgages. Gillian Tett, author of the 2009 book

*Fool's Gold*, describes how initially this was an innocuous innovation designed as an end run around the Basel capital requirements. Since taking on such mortgage debts seemed all but totally safe, the capital requirement for holding them was very small. There was only one question: who was going to hold the super-senior tranche, the remaining fraction? This tranche, it was thought, would always pay at par, so it would not have to pay much added interest.

Indeed, this is the same question that faces businesspeople in all walks of life. Demolitionists, for example, who take down buildings to make way for newer ones, are an important element of our economy, and they illustrate well the shortcomings of unregulated capitalism. Money can be made in demolition if one just demolishes the building and sells off the scrap. But if one has to take care of the asbestos and other environmental issues, by legal means, well, then it becomes difficult. So there is a powerful incentive for demolitionists to do something antisocial and illegally dump the asbestos, and a tendency all over the world for demolitionists to be crooked. Honest ones generally cannot survive, unless there are regulators watching the industry very closely. Unfortunately, finance bears a resemblance to demolition in this respect. In the early stages of the current financial crisis, financial companies were able to insure the super-senior tranche. There were no problems. But then this kind of mortgage securitization became more widespread, demanding more and more placement of the securities in investor portfolios. They were still able to sell the standard tranches at prices that made it worthwhile, but not the super-senior tranche. And, gradually, the banks and the shadow banks (which also borrow short but hold long-term assets) came to think that their strategy was riskless; but in fact they were taking on more and more of this risk. The position of the bankers was very much like that of the demolitionists. They faced a tough choice. There was a lot of money to be made in packaging and selling off mortgage securities, except that it was difficult to get rid of the super-senior tranche at a price that would make it worthwhile. The choices were either to play the game, and take the risk, or not to enter the market. The dilemma was expressed most vividly by Charles Prince, then the CEO of CitiGroup, in the *Financial Times* in the summer of 2007: "When the music stops, in terms of liquidity, things will be complicated. But as long as the music is playing, you've got to get up and dance. We're still dancing."[2]

There is a simple lesson that comes in loud and clear, not just from the case of the demolitionists and asbestos, but from the collapse of the financial industry. In the case of getting rid of the asbestos, if no one is watching how the asbestos is disposed of, then it will be disposed of in the cheapest way. The same thing was true in the financial industry. Neither the investors nor the public was watching how the toxic part of the securitizations was being disposed of.

The public, and the regulators who were supposed to act on their behalf, had failed to understand a fact of life that is totally obvious to everyone who has played a serious team sport: there have to be rules and there has to be a referee who enforces them—and a good and conscientious referee at that. Otherwise there will be random cheating that destroys the sense of the game, and dangerous and aggressive play, so that many people will get hurt and the game will cease to reward good play.

Up until the 1980s this regulatory principle seemed to have been well understood by those who had gone through the Great Depression, with respect to financial markets. This generation appreciated the damage that could be done by letting financial markets loose and leaving them unguarded. But with time and the continued prosperity of the years after World War II, this great lesson was forgotten. And people came up with a new story about how the economy worked: that private markets, without regulation, give us the best of all possible worlds. They forgot about the soft underbelly of capitalism. Private enterprise needs to be watched quite closely, especially where it is hard to know if toxic waste is being disposed of safely. Indeed, there was so little regulation of financial markets that even today there are no good standard statistics that summarize the volumes of complicated securities traded and, more importantly, still outstanding. People had taken the "invisible hand" too seriously, and enshrined it with a mythology, like that embodied in *The Apprentice,* that made it central to our culture.

To continue the metaphor of the referee at the sports event, they took the good advice that they should not be stopping the game constantly for minor infractions. The game has to go on. But they also took that advice to mean that they should completely relax and look the other way. That was a mistake. It led to a changed story of the game, to a wild free-for-all. And more people are now concluding that maybe they don't want to play.

Indeed, our analogies and our picture of capitalism—the confidence, the role of corruption and bad faith, the role of stories in the working of the economy—seem to exactly fit the mania and the subsequent panic.

## What Should We Do about It?

In the book, we talk about the role of government. Our view is that capitalist societies have problems if they are not watched over. The cycles of overoptimism and overpessimism that translate into excesses of speculative boom and bust give the government a role. Its first role is to see that the rules of financial markets make the best trade-off between allowing markets to roam free, with all the benefits of the creative animal spirits of capitalism, and reining the markets in, when those animal spirits get too wild. Furthermore, if, as now, the economy has gone too far and is in cyclical overreaction, it is also the role of the government to repair the damage, as best as it can.

In *Animal Spirits* we explain that, with the collapse of the credit markets, we should aim for two targets. The first is an aggregate demand target. Conventional fiscal and monetary policy should aim for full-employment levels of demand. But, additionally, with the collapse of investor trust, credit markets, which fulfill an important economic role, also need prosthetic help from the government.

How well are these targets being met? Let us consider the example of the United States. The Obama administration and the Federal Reserve have taken measures aimed precisely at those two targets. The first of these has been the stimulus package. The second has been the Fed's expansion of credit in a variety of different ways, which can be summarized by a glance at the Fed balance sheet, then and now. If we look at the Fed balance sheet in August 2007, which is the exact onset of the crisis, it had assets of about $850 billion. Most of it was in treasury bonds. Now, two years later, the Fed has assets just shy of $2 trillion. It has about the same amount of treasury securities as it did before. But it also has $550 billion of mortgage-backed assets; about $360 billion of credits against collateral that it has given, sometimes in diverse and inventive ways (such as in auction); $60 billion in portfolio holdings of AIG and Bear Stearns (called Maiden Lane I, II, and III—never say that central bankers have no sense of humor!); and $150 billion of foreign-related securities, including $70 billion of liquidity swaps with other central banks. Two years ago, the amounts held in all of the items other than the treasury bills were either literally zero, or, relative to the total balance sheet, small change. This increase in the balance sheet by $1.15 trillion, most of it of unusual forms, represents the sort of aggressiveness that we had in mind when we said that the government itself would need to play a major role in replacing the credit markets, which were collapsing in the fall of 2008.[3]

*Animal Spirits* was written at a high level of generality. It does not simulate economic models; it does not examine the precise nature of financial markets. One might think that we would therefore have little to say about economic policy. But surprisingly—perhaps even to us, its authors—the book seems to have many very specific implications for economic policy, just as the unadulterated "invisible hand," free market story of the past generation seemed to have many consequences (not all of them benign) for economic policy. Probably the most important decision for any journey is where you want to go: *Animal Spirits*, with its story about how capitalism works, tells us that.

As we write this in October 2009, we are afraid that the optimism, even if still a bit guarded, reflects an Indian summer. We do not know what lies ahead. We go along with those who consider it a good sign, at the time of this writing, that there are "green shoots" of recovery, and that forecasters are talking about growth of GDP sometime in the near future. It would be far worse if people were gloomier.

But the *Animal Spirits* view of confidence, both overconfidence and underconfidence, makes us wary. It tells us that we do not know what lies ahead. And now should be the time when we are making plans for what happens if there are future shocks: if there are future Lehman Brothers, future massive declines in the stock market, yet more unanticipated bankruptcies. In the United States, for example, we fear that neither the Congress nor the Obama administration is now readying the public for the possible necessity of further stimulus packages, or for further dramatic action by the Federal Reserve to support credit markets if that should become necessary.

There are a few steps that we think should be taken now, in the United States and in other countries as well:

1. *The Cat in the Hat.* This book tells us the stance with which we should approach the current state of aggregate demand and credit markets. We should approach them as did the Cat in the Hat in the beloved 1958 Dr. Seuss children's book.[4] In this fanciful story, the Cat came by

to solve the mysterious problem of the ring in the bathtub, which had been spreading like an epidemic to the wall, to the clothes, even to the snow outside. He tried Plan A, and then Plan B, and then Plan C, and then even Plan D. If we, like the Cat, find that these are not working, we need to go to Plan E, and if that does not work we should go on down the alphabet, until we find something that does. There is one goal: we need to get the economy working again.

What does this mean practically? It means that governments seem to have used up their political capital in the measures that have already been taken. The public is now wary of future large-scale endeavors. These were all urgently needed. Perhaps they were even underdone. But we need to preserve our willingness to let the Cat do more tricks. *Animal Spirits* says that if new shocks occur, and especially if new shocks occur to confidence, then more new, bold measures should be taken. *Animal Spirits* then tells us—the public and the government— not only why we got into the current mess. It also tells us that although this may be a time for a sigh of relief—as it appears that things are not for sure going to be as bad as we thought a few months ago—it is not a time for relaxed vigilance.

2. *Microeconomic Reforms. Animal Spirits* also tells us that now should be a time of urgency for microeconomic reforms, in at least three different areas:

- *Financial Regulation.* We have now seen that the previous system of regulation did not ensure that financial institutions would not go bankrupt like a row of falling dominoes in the face of systemic risk. There were insufficient safeguards to make sure that those who promised to take up risk had the capital to pay up when confidence failed. It can only be surmised that the regulators were asleep at the switch, dozing off in the confident but wrong-minded notion that capitalist markets would police themselves because people would watch out for their own interest. Stricter regulation is needed; at the same time, however, any new financial rules have to be open to genuine financial innovation.
- *Bankruptcy Law.* This should be a major agenda pursued by governments around the world. Some enterprises seem to have remarkably little difficulty going into bankruptcy, and then emerging out of it after a reorganization of debts and (sometimes) labor

contracts. In the United States, Chapter 11 of the bankruptcy code allows them to continue to operate, and the difference between the bankrupt operations and the solvent ones seems to be almost negligible.

But this is not the case with financial institutions, and for good reason. Financial institutions tend to borrow short and lend long. When they go bankrupt everyone knows that it is a game of musical chairs. The last person to get out will be left without anything. So everyone rushes for the door. When financial institutions are bankrupt either they are taken over by another financial firm that wants the good will and the accounts, or they cease operation entirely. In some cases the Federal Deposit Insurance Corporation has standing to take over, and to take care of the debts as deemed appropriate, usually under the condition that it minimize the cost of the bailout. When the firm goes to bankruptcy court, the people with standing are the creditors. The public's interest is not considered. Indeed, this is the major problem of overconfidence–underconfidence cycles. In the downturn, the bankrupt firms close, and, in the case of financial institutions, this means that the credit that they had previously been supplying dries up. There needs to be a reconsideration of bankruptcy law, to take special account of the fact that the public, and perhaps also the employees of the bankrupt firm, have an interest. Indeed, it was the discontinuity involved in financial bankruptcy that led to the onset of the current crisis. It made a world of difference whether Lehman Brothers was bankrupt or not—and would have done so even if the firm had been only one dollar in the red.

- *Equity.* For a long time now the disparity of income between the rich and the poor in most countries of the world has been growing. The natural response to such an increase in income of the rich relative to the poor should have been increases in tax rates for the rich, and decreases for the poor. Instead, remarkably, especially during the George W. Bush administration, taxation for the rich declined massively in the United States, with only very small declines for the poor.

  There might be no problem with such a dispersion of incomes if we felt that the rewards reflected relative contributions to society. Surely those who invented the Internet and Kindle are deserving of our praise, and perhaps high monetary rewards as well. But, on the contrary, what we see is that hedge fund managers and investment bankers are taking home pay that dwarfs even that of the CEOs of large manufacturing corporations. In *Animal Spirits* we take seriously the importance of fairness and equity. The current anger at the disparity between rewards and contributions deserves attention.

In the current macroeconomic slump, we see the problem of getting the world economy securely back to work again as the first priority. On our book tour in the United States we witnessed the great anger of the public against Wall Street, and especially against bonuses to those whose firms had benefited from the TARP bailout. Although we sympathize with those who feel this anger, the direct economic consequences of the bailout, which are a tidy sum in the billions, are still small change compared to the losses— estimated to be in the trillions or tens of trillions—from the even deeper recession or depression that would have resulted had the bailout not been passed. We are afraid that this anger, targeted especially at those who are working to keep credit markets functioning, will derail significant future plans to stimulate macroeconomic demand and credit, if and when they become necessary. More than that, we believe that it is important for workers and citizens to feel that they live in a just society. For this reason, now is also a time to construct plans to do what can be done to increase the concordance between monetary rewards and social contribution.

*Animal Spirits* will not answer all of the tough questions now facing our economy. But it does give a picture of how a capitalist economy works, especially at the macro level. We consider specifically eight questions about the working of the economy, in successive chapters of Part Two of the book. This gives the background that is necessary to take on other questions about macroeconomic policy, finance, bankruptcy law, equity, and other subjects as well, and to begin to answer them.

Animal spirits—our sense of confidence, of fairness, of good faith, of realistic valuations—drive the economy. Regulatory policy should dampen—even if it cannot prevent altogether—the financial market excesses caused by errant animal spirits. In the current crisis regulatory policy went astray, so that governments now must revamp the rules that govern their financial markets. Also, they must limit, as best they can, the resultant bust. Continued full employment is the goal. The United States made that goal clear for itself in the Employment Act of 1946: "It is the responsibility of the Federal government . . . to use all practicable means . . . to promote maximum employment, production, and purchasing power." Governments everywhere must keep their eye on that ball.

# Preface

Life occasionally has its revelatory moments. In Henry James' *The Golden Bowl*, it was just a glance—and then the American heiress knew that her suspicions were accurate: her husband and her father's wife were intimate.[1] For the world's economy, September 29, 2008, was such a defining moment. The U.S. Congress had refused (although it later reversed itself) to pass the $700 billion bailout plan proposed by Treasury Secretary Henry Paulson. The Dow Jones stock market index dropped 778 points. Stock markets fell throughout the world. Suddenly what had seemed only a remote possibility—a repeat of the Great Depression—was now a real prospect.[2]

The Great Depression was the tragedy of the past century. In the 1930s it led to joblessness around the world. And then, as if the Depression itself had not caused enough suffering, the power vacuum it created led to World War II. More than 50,000,000 died prematurely.[3]

A repeat of the Great Depression is now a possibility because economists, the government, and the general public have in recent years grown complacent. They have forgotten the lessons of the 1930s. In those hard times we learned how the economy really works. We also learned the proper role of government in a robust capitalist economy. This book recovers those lessons, while also giving them a modern slant. To see how the world economy got into its current bind, it is necessary to understand those lessons. More important still, we must understand them in order to know now what is to be done.

In the middle of the Great Depression, John Maynard Keynes published *The General Theory of Employment, Interest and Money*. In this 1936 masterwork Keynes described how creditworthy governments, like those of the United States and Great Britain, could borrow and spend, and thus put the unemployed back to work. This prescription was never systematically implemented during the Depression itself. It was not until it was over that economists began to give clear guidance to politicians. So leaders muddled through. In the United States, for example, both Herbert Hoover and Franklin Roosevelt did engage in some deficit spending. For the most part they had the right intuitions, although they were frightfully confused, and their policies mostly led in the right direction. But, because they had no guidelines, they lacked the confidence to pursue those policies far enough.

When Keynesian borrowing and spending finally took place—to fight the war—unemployment vanished. By the 1940s Keynes' prescription had become so standard that it was adopted in countries all over the world and even enshrined into law. In America the Employment Act of 1946 made the maintenance of full employment a federal responsibility.

Keynesian principles regarding the role of fiscal and monetary policy in fighting recessions became fully incorporated into the thinking of economists and politicians, of academics, and of some of the general public. Even the late Milton Friedman has been quoted as saying "We are all Keynesians now"—although he later disavowed his statement.[4] And Keynesian macroeconomic policies have largely worked. Yes, there have been ups and downs. Yes, there have been some major upheavals, such as Japan in the 1990s, Indonesia after 1998, and Argentina after 2001. But a bird's-eye view of the world economy suggests that the entire postwar period has been, and continues to be, a success. Country after country has maintained something like full employment. And now that China and India have moderated their socialist leanings, they too, with their vast populations, have begun to experience economic prosperity and growth.

But beyond the usefulness of deficit finance to get out of recessions, another more fundamental message of *The General Theory* was cast aside. This was Keynes' deeper analysis regarding how the economy works and the role of government within it. In 1936, when *The General Theory* was published, on one end of the political-economic spectrum were those who thought that the old, pre-Keynesian, economics had gotten it right. According to this classical economics, private markets, of their own accord and with no government interference, would, "as if by an invisible hand," assure full employment. According to the classical logic in its simplest form, if a worker was willing to work for less than she was able to produce, an employer could make a profit by giving her a job. The folks with these views urged the balancing of budgets and insisted on minimal government regulation. On the other end of the spectrum in 1936 were the socialists. They thought that recovery from the joblessness of the 1930s could be accomplished only if the government took over business. It would then eliminate joblessness by doing the hiring itself.

But Keynes took a more moderate approach. In his view the economy is not just governed by rational actors, who "as if by an invisible hand" will engage in any transaction that is to their mutual economic benefit, as the classicists believed. Keynes appreciated that most economic activity results from rational economic motivations—but also that much economic activity is governed by *animal spirits*. People have noneconomic motives. And they are not always rational in pursuit of their economic interests. In Keynes' view these *animal spirits* are the main cause for why the economy fluctuates as it does. They are also the main cause of involuntary unemployment.

To understand the economy then is to comprehend how it is driven by the animal spirits. Just as Adam Smith's invisible hand is the keynote of classical economics, Keynes' animal spirits are the keynote to a different view of the economy—a view that explains the underlying instabilities of capitalism.[5]

Keynes' claim about how animal spirits drive the economy brings us to the role of government. His view of the government's role in the economy was very much like what we are told in the parenting advice books.[6] On the one hand, they warn us not to be too authoritarian. The children will be superficially obedient, but when they become teenagers they will rebel. On the other hand, these books tell us not to be too permissive. In this case they have not been taught to set proper limits for themselves. The advice books then tell us that appropriate child rearing involves a middle road between these two extremes. The proper role of the parent is to set the limits so that the child does not overindulge her animal spirits. But those limits should also allow the child the independence to learn and to be creative. The role of the parent is to create a *happy home*, which gives the child freedom but also protects him from his animal spirits.

This happy home corresponds exactly to Keynes' position (and also our own) regarding the proper role of government. Capitalist societies, as correctly seen by the old economics, can be tremendously creative. Government should interfere as little as possible with that creativity. On the other hand, *left to their own devices*, capitalist economies will pursue excess, as current times bear witness. There will be *manias*. The manias will be followed by *panics*.[7] There will be joblessness. People will consume too much and save too little. Minorities will be mistreated and will suffer. House prices, stock prices, and even the price of oil will boom and then bust. The proper role of the government, like the proper role of the advice-book parent, is to set the stage. The stage should give full rein to the creativity of capitalism. But it should also countervail the excesses that occur because of our animal spirits.

Speaking of excesses, the current economic crisis has been astutely explained by George W. Bush: "Wall Street got drunk." But an explanation of why Wall Street got drunk, why our government set the preconditions that allowed it to get drunk and then sat idly by while it overindulged, must come from a theory of the economy and of how it operates. It comes from the steady emasculation of Keynes' *General Theory*—which began soon after its first publication and then was intensified in the 1960s and 1970s.

Following the publication of *The General Theory*, Keynes' followers rooted out almost all of the animal spirits—the noneconomic motives and irrational behaviors—that lay at the heart of his explanation for the Great Depression. They left just enough animal spirits to yield a Least-Common-Denominator theory that minimized the intellectual distance between *The General Theory* and the standard *classical* economics of the day. In this standard economic theory there are no animal spirits. People act only for economic motives, and they act only rationally.

Keynes' followers adopted this "banality" (as it has been described by Hyman Minsky) for two good reasons.[8] The first was that the Depression was still raging, and they wished to make converts as rapidly as possible to his message about the role of fiscal policy. They would make the maximum number of converts by coming as close as possible to the existing theory. And such minimal deviation was useful for another reason. It enabled the economists of the time to understand the new theory in terms of the old.

But this short-term solution has had long-term consequences. The watered-down version of *The General Theory* gained almost universal acceptance in the 1950s and 1960s. Yet this reduced version of Keynesian economics was also vulnerable to attack. During the 1970s a new generation of economists arose. In their critique, called the New Classical Economics, they saw that the few animal spirits that remained in Keynesian thought were too insignificant to have any importance in the economy. They argued that the original Keynesian theory had not been watered down enough. In their view, now the centerpiece of modern macroeconomics, economists should not consider animal spirits at all. So, not without a little irony, the old pre-Keynesian classical economics, without involuntary unemployment, was rehabilitated. The animal spirits had been relegated to the dustbin of intellectual history.

This New Classical view of how the economy behaves was passed from the economists to the think tankers, policy elites, and public intellectuals, and finally to the mass media. It became a political mantra: "I am a believer in free markets." The belief that government should not interfere with people in pursuit of their own self-interest has influenced national policies across the globe. In England it took the form of Thatcherism. In America it took the form of Reaganism. And from these two Anglo-Saxon countries it has spread.

This permissive-parent view of the role of government replaced the Keynesian happy home. Now, three decades after the elections of Margaret Thatcher and Ronald Reagan, we see the troubles it can spawn. No limits were set to the excesses of Wall Street. It got wildly drunk. And now the world must face the consequences.

It has been a long time since we discovered how it was possible for a government to offset the rational and irrational shocks that occur to capitalist economies. But as Keynes' legacy and the role of government have been challenged, the system of safeguards developed from the experience of the Great Depression has been eroded. It is therefore necessary for us to renew our understanding of how capitalist economies—in which people have not only rational economic motives but also all kinds of animal spirits—really work.

This book, which draws on an emerging field called behavioral economics, describes how the economy really works. It accounts for how it works when people really are *human,* that is, possessed of all-too-human animal spirits. And it explains why ignorance of how the economy really works has led to the current state of the world economy, with the breakdown of credit markets and threat of collapse of the real economy in train.

With the advantage of over seventy years of research in the social sciences, we can develop the role of animal spirits in macroeconomics in a way that the early Keynesians could not. And because we acknowledge the importance of animal spirits, and accord them a central place in our theory rather than sweep them under the rug, this theory is not vulnerable to attack.

This theory is especially needed in the context of the current recession. Above all, policy makers must know what to do. But the theory is also needed by those who already have the right intuitions, such as Federal Reserve Chairman Ben Bernanke. Only with the clear understanding it provides will they have the confidence and also the intellectual legitimacy to pursue their instincts for the truly aggressive measures needed to deal with our current economic crisis.

# Acknowledgments

Our first debt of gratitude is to Peter Dougherty, director of Princeton University Press, who has provided us with wisdom and consistent guidance throughout the years we have worked on this book. We have also benefited from his personal perspective on the economics literature and its broad implications.

We are especially grateful to those economists who have participated in the Behavioral Macroeconomics workshops (later called the Macroeconomics and Individual Decision Making workshops) that the two of us have been organizing at the National Bureau of Economic Research since 1994. These took place with the support of the behavioral economics program of the Russell Sage Foundation until 2004, and since then they have been supported by the Federal Reserve Bank of Boston.

This book incorporates ideas first published in our separate journal articles with various co-authors. Those co-authors include John Campbell on asset price volatility; Karl Case and Allan Weiss on housing; William Dickens and George Perry on inflation-unemployment trade-offs; Rachel Kranton on minority poverty; Paul Romer on bankruptcy and looting; and Janet Yellen on fairness in wages and unemployment. We are also greatly indebted to three referee reports on a prior version of the manuscript in 2003. Those reports suggested that we undertake a project much more ambitious than we ourselves had originally planned. We are also indebted to the four referees of the nearly completed manuscript in 2008.

We are very grateful for the invaluable help we have received from our research assistants Santosh Anagol, Paul Chen, Stephanie Finnel, Diego Garaycochea, Joshua Hausman, Jessica Jeffers, Mark Schneider, Hasan Seyhan, Ronit Walny, and Andy Di Wu, as well as from Carol Copeland, a most loyal administrative assistant.

We are grateful for many comments offered by students in Robert Shiller's Economics 527 / Law 20083 / Management 565 course, part of the macroeconomics sequence at Yale University, in which, over the course of five consecutive years, succeeding drafts of this book were used as a textbook.

Robert's wife, Virginia Shiller, a clinical psychologist, has been influential in impressing upon her husband the significance for economics of various principles of human psychology and has helped temper his technical impulses to make sure there is always a connection to economic reality. We both have sons who are emerging scholars and who have offered comments on the book.

George Akerlof thanks the Canadian Institute for Advanced Research and the National Science Foundation (grant SES 04-17871) for generous financial support.

We also thank Edward Koren, whose drawings, wordlessly and succinctly, capture the spirit of this book.

*Animal Spirits*

# Introduction

TO UNDERSTAND HOW economies work and how we can manage them and prosper, we must pay attention to the thought patterns that animate people's ideas and feelings, their *animal spirits*. We will never really understand important economic events unless we confront the fact that their causes are largely mental in nature.

It is unfortunate that most economists and business writers apparently do not seem to appreciate this and thus often fall back on the most tortured and artificial interpretations of economic events. They assume that variations in individual feelings, impressions, and passions do not matter in the aggregate and that economic events are driven by inscrutable technical factors or erratic government action. In fact, as we shall discover in this book, the origins of these events are quite familiar and are found in our own everyday thinking. We started work on this book in the spring of 2003. In the intervening years the world economy has moved in directions that can be understood only in terms of animal spirits. It has taken a rollercoaster ride. First there was the ascent. And then, about a year ago, the fall began. But oddly, unlike a trip at a normal amusement park, it was not until the economy began to fall that the passengers realized that they had embarked on a wild ride. And, abetted by this obliviousness, the management of this amusement park paid no heed to setting limits on how high the passengers should go. Nor did it provide for safety equipment to limit the speed, or the extent, of the subsequent fall.

What had people been thinking? Why did they not notice until real events—the collapse of banks, the loss of jobs, mortgage foreclosures—were already upon us? There is a simple answer. The public, the government, and most economists had been reassured by an economic theory that said that we were safe. It was all OK. Nothing dangerous could happen. But that theory was deficient. It had ignored the importance of ideas in the conduct of the economy. It had ignored the role of *animal spirits*. And it had also ignored the fact that people could be unaware of having boarded a rollercoaster.

## What Have People Been Thinking?

Traditional economics teaches the benefits of free markets. This belief has taken hold not just in the bastions of capitalism, such as the United States and Great Britain, but throughout the world, even in countries with more established socialist traditions, such as China, India, and Russia. According to traditional economics, free market capitalism will be essentially perfect and stable. There is little, if any, need for government interference. On the contrary, the only risk of major depression today, or in the future, comes from government intervention.

This line of reasoning goes back to Adam Smith. The basis for the idea that the economy is essentially stable lies in a thought experiment which asks: What do free, perfect markets imply? The answer: If people rationally pursue their own economic interests in such markets, they will exhaust all mutually beneficial opportunities to produce goods and exchange with one another. Such exhaustion of opportunities for mutually beneficial trade results in full employment. Workers who are reasonable in their wage demands—those who will accept a wage that is less than what they add to production—will be employed. Why? If such a worker were unemployed, a mutually beneficial trade could be arranged. An employer could hire this worker at the wage she requires and still have some spare extra output for a larger profit. Of course some workers will be unemployed. But they will be unable to find work only because they are engaged in a temporary search for a job or because they insist on pay that is unreasonably high—greater than what they add to production. Such unemployment is voluntary.

There is a sense in which this theory about the economy's stability is remarkably successful. For example, it explains why most people who seek work are employed most of the time—even in the troughs of severe depressions. It may not explain, for example, why 25% of the U.S. labor force was unemployed in 1933 at the height of the Great Depression, but it does explain why, even then, 75% of the workers who sought jobs were employed. They were engaging in the mutually beneficial production and trade predicted by Adam Smith.

So, even at its worst, this theory deserves high marks—at least by the criterion of a schoolboy we once overheard at a restaurant. He was complaining about the C he had received on a spelling test—despite the fact that 70% of his answers were correct. Furthermore the theory does so well even in its worst prediction in two hundred years. Most of the time—as now, when the U.S. unemployment rate is still 6.7% (although rising)—it predicts remarkably accurately. Consider yet again the Great Depression. Few people ask why *employment* was as *high* as 75% in 1933. Instead the common question is why 25% of the labor force was *unemployed*. To our mind macroeconomics concerns departures from full employment. Failure to be at such full employment must then result from a *departure* from the classical model of Adam Smith.

We do believe, like most of our colleagues, that Adam Smith was basically right regarding why so many people are employed. We are also willing to believe, with some qualifications, that he was essentially correct about the economic advantages of capitalism. But we think that his theory fails to describe why there is so much variation in the economy. It does not explain why the economy takes rollercoaster rides. And the takeaway message from Adam Smith—that there is little, or no, need for government intervention—is also unwarranted.[1]

## *Animal Spirits*

The thought experiment of Adam Smith correctly takes into account the fact that people rationally pursue their economic interests. Of course they do. But this thought experiment fails to take into account the extent to which people are also guided by noneconomic motivations. And it fails to take into account the extent to which they are irrational or misguided. It ignores the *animal spirits*.

In contrast, John Maynard Keynes sought to explain departures from full employment, and he emphasized the importance of animal spirits. He stressed their fundamental role in businessmen's calculations. "Our basis of knowledge for estimating the yield ten years hence of a railway, a copper mine, a textile factory, the goodwill of a patent medicine, an Atlantic liner, a building in the City of London amounts to little and sometimes to nothing," he wrote. If people are so uncertain, how *are* decisions made? They "can only be taken as a result of animal spirits." They are the result of "a spontaneous urge to action." They are *not*, as rational economic theory would dictate, "the outcome of a weighted average of quantitative benefits multiplied by quantitative probabilities."[2]

In the original use of the term, in its ancient and medieval Latin form *spiritus animalis*, the word *animal* means "of the mind" or "animating." It refers to a basic mental energy and life force.[3] But in modern economics *animal spirits* has acquired a somewhat different meaning; it is now an economic term, referring to a restless and inconsistent element in the economy. It refers to our peculiar relationship with ambiguity or uncertainty. Sometimes we are paralyzed by it. Yet at other times it refreshes and energizes us, overcoming our fears and indecisions.

Just as families sometimes cohere and at other times argue, are sometimes happy and at other times depressed, are sometimes successful and at other times in disarray, so too do whole economies go through good and bad times. The social fabric changes. Our level of trust in one another varies. And our willingness to undertake effort and engage in self-sacrifice is by no means constant.

The idea that economic crises, like the current financial and housing crisis, are mainly caused by changing thought patterns goes against standard economic thinking. But the current crisis bears witness to the role of such changes in thinking. It was caused precisely by our changing confidence, temptations, envy, resentment, and illusions—and especially by changing stories about the nature of the economy. These intangibles were the reason why people paid small fortunes for houses in cornfields; why others financed those purchases; why the Dow Jones average peaked above 14,000 and a little more than a year later fell below 7,500; why the U.S. unemployment rate has risen by 2.5 percentage points in the past twenty-four months, with the end of this rise not yet in sight; why Bear Stearns, one of the world's leading investment banks, was only (and barely) saved by a Federal Reserve bailout, and why later in the year Lehman Brothers collapsed outright; why a large fraction of the world's banks are underfunded; and why, as we write, some of them are still tottering on the brink, even after a bailout, and may yet be the next to go. And we know not what is yet to come.

## Macroeconomics with and without Animal Spirits

Of course there is a rich body of macroeconomics that explains why there are fluctuations in the economy. Indeed that is what the macroeconomics textbooks are all about. We will give just two examples. In the post–World War II period, economists felt that they could explain deviations from full employment by a single type of animal spirit: that workers dislike money wage cuts, and that employers are therefore reluctant to make them.[4] This tradition then morphed into a slightly more sophisticated explanation for why wages are slow to change. It explains fluctuations in employment arising from shifts in demand as due to the fact that wages and prices are not all set simultaneously. This concept in macroeconomics is known as "staggered contracts."[5] The macro textbooks are full of many other departures from the simple thought experiment of Adam Smith, in which there is always a meeting of minds and contracts are negotiated between rational people motivated purely by economic interests.[6]

And that leads us to the philosophical difference between this book and standard economics texts. This book is derived from a different view of how economics should be described. The economics of the textbooks seeks to minimize as much as possible departures from pure economic motivation and from rationality. There is a good reason for doing so—and each of us has spent a good portion of his life writing in this tradition. The economics of Adam Smith is well understood. Explanations in terms of small deviations from Smith's ideal system are thus clear, because they are posed within a framework that is already very well understood. But that does *not* mean that these small deviations from Smith's system describe how the economy really works.

Our book marks a break with this tradition. In our view economic theory should be derived not from the minimal deviations from the system of Adam Smith but rather from the deviations that actually do occur and that can be observed. Insofar as animal spirits exist in the everyday economy, a description of how the economy really works must consider those animal spirits. That is the aim of this book.

In producing such a description, we think that we can explain how the economy works. This is a subject of permanent interest. But, writing as we are in the winter of 2008–9, this book also describes how we got into the current mess—and what we need to do to get out of it.

## How the Economy Really Works and the Role of Animal Spirits

Part One of this book will describe five different aspects of animal spirits and how they affect economic decisions—*confidence, fairness, corruption and antisocial behavior, money illusion,* and *stories:*

- The cornerstone of our theory is *confidence* and the feedback mechanisms between it and the economy that amplify disturbances.

5

- The setting of wages and prices depends largely on concerns about *fairness*.
- We acknowledge the temptation toward *corrupt and antisocial behavior* and their role in the economy.
- *Money illusion* is another cornerstone of our theory. The public is confused by inflation or deflation and does not reason through its effects.
- Finally, our sense of reality, of who we are and what we are doing, is intertwined with the story of our lives and of the lives of others. The aggregate of such *stories* is a national or international story, which itself plays an important role in the economy.

Part Two of this book describes how these five animal spirits affect economic decisions, demonstrating how they play a crucial role in answering eight questions:

1. Why do economies fall into depression?
2. Why do central bankers have power over the economy, insofar as they do?
3. Why are there people who can't find a job?
4. Why is there a tradeoff between inflation and unemployment in the long run?
5. Why is saving for the future so arbitrary?
6. Why are financial prices and corporate investments so volatile?
7. Why do real estate markets go through cycles?
8. Why does poverty persist for generations among disadvantaged minorities?

We see that animal spirits provide an easy answer to each of these questions. We also see that, correspondingly, none of these questions can be answered if people are viewed as having only economic motivations which they pursue rationally—that is, if the economy is seen as operating according to the invisible hand of Adam Smith.

Each of these eight questions is fundamental. They would occur to anyone with a natural curiosity regarding the economy. In providing natural, satisfactory answers to all of them, our theory of animal spirits describes how the economy works.

In answering these questions, in telling how the economy really works, we accomplish what existing economic theory has not. We provide a theory that explains fully and naturally how the U.S. economy, and indeed the world economy, has fallen into the current crisis. And—of perhaps even greater interest—such a theory then allows us to understand what needs to be done to extricate ourselves from the crisis. (We present our analysis and recommendations in the postscript to Chapter 7, the chapter dealing with the powers of the Federal Reserve.)

*Part One*

# Animal Spirits

# ONE

# Confidence and Its Multipliers

ONE OF US (Akerlof) remembers a dinner conversation a few years ago. During the housing boom a distant relative from Norway—by marriage by marriage by marriage, known only from a brief encounter at a family wedding—had reportedly bought a house in Trondheim, for more than $1 million. That seemed like a lot of money—perhaps not for New York, Tokyo, London, San Francisco, Berlin, or even for Oslo—but certainly for Trondheim, up the Norwegian coast, on the edge of settlement, and vying for the title of world's most northern city. Nor was it a mansion. This thought remained quietly parked in Akerlof's brain, classified along with other observations that property values were high in Scandinavia.

Recently Akerlof told his co-author, Shiller, that he had been wondering if he should have given more thought to the Trondheim story. We discussed the matter. This seems to have been a mental lapse, accepting this story of the high price as nothing more than an insignificant oddity. On the contrary, Akerlof should have seen it as an incongruity requiring active thought, to be resolved within the context of a larger view of the markets.

We decided that this little story is worth pondering at greater length—for the insight it offers into the thought patterns that underlie the booms and busts that characterize the business cycle, and, notably, the twin crises of confidence and credit that currently envelop much of the world.

## Confidence

The newspapers and the pundits tell us when the economy goes into recession that it is necessary to "restore confidence." This was J. P. Morgan's intention after the stock market crash of 1902 when he put together a bankers' pool to invest in the stock market. He employed the same strategy in 1907.[1] Franklin Roosevelt analyzed the Great Depression in similar terms. "The only thing we have to fear," he declared in his first inaugural address in 1933, "is fear itself." Later in the same speech he added: "We are stricken by no plague of locusts." Ever since the founding of the U.S. republic, business downturns have been proclaimed as the result of a loss of confidence.

Economists have a particular interpretation of the meaning of the term *confidence*. Many phenomena are characterized by two (or possibly more) equilibria. For example, if no one rebuilds his house in New Orleans after Hurricane Katrina, no one else will want to rebuild. Who would want to live in desolation, with no neighbors and no stores? But if many people rebuild in New Orleans, others will also want to. Thus there may be a good—rebuilding—equilibrium, in which case we say that there is confidence. And there may also be a bad—non-rebuilding —equilibrium, with no confidence. In this view there is nothing more to confidence than a prediction, in this case regarding whether or not others build. A confident prediction is one that projects the future to be rosy; an unconfident prediction projects the future as bleak.

But if we look up *confidence* in the dictionary, we see that it is more than a prediction. The dictionary says that it means "trust" or "full belief." The word comes from the Latin *fido*, meaning "I trust." The confidence crisis that we are in at the time of this writing is also called a *credit crisis*. The word *credit* derives from the Latin *credo*, meaning "I believe."

Given these additional shades of meaning, economists' point of view, based on dual equilibria or rosy versus bleak predictions, seems to miss something.[2] Economists have only partly captured what is meant by *trust* or *belief*. Their view suggests that confidence is rational: people use the information at hand to make rational predictions; they then make a rational decision based on those rational predictions. Certainly people often do make decisions, confidently, in this way. But there is more to the notion of *confidence*. The very meaning of trust is that we go beyond the rational. Indeed the truly trusting person often discards or discounts certain information. She may not even process the information that is available to her rationally; even if she has *processed* it rationally, she still may not *act* on it rationally. She acts according to what she *trusts* to be true.

If this is what we mean by *confidence*, then we see immediately why, if it varies over time, it should play a major role in the business cycle. Why? In good times, people trust. They make decisions spontaneously. They know instinctively that they will be successful. They suspend their suspicions. Asset values will be high and perhaps also increasing. As long as people remain trusting, their impulsiveness will not be evident. But then, when the confidence disappears, the tide goes out. The nakedness of their decisions stands revealed.

The very term *confidence*—implying behavior that goes beyond a rational approach to decision making—indicates why it plays a major role in macroeconomics.[3] When people are confident they go out and buy; when they are unconfident they withdraw, and they sell. Economic history is full of such cycles of confidence followed by withdrawal. Who has not taken a hike and come across a long-abandoned railway line—someone's past dream of a path to riches and wealth? Who has not heard of the Great Tulip Bubble of the seventeenth-century Netherlands—a country famous, we might add, for its stalwart Rembrandt burghers and often caricatured as the home of the world's most cautious people. Who does not know that even Isaac Newton—the father of modern physics and of the calculus—lost a fortune in the South Sea bubble of the eighteenth century?

All of which takes us back to Trondheim. Akerlof had stored the observation prompted by his relative's million-dollar home in the wrong place in his brain. He should have seen that home prices in Trondheim were not merely indicative of curiously high real estate prices in Scandinavia; they were part of a worldwide real estate bubble. He had been too trusting.

But that takes us even further back, to Keynes' passage about animal spirits. When people make significant investment decisions, they must depend on confidence. Standard economic theory suggests otherwise. It describes a formal process for making rational decisions: People consider all the options available to them. They consider the outcomes of all these options and how advantageous each outcome would be. They consider the probabilities of each of these options. And then they make a decision.

But can we really do that? Do we really have a way to define what those probabilities and outcomes are? Or, on the contrary, are not business decisions—and even many of our own personal decisions about which assets to buy and hold—made much more on the basis of whether or not we have confidence? Do they not involve decision-making processes that are closer to what we do when we flip a pancake or hit a golf ball? Many of the decisions we make—including some of the most important ones in our lives—are made because they "feel right." John F. "Jack" Welch, the long-time CEO of General Electric and one of the world's most successful executives, claims that such decisions are made "straight from the gut." (We shall revisit him later.) But at the level of the macroeconomy, in the aggregate, confidence comes and goes. Sometimes it is justified. Sometimes it is not. It is not just a rational prediction. It is the first and most crucial of our animal spirits.

## The Confidence Multiplier

The most basic element of Keynesian economic theory is its notion of the *multiplier.* The concept, originally proposed by Richard Kahn as a sort of feedback system, was adopted by Keynes and became the centerpiece of his economic theory.[4] Within a year of the publication of Keynes' *General Theory,* John R. Hicks published a quantitative interpretation of Keynes that emphasized a rigid multiplier and the interaction of its effects with interest rates. Hicks' version soon superseded Keynes' original as the authoritative embodiment of Keynesian theory.[5] Keynes was ruminating, discursive, disjoint, impenetrable, but nevertheless provocative and amusing; Hicks was orderly, efficient, and logically complete. Hicks' version won the day. He is not as famous as Keynes, for he is often viewed as a mere interpreter of Keynes' genius. But in terms of the history of thought, the "Keynesian revolution" was just as much a "Hicksian revolution."

But we believe that the Hicksian embodiment of Keynes' notions is too narrow. Instead of the simple multiplier that Hicks focused on, we should look at an allied concept, which we call the *confidence multiplier.*

The Keynesian multiplier, taught for generations to millions of undergraduates, works as follows. Any initial government stimulus, say a program of increased government expenditure, puts money into people's hands, which they then spend. The initial government stimulus is the first round. Each dollar spent by the government ultimately becomes income to some people, and, once it has been put into their hands, they spend some fraction of it. That fraction is called the marginal propensity to consume (MPC). Thus the initial increase of expenditures feeds back into a second round of expenditures, made by people, not the government. This then feeds back again into income for yet more people, in an amount equal to the MPC dollars. These people in turn spend a fraction of the MPC, called the MPC squared dollars. This is the third round. But the story is not over yet. Round after round of expenditure follows, and so the sum of the effects of the initial expenditure of a single dollar by the government may be represented as $\$1 + \$MPC + \$MPC^2 + \$MPC^3 + \$MPC^4$. . . . The sum of all these rounds is not infinite; it is in fact equal to $1/(1 - MPC)$, a quantity that is called the *Keynesian multiplier*. But the sum may be much larger than the original government stimulus. If the MPC is, say, 0.5, the Keynesian multiplier is 2. If the MPC is 0.8, the Keynesian multiplier is 5.

That idea was captivating for many people when Keynes articulated it in his 1936 book, and it was seized upon by Hicks in 1937. It was interpreted as explaining the mystery of the Great Depression. The Depression had been so puzzling because people could see no readily comprehensible cause for such an important event. The multiplier theory explained that a small dip in expenditure could have greatly magnified effects. If there were a small but substantial decline in consumption expenditures because people overreacted in fear to a stock market crash, such as the one of 1929, then this would act just like a *negative* government stimulus. For each dollar that people cut their consumption, there would be another round of expenditure cuts, then another and then another, resulting in a much larger decline in economic activity than would be attributable to the initial shock. A depression could come about over the course of several years, as the multiple rounds of negative expenditure hits put businesses further and further into the red. The theory won widespread acclaim—if not immediate policy implementation—for it sounded like just what was happening to businesses as the Depression increasingly deepened from 1929 to 1933.

Keynes' multiplier theory also won popularity among econometricians because it could be quantified and modeled. Authoritative statistics on national consumption and income became available at around the same time as Keynes' *General Theory* and Hicks' interpretation of it were first published, and they provided the data sets for their analysis. The first estimates of national consumption data were published by the Brookings Institution in 1934.[6] The U.S. National Income and Product Accounts were developed and put into a framework amenable to Keynesian-Hicksian theory by Milton Gilbert in the early 1940s.[7] To this day the U.S. government, like the governments of other major countries, still produces national income and consumption data in accordance with the demands of this theory. Surprising as it may seem, given the huge volume of economic literature, no other macro-economic model after that of Hicks has had such authority to dictate major changes in the way national data are collected. In a sense it is the data that dictate the theory that serves as the basis for formal modeling—for the data we have today were generated with but one theory in mind.

The creation of the data sets led to the development of large-scale computer simulation models for the economies of the countries of the world. This modeling started when Jan Tinbergen developed an econometric model of the Dutch economy in 1936 and a forty-eight-equation model of the U.S. economy in 1938. In 1950 Lawrence Klein developed another model of the U.S. economy, which grew over subsequent decades into the enormous Project Link, which linked together econometric models of every major country of the world, composed of thousands of equations. Such models have only a minimal role for animal spirits, and Keynes himself was skeptical of them.[8]

But it is possible to conceive of a role for confidence within these models. We usually think about multipliers only with respect to conventional variables that can be easily measured. But the concept applies equally well to variables that are not conventional and that cannot be measured so easily. Thus there is not only a consumption multiplier, an investment multiplier, and a government expenditure multiplier, which represent the change in income that occurs when there is, respectively, a $1 change in consumption, investment, or government expenditure. There is also a confidence multiplier. That represents the change in income that results from a one-unit change in confidence—however it might be conceived or measured.

We can also think of the confidence multiplier, like the consumption multiplier, as resulting from different rounds of expenditure. Here the feedbacks are more interesting than in our earlier simple example of rounds of consumption expenditure. Changes in confidence will result in changes in income and confidence in the next round, and each of these changes will in turn affect income and confidence in yet further rounds.

For a long time now there have been survey measures of "confidence." The best known of these is the Michigan Consumer Sentiment Index, but there are others. Some statisticians have developed models that test for feedback from confidence to gross domestic product (GDP) using these data. There is little doubt that such measured confidence is a predictor of future expenditure. Causality tests for several countries suggest that current measured "confidence" does feed future GDP, and this result would seem to confirm the feedback implicit in the confidence multiplier.[9] Other statisticians have performed similar analyses using credit quality spreads, measured as the difference between interest rates on risky debt and interest rates on less risky debt, interpreting these as measures of confidence and testing whether they feed into, and help predict, GDP.[10] But we believe that such tests are actually of limited value. Even when such results are obtained strongly, that does not necessarily imply that animal spirits are playing a role. Why not? Because the measure of confidence may not be measuring them. Instead they may only be reflecting consumers' expectations regarding current and future income.[11]

And of course we would expect them to be predictive of future expenditure and income. It is also difficult to measure the effects of confidence on income because we conceive of this channel as being of much greater importance at some times than others. We conceive of the link between changes in confidence and changes in income as being especially large and critical when economies are going into a downturn, but not so important at other times. It is in such terms that Olivier Blanchard has characterized the 1990–91 recession in the United States (sometimes called the Kuwaiti recession because of the role played by the increase in oil prices in the wake of the invasion of Kuwait by Saddam Hussein). Blanchard believes that the confidence index indicates that this is exactly what happened. He found a very large, otherwise unpredictable shock to the Michigan Consumer Sentiment Index prior to the recession. He interprets that as due to a wave of pessimism that followed the Kuwaiti invasion. This loss in confidence was then followed by a significant reduction in consumption.[12]

The presence of confidence has a further implication for multipliers. Other multipliers are also highly dependent on the level of confidence. An illustration from the current economy (as of November 2008) indicates why. Low confidence has caused credit markets to freeze up. Lenders do not trust that they will be paid back. Under the circumstances those who want to spend find it difficult to obtain the credit they need; those who supply the goods find it difficult to obtain the working capital they need. As a result the usual fiscal multipliers, from increased government expenditures or from decreased taxes, will be smaller—probably much smaller.

In the postscript to Chapter 7 we recommend that, in addressing the current crisis, the government have two targets. The first such target—and the only one that would be needed in a normal recession—would be a monetary policy and a fiscal policy that would be jointly sufficient to return the economy to full employment. But because of the severe credit crunch, which has been induced by the low state of confidence, such a stimulus is not enough. Indeed, in the face of the credit crunch, it might take very large increases in government expenditures or tax reductions to reach full employment. So we argue that government macroeconomic policy should have a second, intermediate target. Credit flows should also be targeted at the level that would normally prevail at full employment. In the postscript to Chapter 7 we shall describe how the Federal Reserve has developed clever schemes that could enable it to achieve such a target even in these dire times. Achieving this target would replace the credit flows that have disappeared because of the sudden decrease in confidence.

# TWO

# Fairness

ALBERT REES WAS a man of judgment and wisdom. He also had a perfect career. He was born in 1921, was an undergraduate at Oberlin, and then went on for a Ph.D. at the University of Chicago, where, as a mark of unusual favor, he was asked to stay. He rose through the ranks, as assistant professor, associate professor, full professor, and even department chairman. His field was labor economics. He wrote the influential book *The Economics of Trade Unions.*[1] In 1966 he left Chicago for Princeton, and shortly thereafter he began taking on increasing administrative responsibilities. He was eventually tapped by President Gerald Ford to be the director of the Council on Wage and Price Stability. He later returned to Princeton, where he became provost, and finally he served as president of the Alfred P. Sloan Foundation.

Shortly before his death, Rees wrote a paper for a conference in honor of his old friend Jacob Mincer, also a distinguished labor economist of the Chicago School. (Rees himself had been honored by a similar conference three years earlier.) He used this occasion to look back on his former life as an economist. He made a remarkable confession: that in his later life as an administrator he discovered a devastating omission from his earlier analyses. As an administrator he constantly had to decide what was and was not fair. Yet as an economist the concept of fairness had been totally absent from his analysis.

Here are his own words:

> The neoclassical theory of wage determination, which I taught for 30 years and have tried to explain in my textbook . . . has nothing to say about fairness. . . . Beginning in the mid-1970s, I began to find myself in a series of roles in which I have participated in setting or controlling wages and salaries. These included sitting on three wage stabilization bodies during the Nixon and Ford administrations, as a director of two corporations, as a provost of a private university, as a president of a foundation, and as a trustee of a liberal arts college. In one of the corporations I serve as chairman of the compensation committee.

In none of these roles did I find the theory that I taught so long to be the slightest help. The factors involved in setting wages and salaries in the real world seemed to be very different from those specified in the neoclassical theory. The one factor that seemed to be of overwhelming importance in all these situations was fairness.[2]

## The Importance of Fairness

The quote from Rees in one sense exaggerates the extent to which fairness has been ignored by economists. Economists, like everyone else, know how seriously people take fairness; as parents, they too have witnessed those awful fights among the back-seat passengers. Economists, like everyone else, are familiar with the biblical version of a food fight: how Joseph's father preferred him to his brothers and gave him a coat of "many colors" and how his jealous brothers responded.[3] They first cast him into a pit, intending to leave him there to die, but then, on second thought, more profitably sold him to slavers bound for Egypt.

Economists have written many articles—we reckon them in the thousands—regarding fairness. Indeed there is even a whole series on the subject of being *fair* by an author whose surname has that exact pronunciation—Ernst Fehr.

But there is a larger, more general sense in which Rees' epiphany gets it right, both for himself and for economics as a whole. However many articles there have been on fairness, and however important economists may consider fairness, it has been continually pushed into a back channel in economic thinking. Just look at the textbooks. Though some do mention fairness as a motive, they still demote it to end-of-chapter, back-of-the-book status. It is reserved for those sections that students know they can skip when studying for the exam, while the professors who assign the textbook can assure themselves that, yes, it really does cover everything—it *even* covers *fairness.*

But fairness may be just as important as the economic motivations that are given prime time. Are concerns about fairness of comparable, or even greater, importance, than strictly economic concerns? Do considerations of fairness or social expectation trump the consequences of strictly economic motivations? To pose such questions would challenge the place of fairness in those back-of-the-book chapters.

Of course there is a further reason why no textbook has posed these questions. Economics textbooks are supposed to be about *economics*, not about psychology, anthropology, sociology, philosophy, or whatever branch of knowledge teaches us about fairness. Those who assign the economics textbooks want to teach their special expertise. Pure economic theory is indisputably valuable in a wide range of applications, and so there is a natural tendency to focus on that magnificent theory—even if it doesn't fit some other very important applications. Focusing exclusively on the rational theory leads to an elegant presentation. It would violate the etiquette of textbooks to mention that some other factor, outside the formal discipline of economics, is the fundamental cause of certain major economic phenomena. It would be like burping loudly at a fancy dinner. It is just not done.

## *Questionnaires*

But studies of fairness do indicate the strong possibility that such concerns will override the effects of rational economic motivation. One of our favorite studies comes from a team consisting of a psychologist, Daniel Kahneman, and two economists, Jack Knetsch and Richard Thaler.[4] The study asked respondents about their reactions to a number of vignettes. Was the action taken *acceptable* or *unfair*?

The first question, dealing with the price of snow shovels after a snowstorm, illustrates the method and the answers. According to the vignette, there has been a snowstorm, and the local hardware store has increased the price of snow shovels. Is that acceptable or unfair? According to elementary economics such a distinction would be irrelevant: the rise in demand (because people now have to shovel out their driveways and sidewalks) should entail a rise in price. But 82% of the respondents thought that an increase in the price of snow shovels from $15 to $20 in the wake of a storm would be unfair. The hardware store, which had experienced no increase in its own cost to purchase the snow shovels, would be taking advantage of its customers' hard luck. Indeed Home Depot appears to have reacted to such sentiments after Hurricane Andrew in 1992. It avoided charges of price gouging by absorbing a large fraction of its increased costs for plywood.[5]

The responses to another Kahneman, Knetsch, and Thaler vignette illustrate further how considerations of fairness can trump economic motivations:

You are lying on a beach on a hot day. All you have to drink is ice water. For the past hour you have been thinking that you would like to drink a nice cold bottle of your favorite brand of beer. A companion gets up to make a phone call and offers to bring back a beer from the only nearby place where the beer is sold [a fancy resort hotel, a rundown supermarket]. He says that the beer might be expensive so he asks you how much you would be willing to pay for the beer. He says he will buy the beer if it costs as much or less than the price you state, but if it costs more than the price you state he will not buy it. You trust your friend and there is no chance to bargain with the [bartender, store owner]. What price do you state?[6]

On average respondents had a reservation price for the beer that was higher when it came from the swanky hotel than from the run-down grocery store. They were, on average, willing to pay 75% more.

The situation may be totally prosaic, but the responses have far-reaching consequences. They demonstrate that considerations of fairness can override rational economic motivation. If respondents are considering only how much the beer would add to their enjoyment of lying on the beach, they should pay the same amount for it, whether it comes from the hotel or from the grocery store. They will forgo that extra enjoyment if the grocery store charges "too much." It cannot be because they are unwilling to sacrifice the extra money for the beer; they are willing to pay it to the hotel bartender. It must be because they think it would be unfair for the grocery to charge a price that is more than their maximum.

## Experiments

Economic experiments offer another demonstration of the role of fairness. There are many, many different experiments, but our very favorites are those of Ernst Fehr and Simon Gächter.[7] They made an innovation to a game commonly played in experimental laboratories to test subjects' cooperation and trust of one another. In the plain vanilla version of this game subjects have the opportunity to put some money into a "pot," which will be augmented and then shared with the rest of the group. If everyone acts cooperatively the returns for the whole group are the greatest. But at the same time there is an incentive to act selfishly: I achieve the best outcome for myself if *everyone else* puts his money into the pot—to be augmented and shared—but *I* act selfishly.

There is a standard wisdom about the outcomes of such games: experimental subjects initially play such games with some degree of cooperation, but if the games are repeated they first learn that some other players are defectors and then they themselves increasingly defect. After many repetitions of the game all players are playing selfishly. The behavior pattern is very basic: it has been documented in monkeys as well as in humans.[8]

But Fehr and Gächter had an idea. They made a slight modification to the game to determine what would happen if players could punish those who played noncooperatively. They conjectured that subjects would punish even if they had to pay to do so. That is exactly what they found: subjects were willing to pay to punish those who acted selfishly, even though there was an individual cost to inflicting such punishments. Interestingly they also found that the possibility of punishment greatly reduced selfish behavior. Even after numerous repeated games, many players were still putting money into the pot.

Of course payments for the opportunity to punish indicate that subjects care about fairness. They are angry when other subjects are selfish. With another set of co-authors Fehr asked subjects to play similar games while their brains were being PET-scanned.[9] Engaging in such punishment appears to make the subjects happy: it activates an area of the brain, the dorsal striatum, that "lights up" in anticipation of many different types of rewards.[10]

## Theories of Fairness

The most basic economics is a theory of exchange: it describes who trades what to whom in which markets. But there is also a sociological theory of exchange. This theory differs from the economic theory primarily in the central role it accords to fairness. It depends upon notions of what is fair and what is unfair.

Sociology needs a different theory since sociologists have a more general notion of exchange than economists. Not only do they want to explain who trades what in which markets, they also want to explain nonmarket exchanges, within the firm, between friends and acquaintances, and within the family. The sociologists say that, when transactions are not fair, the person on the short end of the transaction will be angry. The impulses released by that anger force exchanges to be fair.

The social psychological theory of exchange is called *equity theory*. It holds that on either side of an exchange the inputs should equal the outputs.[11] This of course sounds like what happens in any market situation. For example, at the supermarket the store gives you the groceries; you give them the value of those goods. Sociologists thus say that their theory is motivated by economists (and it is perhaps a bit tainted in their eyes for that reason).

But there is a world of difference between the two theories, because what an economist would put into the valuation of the input on either side of the exchange—which is only the monetary value of the exchange —is very different from what sociologists put into the valuation of the inputs and the outputs. Those inputs include subjective evaluations, such as whether the person on either side of the transaction is of high status or low status.

An early version of exchange theory comes from Peter Blau's study of government agents involved in complex litigation.[12] The official rules said that they could seek assistance only from their supervisors. Of course the agents did not want to go constantly to their supervisors for help. Not only would they be a nuisance, but they would also be admitting their own lack of knowledge and independence. So they systematically violated the rules; they consulted among themselves.

Blau observed the pattern of these consultations and explained it in terms of equity theory. He noticed that the agents had different levels of expertise. It rarely happened, as one might suppose, that low-expertise agents sought advice from those with high expertise. Instead the low-expertise agents gave and received advice from their peers, who also had low expertise. And similarly, high-expertise agents gave and received advice from others with high expertise. Why did this occur?

Because the low-expertise agents had only limited currency to trade. They could offer their gratitude and thanks; and on the rare occasions when they sought advice from high-expertise agents, that is what they did. Such gratitude may be initially rewarding, but it eventually wears thin. It also becomes wearing to give. So low-expertise agents might have initially sought the advice of more knowledgeable agents, but they rarely returned. In contrast, with their peers, the exchange took place with trades of comparable value.

When subjective elements enter this evaluation, such as the values of ingratiation and thanks, this becomes a theory of fair exchange. The gratitude expressed by the low-expertise agents for their trades with the high-expertise agents, when they occur, makes the transactions fair. The inputs on the one side of the exchange are equal in value to the outputs on the other side. The theory explains why those of low status (for example, blacks and women in traditional societies) are subservient. To equalize the subjective and objective inputs and outputs in the exchange, they have to give more than those of higher status.

## Norms and Fairness

While equity theory may explain what is fair in some types of exchange, there is a broader, more general, theory of fairness. Sociologists would say that there are *norms,* which describe how people think that they and others should or should not behave. One of us (Akerlof) has written extensively on this subject with Rachel Kranton.[13] We have shown that a great deal of what makes people happy is living up to what they think they should be doing. In this sense most of the time people want to be fair. They consider it an insult if others do not think they are fair. At the same time, people also want others to live up to what they think those others should be doing. People get upset (think of Fehr's experimental subjects and their desire to punish) when they think others are not being fair.

Fairness then involves bringing into economics these concepts of how people think they and others should or should not behave.

## Fairness and the Economy

Considerations of fairness are a major motivator in many economic decisions and are related to our sense of confidence and our ability to work effectively together. Current economics has an ambiguous view of fairness. While on the one hand there is a considerable literature on what is fair or unfair, there is also a tradition that such considerations should take second place in the explanation of economic events.

We insist that if such motivations are to be given lower status in economic argument, then justification must be given. On the contrary, we think phenomena as basic as the existence of involuntary unemployment and the relation between inflation and aggregate output can be easily explained when fairness is taken into account. Indeed when fairness is not taken into account they remain puzzles, as we shall discuss in greater detail in Part Two of this book, in Chapters 8 and 9.

# THREE

# Corruption and Bad Faith

IF WE WISH to understand the functioning of the economy, and its animal spirits, we must also understand the economy's sinister side—the tendencies toward antisocial behavior and the crashes and failures that disrupt it at long intervals or in hidden places. Some economic fluctuations may be traced to changes over time in the prominence, and the acceptability, of outright corruption. Even more significantly, there are changes over time in the prevalence of bad faith—economic activity that, while technically legal, has sinister motives.[1]

The exponents of capitalism wax poetic over the goods it provides.[2] It produces whatever can be turned out at a profit. Thus the urbanologist Jane Jacobs sees architectural poetry in the variety and excitement of cityscapes that are the creation of individual private entrepreneurs.[3] At the time of Mikhail Gorbachev's *apertura*, Gary Becker, the intellectual heir to Milton Friedman's legacy at the University of Chicago, described the Yellow Pages to Muscovites. These volumes themselves are a result of free enterprise and an indication of the bounty of capitalism, with their alphabetical listings of its many offerings. A friend of ours opined that capitalism was about *chocolate milk*. The commissars of Soviet Moscow would never have deigned to produce chocolate milk. (Of course even if chocolate milk captures the *economic* differences between capitalism and communism, it does not speak to the differences in *political* freedoms, nor to the atrocities of Stalin, Mao, Pol Pot, Ceauşescu, Kim Il Sung, and many others.)

But the bounty of capitalism has at least one downside. It does not automatically produce what people really need; it produces what they *think* they need, and are willing to pay for. If they are willing to pay for real medicine, it will produce real medicine. But if they are also willing to pay for snake oil, it will produce snake oil. Indeed nineteenth-century America had a whole industry devoted to fraudulent patent medicines. To take just one example, William Rockefeller, the father of John D. Rockefeller, was an itinerant huckster. He would roll into town in his buggy, distribute flyers and hire criers announcing his arrival, give a lecture on his miracle cures in the town square, and then hold court for customers in a hotel suite.[4] Rockefeller Senior seemed to have a natural talent for deception. His son transformed his genetic legacy into something more constructive, if highly controversial.

The need for consumer protection is always a cause of some importance, but for a variety of reasons it is not the Achilles heel of capitalism. Consumers are sufficiently knowledgeable that, for the most part, they do not buy things frivolously. Most of their purchases are recurring, and they learn quickly if a product does not produce results. Retail stores also certify, at least to some extent, what they sell. In addition there are government safeguards. These are particularly important in cases in which the consumer cannot easily assess a product's attributes. Many products are subject to safety requirements that are a matter of law. For example, building codes protect homeowners from shoddy workmanship hidden behind the walls.

But there is one field in which consumer protection is especially needed, and in which it is especially difficult to provide. This is in the area of securities, which represent people's savings for the future. There is a myth (probably not true) that in the old days there was no need for such protection, since there would have been a coincidence between savers and investors. The farmer desirous of future income would invest in his own farm. He knew better than anyone else the trade-off between the sacrifices he might make today and the increase in his output tomorrow. But today most workers do not work for themselves, and the major means by which they put something away for the future is to acquire such financial assets as stocks, bonds, claims to retirement funds, and life insurance. The physical nature of these assets testifies to their insubstantiality: they are no more than pieces of paper, representing implicit promises of future payments.

There is something inherently unknowable about the worth of most of these sources of savings in the modern economy. Because of economies of scale, capitalist enterprises have grown immensely large and complex. People would be reluctant to invest in such enterprises if those investments also carried the downside risk of paying the firms' debts. So capitalism has come to the rescue with a specific invention: limited liability. In a limited liability corporation the most that shareholders can lose is what they have put into the shares themselves.

Such limited liability works pretty well. On the one side it protects the shareholders. Initially it induces them to invest in risky endeavors;

it also allows them later to sell their stakes to others, who also will not have to suffer the downside risk. One might think that the limited liability enjoyed by the owners of corporations might discourage the firms' creditors. But in most situations the discouragement is fairly slight. Why? Because the creditors will only incur a problem with recovering what is owed them in the extreme case that the firm goes bankrupt. If the shareholders have put in enough equity this risk is fairly small—in some cases it is even negligible. And there are precise measures that give a good indication of just how far the firm may be from bankruptcy. These are the accounting measures of assets and liabilities and of net profits.

There is a reason why these measures are useful in the protection of the creditors and stockholders. The assets minus the liabilities, if correctly accounted, indicate the margin of the firm relative to the payouts it is slated to make for credit. The profits net of dividends indicate the rate at which there is an addition or depletion of this net asset position. One measure indicates how far the firm is from bankruptcy; the other, the rate at which it is moving away from it or toward it.

But when there is false accounting, the sale of assets resembles the sale of snake oil. Just as it is possible to hawk a fraudulent medicine by claiming that it does something that it will not do, it is also possible to hawk stocks, bonds, or credit by misrepresenting the corporate books. Insofar as the books are cooked, the stock-buying public that relies on the accounting numbers to assess the firm's financial position will pay more for the owners' shares than they are worth. On the one hand they may believe that the excess of assets over liabilities is greater than it really is. On the other hand they may project into the future profits that are artificially high. The owners of shares, and of options to purchase those shares, can then cash in on the gullibility of those who were so foolish as to believe the false accounting.

A bit of very elementary theory describes when it pays firms to create snake oil and when it does not.[5] Consider a firm that has a slated stream of dividends. Economists would say that, in a competitive market, the price of the shares is the sum of the values of those future payments, once they are duly discounted for the fact that they are taking place in the future and also for the risk entailed. In the normal course of the operation of a firm this should be its value, if stock markets arbitrage efficiently, and also if its owners let the firm stay in business and continue to hold its shares.

But an alternative strategy is sometimes yet more profitable than holding on and keeping the business afloat. If the firm could jigger its accounting in such a way that its owners could take more money out of the firm than the discounted value of its future profits, that would be even better for them than simply holding on to their shares. One way of achieving such an enhanced payout is to kite, or inflate, the value of the shares and then sell them, letting the new owners sit on the snake oil they have acquired. But this is only one of the ways to creatively use accounting. Another is to sell credit, then figure out how to take out the money that the creditors have poured in. There are a large number of ways to take this money out, including salaries, bonuses, sweetheart deals, nepotism, high dividends, and options (which themselves will have kited values because the accounting makes it appear that the firm is doing better than its true performance).

The usual symbols of what makes capitalism work are the go-get-'em CEOs who pride themselves on being aggressive and tough risk-takers. Jack Welch, who reduced the size of General Electric from 411,00 employees to 299,000 in five short years, was dubbed "neutron Jack" after the neutron bomb.[6] He is not apologetic. Nor, according to the precepts of capitalism, should he be. On the contrary, he has only done his duty, which is to maximize GE's profits. But it is precisely because there are these CEOs, so unapologetic about making a buck for themselves and for their companies, that there is a need for a counterbalance, to ensure that all of this energy does not spill over into dishonesty. This counterbalance comes in the form of accountants, so well known for their stable personalities and their probity. A psychological study of the personalities of accountants found that they are oriented toward "facts and details," are "skeptical and critical" by nature, and like to "work in a steady, orderly manner."[7] They too are the heroes of capitalism. They are the cool-minded sheriffs of its Wild West.

## Examples from the Past Three Recessions in the United States

Each of the past three economic contractions in the United States—the recession of July 1990 to March 1991, the recession of March to November 2001, and the recession that began in December 2007—involved corruption scandals. Scandals played a role in determining the severity of each of these recessions. Let us consider the role of corruption and its lesser counterpart, bad faith, in each of them. These will serve as examples of the role of corruption in recessions anywhere: in our opinion the United States actually has less of a problem with corruption than most countries.

Corruption scandals are always tremendously complicated. Yet they are also tremendously simple. They are simple because they always involve the violation of elementary principles of accounting regarding how much money can legitimately be taken. They are complicated precisely because the participants seek to shroud in complexity the violation of these simple principles.

## Savings and Loan Associations and the Recession of 1991

All public corporations involve the managing of other people's money. There is therefore always the opportunity for the managers to pocket the money and run. But the opportunities are not always equally big. When they are big, we see consequences for the whole economy. One example of this occurred in the savings and loan (S&L) crisis, which was a factor in the recession of 1990–91. (The loss in confidence in the wake of the first Iraq war and the spike in oil prices that preceded it were more important factors.)

In the United States, S&Ls act as banks that lend money primarily for mortgages. The S&L crisis began in the 1980s after the Garn–St. Germain Depository Institutions Act of 1982 deregulated the S&Ls. The act allowed them to lend much more aggressively but left in place the government as guarantor of their deposits—a sure prescription for disaster if anyone is tempted to engage in questionable lending. The deregulation created opportunities for corruption, which were rapidly exploited by certain S&Ls, which made bad loans and subsequently failed. The resulting crisis culminated with the creation of the Resolution Trust Corporation, founded in August 1989 to deal with the insolvent S&Ls.

There is always a possibility for accounting abuse if the owners or managers of firms with low equity find it more profitable to siphon money out through sweetheart deals than to stay in business and produce a product or service that people really want. S&Ls were an especially appealing target for such abuse, because the government had set itself up to be the fall guy. Thanks to government-sponsored deposit insurance, the creditors of the S&Ls, who were the depositors, did not need to worry about the institutions' creditworthiness. If something went wrong the government would hold the bag. It did—to the tune of $140 billion.[8]

The 1980s saw conditions in which such deals became endemic. As the economy entered the decade, S&Ls had granted a large number of mortgages at fixed interest rates. But then inflation rose, and so did interest rates in general. That meant that the cost of obtaining funds had become greater than the receipts that the S&Ls were taking in from their mortgages. With proper accounting these S&Ls would be bankrupt.[9]

But acknowledging the S&Ls' bankruptcy would be an embarrassment for the government. Such an admission would require that the institutions be immediately bailed out. So clever accounting practices were instituted to allow the S&Ls to stay in business. But most of them could now be purchased for a song because their net worth was at best barely positive, and in most cases it was in fact negative.

It should come as no surprise that the scandals that followed took many different forms. The S&Ls were not worth anything as going enterprises—but they were worth a great deal for whatever sweetheart deals their owners could make. Such deals could involve real estate, with receipt of kickbacks from developers, or they could involve the purchase of risky but high-paying assets. The most inventive user of S&L sweetheart money was the junk bond impresario Michael Milken.

Up until the 1980s the prevailing wisdom among economists had been that it was very difficult, if not impossible, to engage in a profitable hostile takeover bid. If the firm was undervalued before the bid was made, the bid itself would cause it to rise in value. By the time the deal was closed, the surplus for the bidder would be insufficient to pay the transaction costs of the takeover.[10]

But Milken found a way to drastically reduce the cost of takeovers. He would enable deals to go through at near-lightning speed by using other people's money. This money came straight from the S&Ls through their purchase of Milken's junk bonds. If Milken or a Milken-connected enterprise made a hostile bid for a firm, it very much helped that he could guarantee a large part of the purchase through the sale of junk bonds. The S&Ls themselves did not need to be compensated—but their owners would receive "private prerogatives" from the sale, ensuring the smooth continuation of this practice. They would, for example, be given a form of option called a warrant, enabling them to buy the shares of the firm at a specified price. Milken is known to have allocated to himself quite a few warrants in these deals.[11]

Corporate executives discovered that they could take their firms private, floating large quantities of debt (as junk bonds) to pay off the stockholders. If the firms that had been taken private could pay off the junk bonds, these executives would be rewarded enormously. It was not long before the scale for executive pay had shifted dramatically upward. Graef Crystal, a leading consultant to executives on *their* compensation, was so appalled by the changes that he wrote a book entitled *In Search of Excess*.[12] A new era of inequality, with new standards, had begun.

It could be that the timing of Milken's exploits and the beginning of the new inequality were merely coincidental. Ronald Reagan was elected president, with a new philosophy of the role of government, in 1980. It could be that Milken was only the first harbinger of a historical shift that was bound to occur one way or another.

But the more or less simultaneous advent of junk bonds, hostile takeovers, and massive increases in executive pay does highlight the fragility of capitalism. A very small number of non-arms-length transactions allowed deals to take place that economists just a few years earlier—envisioning financiers as following the conventional rules— would have thought impossible.

This fragility was particularly clear in Texas, where the S&L scandals were especially virulent. There the price of real estate soared. Those who were in the legitimate real estate business knew what was happening and faced a dilemma. Should they get out of the business, or should they continue, knowing that prices were vastly inflated? For legitimate builders and developers it was a tough decision.

The S&L crisis was ultimately responsible for a considerable amount of the economic turmoil that disturbed the economy during the recession of 1990–91 and for the slow recovery that followed it, lasting until 1993. The spectacle of the Resolution Trust Corporation sifting through the wreckage of S&L after S&L, and of the difficulties that the Resolution Funding Corporation faced in auctioning off bonds to finance its efforts, filled the news. The head of the General Accounting Office told the Senate Banking Committee in 1990: "It's my very strong feeling that right now we have a banking system that doesn't enjoy a whole lot of confidence."[13] Confidence suffered even more when the chairman of the Federal Deposit Insurance Corporation (FDIC) asked for federal money to continue bailing out failed banks. The crisis affected real estate prices, which dropped 13% in real terms from the peak in the last quarter of 1989 to the trough in the first quarter of 1993.[14] Through those prices it affected the construction industry and in turn other industries. It affected the stock market and our trust in the whole financial sector. It affected investor confidence and the willingness to go forward with all manner of economic activities. And it all began with widespread activities that were decidedly corrupt.

## Enron and the Recession of 2001

The recession of 2001 is commonly attributed to the aftermath of the stock market boom of the 1990s. The explanations for the recession were many and varied, however, and the stock market boom and the subsequent market contraction themselves had many causes. Among these were several celebrated cases of corporate corruption—none more prominent than that of the Enron Corporation.

The study of what happened at Enron, how accounting principles were first taken to their limit and then exceeded, could by itself be the foundation for an entire course in the principles of accounting. But— omitting the mix of personalities, the greed, the ambition, the parties, the fast cars, the fast men and women it is still possible to give a short summary.[15]

Jeffrey Skilling, an erstwhile McKinsey consultant, discovered a way in which Enron could book enormous overnight profits. Under a new ruling by the Securities and Exchange Commission—made largely at the urging of Enron itself—long-term contracts for the sale or purchase of natural gas were to be accounted using mark-to-market accounting. That is, at the time these contracts were booked the firm was entitled to book as current profits the expected stream of future earnings over the life of the contract (appropriately discounted, of course, according to the expected future dates of receipt of the earnings). It takes only a moment's thought to figure out how such a regulation could be systematically abused. The future sales prices of gas were fixed, or nearly so, in these contracts. To overestimate current profits, all Enron had to do was to underestimate the future *purchase* price. And Enron's corporate culture offered every possible incentive for such behavior. Those who engaged in trades that contributed to profits were richly rewarded with options and other bonuses.

It is almost surely no coincidence that Enron made an analogous accounting and incentive error in another, very different, segment of the business. In addition to its energy trading, Enron also had a division engaged in the construction of gas-fired electrical generation systems in the developing world. In charge of this unit was a woman of tremendous charm and energy, Rebecca Mark. These projects, involving as they did cooperation between many different people in foreign countries and also an expensive form of fuel, were extremely hard to book. The most famous of them was at Dabhol in India; it promised, at immense cost to its customers, to solve the electrical generation problems of the state of Maharashtra for decades to come.

Once booked, these projects faced further difficulties. They were impossible to carry out at reasonable cost. However, Enron's accounting practices took no notice of this fact. The firm recorded the profits from its generation projects on a mark-to-market basis, and according to the cost assumptions made when the contracts were signed. As soon as the projects were booked, the expected profits went on the record. Those involved in the projects' development were rewarded accordingly —even though the project might still be scuttled and, under the most optimistic scenario, the very first kilowatt-hour was years away. Such projects were booked for vast amounts, and Enron recorded significant current profits from them. When it could not deal with the pie-in-the-sky littering its books, Enron, curiously, did not seek to make up for the overbooked profits. It simply sought strategies to book ever-growing profits, to continue the miraculous uptick that had caught the eye of Wall Street.

The legal methods for kicking the missing profits down the road were soon exhausted, and so Enron resorted to illegal strategies—the accounting equivalent of a perpetual motion machine. The CFO, Andrew Fastow, realized that if he could set up a holding corporation that would buy assets of the parent corporation above their real price, Enron could record as profits the difference between the price paid for the assets and the price at which the assets were booked.

How do you do that? You give the holding corporation already kited Enron stock. To the creditors of the dummy corporation you give guarantees by Enron to make good any losses that might occur. In this way it is possible to remove the missing profits from Enron's ledgers. Indeed such a device can be used to create any amount of profits, since any valuation can be given to the assets that are being purchased. The creditors do not care. They have Enron's guarantees. And the holders of the equity in the dummy corporation wear two hats: they work not just for the dummy corporation but also for Enron. Their compensation does not depend on how well they represent the dummy corporation; it depends on how well they do for Enron. The shareholders took out some profits in the form of options in Enron stock, which was rising because of the deception. And their pay more than compensated them for the 3% of the value of the firm they were required to hold to put the accounts of the dummy corporation off the books of the parent.

Furthermore those responsible for the loans to the dummy corporation were themselves doing the same type of deals as the Enron executives. They received large bonuses for the loans and for consulting work that they booked to Enron. They might care when the scheme crashed, since the highly remunerative game would be over; but it would be others taking the actual losses. Nor did the accountants for Enron, the firm of Arthur Andersen, blow the whistle. They were afraid that if they did so they would lose the rich consulting contracts that Enron was also giving them. It was yet another sweetheart deal.

An economist would describe this situation as an equilibrium. Everyone was following his own self-interest. But the public was buying snake oil. The recession of 2001 offered ample evidence that this equilibrium was by no means mutually beneficial for all concerned.[16] The recession came in the wake of a stock market crash that was connected to a widening public recognition that many companies, particularly the so-called dot-com companies, were indeed selling snake oil.

People became fed up with financial markets in general, and this attitude inhibited the economy far more than any other exogenous factor one can imagine operating at the time. That people were reacting to the corruption and bad faith in the financial markets, and desiring to withdraw from them to such alternative investments as real estate, is apparent in the responses to the questionnaires that Karl Case and one of us (Shiller) have regularly sent out to individual and institutional investors since 1989. Investors in 2001 told us in no uncertain terms that the accounting scandals were a major factor in their withdrawal from the stock market, and also a reason for their newfound faith in the housing market. In the housing market they did not need to trust the accountants.

*Subprime Mortgages and the*
*Recession That Began in 2007*

As this chapter is being written the United States faces another bubble and another round of scandals. Once again we see that the same principles apply.

Over the years from the late 1990s to 2006 U.S. housing prices soared, especially in such markets as Boston, Las Vegas, Los Angeles, Miami, and Washington, D.C.[17] This housing bubble has been associated with a massive increase in subprime lending, from a mere 5% of the mortgage market to approximately 20%, at $625 billion.[18]

The subprime lenders became a major new industry, and one that was not properly regulated. They were replacing the government programs that had loaned to low-income borrowers, under the auspices of the Federal Housing Administration and the Veterans Administration. Under the influence of the Reagan-era faith in private market solutions, the government programs—which had been highly regulated, to the benefit of homeowners—were allowed to languish, and private companies offering similar services—but at high interest rates, or interest rates that would reset upward at a later date—were allowed to flourish.[19]

Many subprime lenders unfortunately issued mortgages that were unsuitable for their borrowers. They openly and prominently advertised their low initial monthly payments, often concealing the higher interest rates that would follow. The lenders were successful in placing these loans among some of the most vulnerable, least educated, and least informed members of society. While such behavior may not have been illegal, we think the more egregious instances definitely deserve to be called corrupt.

These mortgage originators did not generally believe in their own products, and they wanted to dispose of them as quickly as possible. This in turn was made possible by concurrent sweeping changes in the way mortgages were originated and held. In the old days those who originated mortgages, such as the S&Ls, were also those who held them. But there has been a change in the market. Now only rarely do the originators of mortgages—whether mortgage brokers, banks, or other thrift institutions—continue to hold them. Instead the mortgages are sold; indeed the returns from them are often repackaged in a variety of different ways. As part of this repackaging, the different tranches of the mortgage returns are often bundled together and sold in very different slices. Financial markets found that it was possible to sell mortgage *parts*—just as smart grocers had discovered that they could do a brisk business in chicken parts. The ultimate holders of these mortgages are far from the originators, and usually they have little incentive to look into the qualifications of any individual mortgages in their portfolios. They share the gains and the losses with a large number of other buyers.

But if the mortgages, or at least their riskier subprime tranches, carry very high risk, one may ask the natural question: who would buy them? It turns out that once the mortgages were put into packages, a financial miracle occurred. They were taken to rating agencies, who often put their stamp of approval on them. The subprime packages were in fact rated very highly—80% AAA and 95% A or higher. These ratings were in fact so high that they would be bought into by bank holding companies, money market funds, insurance companies, and sometimes even depository banks themselves that would never have touched any of these mortgages individually.

According to Charles Calomiris, two bits of magic enabled the rating agencies to accomplish this hat trick. They attached to the securities a very low expected loss rate due to default, about 6%. This probability of default was based on very recent data, from a period when housing prices had been rapidly rising. Even then the estimates of the expected loss in case of default were meager, between 10% and 20%.[20]

Those who bought these highly rated junk packages had no great incentive to look too carefully at them; they wanted the higher returns from buying into the subprimes to show in their current profits.[21] It takes considerable sophistication to question an AAA rating. Those who packaged the junk of course wanted their fees. And no one wanted to take the responsibility for blowing the whistle on the whole game. If a securities rater gave less favorable ratings, the mortgage packagers might simply take their business elsewhere. There was thus an economic equilibrium that encompassed the whole chain, from the buyers of the properties, to the originators of the mortgages, to the securitizers of the mortgages, to the rating agencies, and finally to the purchasers of the mortgage-backed securities. They each had their own motives. But those at the beginning of the chain—those who took on the mortgages and the houses they could not afford, and those who were the ultimate holders of the debt—were buying a modern form of snake oil.

# The Hedge Funds

One of the great questions of the current downturn, as we are preparing this book for press, is: where are the hedge funds? The typical contract of a hedge fund gives its managers highly questionable incentives.[22] A common compensation system for hedge funds gives managers a fixed percentage of the capital under management, typically 2%, and then 20% of the annual profits. On this basis hedge fund owners have a huge incentive to leverage their holdings as much as possible and to make investments that are extremely risky. Curiously it appears that the hedge funds did not, for the most part, invest heavily in subprime packages.[23] Calomiris claims that, as sophisticated investors, they knew better.[24] But the case of Long Term Capital Management (whose failure we shall discuss in considerably more detail in Chapter 7) tells us that hedge funds, leveraged as they are, can fail in unusual times that fall outside the scope of their hedging models. Right now we do not know whether failure of large hedge funds is the next shoe to drop in the current crisis, or whether they really are what they claim to be. They *claim* to take very little risk; they merely make bets on asset price spreads (or yield spreads) that are too high or too low. It has yet to be seen whether their strategies work only in normal times and then fail in times of crisis, when asset markets are unusually unpredictable.

## Relevance for Our Theory of Animal Spirits

We have seen in the foregoing examples that changes in the nature of predatory activity were related to the last three recessions—the recession of 1990–91, the recession of 2001, and the recession that started after the subprime crisis of 2007. These examples illustrate that the business cycle is connected to fluctuations in personal commitment to principles of good behavior and to fluctuations in predatory activity, which in turn is related to changes in opportunities for such activity.

Why do new kinds of corrupt or bad-faith behavior arise from time to time? Part of the answer is that there are variations through time in the perceived penalties for such behavior. Memories of major government crackdowns against corruption fade over time. In a time of widespread corrupt activity, many people may get the impression that it is easy to get away with it. Everyone else is doing it, it seems to them, and no one seems to be getting punished. To some extent, lowering one's adherence to principles at such times is a perfectly rational thing to do.[25] Lower principles at certain times may also reflect a social osmosis, as information about the probability of punishment for certain kinds of crimes spreads through a net of personal acquaintances, as Raaj Sah has documented.[26] Such a process may be a part of the confidence multiplier, as corruption feeds back into more corruption.

The variation through time in the extent of corruption or bad faith is also to some extent a reflection of the fresh opportunities that arise as new financial inventions of one sort or another appear, or as financial regulations allow innovations to be implemented. These innovations may not be understood initially by the public. This variation also occurs because of cultural changes unrelated to fear of punishment or to changes in technology. These changes are clearly within the realm of pure animal spirits. Culture changes over time to facilitate or to hinder aggressively competitive and predatory activities. Because these cultural changes are difficult to quantify, and fall outside the field of economics, they are rarely connected by economists to economic fluctuations. They should be.

In the United States the 1920s, the Roaring Twenties, was a time when disrespect for the law was widely encouraged by the emerging failure of prohibition, as more and more people frequented speakeasies to drink and to gamble, in flagrant violation of the law.[27] The police were seen as looking the other way, and it began to seem that only fools obeyed the letter of the law. Disrespect for the law became generalized, unrelated to knowledge about the probability of punishment. Literature, including the 1925 novel *The Great Gatsby,* celebrated economic predators. The 1920s were in fact a period of remarkable financial predation, which led years later to public disgust with such dealings and, after 1929 and some further delay, to landmark changes in U.S. laws, including passage of the Securities Act of 1933, the Securities Exchange Act of 1934, the Trust Indenture Act of 1939, and the Investment Company Act of 1940.

The post-1920s cultural change manifested itself in other ways, for instance in leisure activities. In the Depression years of the 1930s, the card game contract bridge, first played in the United States in the late 1920s, blossomed. By 1941, the end of the Great Depression, a survey by the Association of American Playing Card Manufacturers revealed that contract bridge had become the most popular card game in the country, and that 44% of U.S. households played it.[28] Contract bridge is a game played by partners, who must cooperate—a social game that from the beginning was frequently recommended as a way to make friends or even find a beau. It was recommended as a means of learning social skills (though the game occasionally ended friendships or caused divorces). Contract bridge has only rarely been played for money.

Yet in the first decade of the twenty-first century contract bridge is in serious decline, viewed as a game for the elderly, with few younger enthusiasts. In contrast, in recent years poker—and especially its twenty-first-century variation, Texas hold 'em—has surged forward. These games are played by individuals for themselves alone, emphasize a type of deception variously called bluffing and "keeping a poker face," and are generally played for money.

Of course we know there may be no link between what is taking place at the card table and what is taking place in the economy. But if card games played by millions of people shift the role of deception, wouldn't we be naïve simply to assume that such shifts do not also occur in the world of commerce?

# FOUR

# Money Illusion

ONE OF US (Shiller) recently was impressed by a sign on a Boston commuter train: "No Smoking—General Laws Chapter 272, Sec. 43A— Punishable by imprisonment for not more than 10 days or a fine of not more than $50 or both." The two penalties seemed wildly incommensurable.

The sign illustrates the phenomenon known as *money illusion*. It is another missing ingredient in modern macroeconomics. Money illusion occurs when decisions are influenced by nominal dollar amounts. Economists believe that if people were "rational" their decisions would be influenced only by what they could buy or sell in the marketplace with those nominal dollars. In the absence of money illusion, pricing and wage decisions are influenced only by relative costs or relative prices, not by the nominal values of those costs or prices.

Almost surely no one has ever gone to jail for violating Chapter 272, Sec. 43A. Still, the absurdity of the sign on the train stood out for us because it highlighted the fundamental assumption of modern macroeconomics. According to that assumption people do not have money illusion. The sign suggests that, on the contrary, nominal considerations do matter. We learned later that the regulation was first promulgated in 1968, with no provision made for changing the maximum fine as inflation eroded its real value. Since that time the real value of $50 has declined by 80%. At $5 per day in 1968, the cost of avoiding jail was merely low; now it is laughable.

The sign on the train is just the tip of the iceberg of other indicators that the fundamental assumption of macroeconomics—the absence of money illusion—should be challenged.

## The History of Thought on Money Illusion

For a long time economists believed that the economy was rife with money illusion. Then in the 1960s they reversed this view. With only a small amount of evidence, but with powerful notions of how people behave, the economists of the 1960s decided that economic decisions should be viewed as based on rational behavior. And with rational behavior there is no money illusion whatsoever. Furthermore, for reasons we shall explain presently, this switch in viewpoint also changed macroeconomics profoundly.

It is now hard to imagine a time when people were unaware of inflation, and of its effect on their pocketbooks. The great classical economist Irving Fisher is most famous for his theory of interest rate determination. But he also spent a great deal of his professional career devising (or arguing for) what he considered to be the perfect price index. He believed strongly that people often made bad economic decisions because they were unaware of inflation. It was Fisher's personal cause to make the public aware of how the dollar changes in value. This dream has now been realized with the public's and the bond market's awareness of the Consumer Price Index.[1]

Fisher's semipopular 1928 book, *The Money Illusion*, illustrates the types of mistakes that people can make if they remain unaware of price inflation. It is full of vignettes of these mistakes, but Fisher especially relishes the dismal tale of a lady we shall call Cora. Fisher tells of his visit with Cora to her investment adviser. Cora had $50,000 of bonds, which in 1928 would have been a considerable sum. But she had been yet richer twenty years earlier. Over the twenty years since Cora had inherited those bonds, the nominal value of her portfolio was unchanged. But according to Fisher prices had risen almost fourfold.[2] So we see Fisher and the much-chastened Cora in the office of her investment adviser circa 1928. The investment adviser is defending himself. He maintains that he has invested Cora's portfolio conservatively, and with a minimum of risk. But Fisher is angry. He claims that the investment adviser failed to understand the risks of inflation and the changing real value of the dollar. Fisher similarly suggests that Cora was unaware that inflation could occur, and of the possibility that her bonds might fall in real value.[3]

Fisher is not alone, even among the great economists of the past century, in believing that people are vulnerable to such money illusion. Even our hero, John Maynard Keynes, explained income distribution for economies at full employment by assuming that workers fail to negotiate increases in wages to offset inflation.[4]

Thus among old-timers, economists of even the very best pedigree believed strongly that there is a human predisposition toward money illusion. But then opinion among professional economists swung to the opposite extreme. It quickly became taboo to believe in money illusion at all.

## The Tide Changes

In the early 1960s economists believed that there was a trade-off between inflation and unemployment. When labor markets got tight, according to the trade-off theory, workers would ask for higher wage increases. When the economy was close to full employment, prices would also rise, partly because labor would be asking for wage increases, but also because the demand for firms' products would be high as well. Thus economic planners—both those who set monetary policy at the Federal Reserve and those who set fiscal policy at the Department of the Treasury and at the Council of Economic Advisers—viewed macroeconomic policy as a matter of choosing the best point on a trade-off described by a curve. Yes, they could engineer lower unemployment and higher output. But that lower unemployment and higher output would occur at the expense of higher inflation. That trade-off is named the Phillips curve after the New Zealand–born economist A. W. Phillips of the London School of Economics. His 1958 article estimates econometrically the relation between wage inflation and unemployment.[5] This trade-off involves a painful choice. If the unemployment rate reaches the moderately high level of 6.5% in the United States, that means there are ten million people unemployed—a number on the order of the entire population of Greece or Sweden. On the one hand any lowering of that number would be of enormous human value. But on the other hand higher inflation would cause difficulty to folks like Cora, who find it difficult to take account of inflation in their financial decision making.

But the tide has changed, and the recognition of such a trade-off has now diminished. Indeed, as rarely occurs with such events, there was a critical moment: the delivery by Milton Friedman of the presidential address to the American Economic Association in Washington, D.C., on December 29, 1967.[6]

According to the Phillips curves of the early 1960s, the nominal wage increases that people ask for depend only on the level of unemployment. But Friedman changed that notion. He claimed that it was irrational. Workers, he insisted, do not bargain for nominal wages. That would entail money illusion. Instead they bargain for *real* wages. This means that in addition to the wage increases that people would make at a given level of unemployment if expected inflation were zero, they will add in their expectations of the rate of inflation. Why? Because both the employers who are buying the labor and the workers who are selling the labor care only about what those wages will buy. They care only about the value of the wages relative to the value of prices. Let's see what this means. Suppose, for example, that workers and their employers would bargain for a wage increase of 2% if the unemployment rate were 5% and expected inflation was zero. Then at that same 5% unemployment rate they would bargain for a wage increase of 4% if expected inflation were 2%, or for 7% if expected inflation were 5%. The general principle is that inflationary expectations will be added one-for-one into the wage bargain.

The same principle applies to price increases, which will also be augmented one-for-one by expected inflation. Why? Neither buyers nor sellers have money illusion. The sellers care only about the relative price they receive for their product, and the buyers care only about the relative price they are paying for it. So inflationary expectations will also be added into price-setting decisions.

Furthermore, Friedman argued, if inflationary expectations are added one-for-one into both wage setting and price setting, there is only one level of unemployment with neither an inflationary nor a deflationary spiral. Suppose we start out with inflationary expectations of zero and suppose also that unemployment is low. At this low level of unemployment, because of both the high demand for labor and the high demand for goods, firms will seek to increase their prices relative to those charged by other firms.[7] That means that price increases must exceed inflationary expectations. But then people will see that inflation was more than they had expected, and they will revise their inflationary expectations upward. While such revisions incorporate their misjudgments of the past, they cause no abatement in the rise in expectations or the rise in inflation. As long as demand is maintained at this high level (that is, as long as unemployment is kept so low), firms will continue to set their prices in excess of expected inflation; the public will continue to revise its inflation expectations upward; and those spiraling inflationary expectations themselves will be continually added one-for-one to wage bargains and to price setting. Symmetrically, according to this same argument, if unemployment is high, inflation will be less than expected, and price and wage inflation will spiral ever downward.

There is, concluded Friedman, only one level of unemployment at which inflation will be neither spiraling upward nor spiraling downward. He called that the natural rate of unemployment.

With this sleight of hand Friedman changed macroeconomics forever. In the absence of money illusion there was no longer a trade-off between the level of inflation and the level of unemployment, to be decided on by monetary and fiscal authorities. Instead, according to Friedman, the role of those authorities should be to stabilize unemployment around the natural rate and to avoid inflationary or deflationary spirals. Furthermore, since there was no long-run trade-off between the level of inflation and the level of unemployment, inflation should be kept conveniently low. There was, after all, little to lose in terms of higher unemployment.

The so-called natural rate theory caught on almost overnight. There were good intellectual reasons for this rapid acceptance. The theory was consistent with economists' growing sense that economics should be more scientific. By scientific they meant that assumed behavior should be derived from the principles of maximization. They also meant that there should be no role for animal spirits. In the case of wage and price setting, there should be no role for money illusion.

But the timing of Friedman's argument was opportune for another reason. Phillips had seen, econometrically, that there was a close fit between the rate of change of nominal wages and the inverse of the unemployment rate for ninety-seven years of British data, between 1861 and 1957. When unemployment rose, inflation fell. There was no adjustment for inflation expectations in his wage equation. However, in the United States in the late 1960s and early 1970s, inflation and unemployment both rose. That seemed to contradict the trade-off between the two that Phillips had found. Natural rate theory offered an explanation for this occurrence: It explained the rise in inflation as the result of the significant oil supply shock that had occurred at the time and also an increase in inflationary expectations, both of which had shifted the Phillips curve outward. It explained the rise in unemployment as the result of a decline in demand.

Furthermore new econometric estimates of Phillips curves that were augmented to include adjustment for inflationary expectations seemed to show that Friedman's theory closely fit the data. They failed to reject Friedman's conjectured one-for-one effect of inflationary expectations on price setting and wage setting.[8] But these estimates were also very imprecise; thus they also failed to reject *economically significant* differences from natural rate theory.[9] But the standard treatment of the Phillips curve ignores this inconvenient truth.

The textbooks thus typically present natural rate theory as a "just-so" story. It goes like this. The previous macroeconomists had posited relations between price changes and unemployment, and between wage changes and unemployment, with no role for inflationary expectations.[10] Friedman perceived that such a theory could apply only if wage and price setters have money illusion; that is, it fails to add inflationary expectations into wage bargains and price setting. Friedman modified the relationship so that wage and price equations would be affected one-for-one by inflationary expectations. Such judicious use of economic theory explained the otherwise mysterious simultaneous increases in inflation and unemployment of the late 1960s and early 1970s. The theory is also consistent with most econometric estimates.

Natural rate theory has become the basis for macroeconomic policy, relied on by almost all of the policy makers at the Fed, the Treasury, and the Council of Economic Advisers. It is commonly accepted theory not just in the United States but in Europe and in Canada as well.

Because the absence of money illusion is the critical assumption underlying natural rate theory, it is also the central assumption of macroeconomics. It is indicative how important it is to macroeconomics that just four years later, James Tobin, an arch foe of Milton Friedman, would declare in his own presidential address to the American Economic Association that "an economic theorist can, of course, commit no greater crime than to assume money illusion."[11] Tobin failed to mention that money illusion had been standard fare just four years earlier. It lay at the heart of the views on macroeconomics of some of the century's leading economists, including Keynes, Paul Samuelson, Robert Solow, Irving Fisher, Franco Modigliani, and Tobin himself.

## Presumption

We see Fisher's and Keynes' unadulterated money illusion as a remarkably naïve belief. It was in need of serious revision. But that does not mean that one should jump to the opposite extreme. It is not necessarily true that, on the contrary, there is no money illusion at all. That is only one possibility. We consider the adoption of natural rate theory, with its outright banishment of money illusion, on the basis of so little evidence, also remarkably naïve. Given its central role in macroeconomics, the theory should have been tested, and retested, and tested some more. Yet, surprisingly, we know of relatively few formal tests of its existence.

Indeed that is why the sign on the train jumped out at us. Indeed when we look for it and think about it in the right way, we see that the economy is full of telltales of money illusion. They suggest that Friedman's natural rate hypothesis, although a first approximation to reality, is not reality itself.

Economic textbooks often introduce the subject of money with a mantra: they declare that money is used as "a medium of exchange, a store of value, and a unit of account." The first two parts of this mantra have been analyzed to death by economists; they lie at the heart of what economists call "the demand for money," which relates how much money people want to hold to both their income and the prevailing interest rate. But economists have paid scant attention to the role of money as a unit of account. Its use as a unit of account means that people think in terms of money. It means that contracts are denominated in money terms. Likewise, accounting is conducted in nominal terms. And many legal provisions, including those underlying tax collection, are also phrased in terms of money.

In each of these cases people could adjust nominal quantities so that the use of money as a unit of account had no effect. In each of these cases there could be automatic adjustment for inflation, for example, by means of indexation or cost-of-living adjustments (COLAs).

According to the language of the economists of yesteryear, money could be just a "veil." That would occur if people saw through inflation and it had no effect on real transactions. That is the view of economists who believe there is no money illusion. That of course is a possibility. But we believe that, in going from nominal dollars to real dollars, something will be lost in translation. Such losses would be the consequences of money illusion.

## *Wage Contracts and Money Illusion*

Economists often express surprise at the small fraction of labor contracts that provide for COLAs (i.e., that include indexation). The best data on this question come from a large sample of Canadian union contracts from 1976–2000.[12] Only 19% of these contracts were indexed. Furthermore, where such indexation did occur, it was far less than one-for-one: COLAs typically kicked in only after inflation had risen by more than a specified target, with no effects of inflation at all up to that level. In roughly a third of these indexed contracts, the actual rate of inflation fell below the threshold.[13] Those who offered, or those who accepted, such contracts must have been thinking at least partially in terms of money rather than in real (indexed) terms. Such asymmetric COLAs are an unambiguous indication of money illusion.

Of course, just because labor contracts are unindexed does not automatically imply money illusion. Wages and prices could take account of inflation, as Friedman suggested, by adjusting one-for-one for expected inflation *when the contract is made* (in contrast to the COLA, which adjusts for actual inflation *after it has occurred*). But, when we think about it, that seems highly unlikely if a COLA agreement has been rejected. It seems to us totally implausible that parties to a wage bargain will reject the opportunity to sign a contract that adjusts perfectly for inflation *as it actually occurs* (a COLA) but then make an exact adjustment for inflation *as it is expected to occur*. The fact that most union contracts do not have COLAs—and that, even when they do have them, those COLAs are far from perfect—should be telling us something. It suggests that exact adjustment for inflationary expectations in wage bargaining is highly unlikely.

There is further evidence of money illusion in wage setting and also in pricing. Resistance to cuts in money wages (known by economists as downward money wage rigidity) is yet another indicator that people do have money illusion.[14] And, just as wage earners seem to resist wage decreases, customers also seem to dislike price increases. Dennis Carlton studied the price rigidity of industrial commodities; he found that the prices of many of these commodities were constant for significant periods, even exceeding a year.[15]

## Debt Contracts and Money Illusion

Not only are most wage contracts expressed in nominal terms without indexation, but this is also the usual form for financial contracts. The typical bond (a bond is a debt contract) issued by government entities in the United States and other countries pays a fixed interest rate until maturity. As inflation changes, the interest rate provided for in most existing bond contracts will not change. Many mortgages carry fixed rates. And even adjustable-rate mortgages, in which the rates adjust with current interest rates, are far from inflation neutral: with inflation-neutral mortgages, the dollar amount of the principal would also rise with the rate of inflation. Thus when inflation occurs, holders of adjustable-rate mortgages are paying back their mortgages, in real terms, at a faster rate.

Once again, if people do not have some form of money illusion we seem to have a paradox. Why should bond contracts and mortgage contracts not be adjusted to inflation as it actually occurs? As in the case of wage contracts, there is the theoretical possibility that when the bond contracts are made the buyers and the sellers adjust for expected inflation. Thus for example nominal interest rates may take into account inflationary expectations. This would be reflected in the prices of bonds, both at their time of issuance and also afterward, when they are traded. But the failure of bond contracts to be indexed (and the fact that mortgage contracts are only partially indexed by means of adjustable rates) leaves us with the same question we asked regarding wages. If the parties to these contracts have eschewed the indexation that would have adjusted for inflation *as it actually occurs,* how likely is it that they would then make the *exactly perfect* adjustments for inflation *as it is expected to occur?*

Once again, given that so much contracting is done in money terms, it seems unlikely that money is just a veil.

## Accounting and Money Illusion

It is said that accounting is the language of business. Managers use accounts of operating income and losses to see whether they are doing "well" and should expand or whether they are doing "badly" and should contract. Accounting is the basis of capital decisions for another reason: outsiders' view of the financial condition of a firm is based on its accounts. Accounting is then the basis for stock prices; it is also the basis on which lenders to the firm decide what interest rate they will charge, or even whether they will lend at all. Accounts are the basis for much of the taxation of a firm as well. The accounts of profit and loss determine the taxes to be levied on profits. They also play a role in determining when, or whether, a firm will be declared bankrupt.

Given the central role of accounting, if accounts are in nominal terms rather than in real terms it should follow that, if decisions are based on them, those decisions also are based on money illusion, since they will be based on the nominal accounts. If that is the case, there will be money illusion.

Since most economic contracts and also most accounts are in nominal terms, it would seem easy to know whether this form of contract affects real decisions. But it turns out that such indications are difficult to find. Why? Because the goals of those who make the decisions, hence the contracts, are complex. Even more important, they are not typically observed. We may observe the outcomes of economic decisions all we want, but we need an intervening theory to tell us what must have been the *motivations* for those decisions.

The economists Franco Modigliani and Richard Cohn have suggested a test.[16] Their test utilizes the known inflationary biases in corporate accounting. They ask whether stock prices reflect profits that are adjusted for inflationary biases or that remain unadjusted. They find that stock prices do not see through the veil of inflation. Once again the assumption of no money illusion seems to be violated.

## Summary

We have seen that one of the most important assumptions of modern macroeconomics is that people see through the veil of inflation. That seems to be an extreme assumption. It also seems totally implausible given the nature of wage contracts, of price setting, of bond contracts, and of accounting. These contracts could easily throw aside the veil of inflation through indexation. Yet the parties to the contracts in most cases choose not to. And these are but a few indications of money illusion. We shall see that taking money illusion into account gives us a different macroeconomics—one that arrives at considerably different policy conclusions. Once again animal spirits play a role in how the economy works.

# FIVE

# Stories

THE HUMAN MIND is built to think in terms of narratives, of sequences of events with an internal logic and dynamic that appear as a unified whole. In turn, much of human motivation comes from living through a story of our lives, a story that we tell to ourselves and that creates a framework for motivation. Life could be just "one damn thing after another" if it weren't for such stories.[1] The same is true for confidence in a nation, a company, or an institution. Great leaders are first and foremost creators of stories.

Social psychologists Roger Schank and Robert Abelson have argued that stories and storytelling are fundamental to human knowledge.[2] People's memories of essential facts are, they argue, indexed in the brain around stories. Facts that are remembered are attached to stories. Other facts may enter short-term memory. But such memories tend not to be influential, and they are eventually erased. For example, each of us has only the foggiest memory of the details of his or her own childhood or, for the older among us, of our own early adult years. Yet we keep in mind a story of those memories, a story that helps define who we are and what our purpose is.

Human conversation, as Schank and Abelson stressed, tends to take the form of reciprocal storytelling. One person tells a story. This reminds the other of a related story. That in turn reminds the first person of a story, and so on and on in a long sequence. We take deep-seated delight in telling a story that provokes a response from another person. Conversation tends to move along, seemingly randomly, from one topic to another. But the process has an underlying design that is key to human intelligence. It not only serves to communicate information in a form that is readily absorbed, it also serves to reinforce memories related to stories. We tend to forget stories that we do not repeat to others.

The organization of memory around stories is revealed most starkly in elderly people who have lost some of their mental acuity, but who sometimes degenerate into telling the same stories again and again, revealing the power of stories to animate human action.

The story-based patterns of human thinking make it difficult for us to comprehend the role of pure randomness in our lives, since purely random outcomes do not fit into stories. In *Fooled by Randomness,* Nassim Taleb makes this point tellingly. He illustrates it through stories of people who make serious mistakes by failing to perceive the utter meaninglessness of certain events. Yet his book itself creatively turns randomness into a story.[3]

In *Love Is a Story: A New Theory of Relationships,* psychologist Robert Sternberg argues that in successful marriages the couples create a shared story. They develop a story around a sequence of shared memories. They interpret their caring for each other and the values embodied in the marriage in light of this story. Sternberg gives a classification of twenty-six different patterns of love stories. Ultimately the success of the marriage depends on the partners' confidence in each other and on how that confidence is symbolically reinforced by repeating the stories.[4]

The National Geographic Society's Genographic Project, which seeks to classify the peoples of the world according to the migration patterns revealed by analysis of DNA, has hit an obstacle. The DNA evidence can be in conflict with the stories that give deep meaning to people's lives. For example, aboriginal peoples often derive a sense of meaning from the notion that they have lived in a specific place since the beginning of time. Hence the dating of their arrival, and the news that they are in fact genetic mixtures, sharing genes with other peoples they care little about, can cause sharp disillusion. Almost every major tribe in North America has declined to take part in the project, and there is significant resistance from indigenous peoples in other parts of the world as well.[5]

Literary analysts have argued that there is a pattern to stories. They claim that a small number of resonant stories have been told and retold throughout human history. Only the names and the details are changed. In 1916 Georges Polti ventured that there are just thirty-six basic dramatic situations.[6] Ronald Tobias wrote in 1993 that there are just twenty fundamental plots, which he titled "quest, adventure, pursuit, rescue, escape, revenge, riddle, rivalry, underdog, temptation, metamorphosis, transformation, maturation, love, forbidden love, sacrifice, discovery, wretched excess, ascension, and descension."[7] These authors have certainly not captured all the variety of human stories, but their various schema are still close enough to reality to have the ring of truth.

## Political-Economic Stories

Politicians are one significant source of stories, especially about the economy. They spend much of their time talking to their public. In doing so they tell stories. And since much of their interaction with the public concerns the economy, so also do these stories.[8]

A good example concerns the waxing and waning of economic confidence in Mexico, as analyzed by Stephanie Finnel. She finds that economic confidence in Mexico over the past fifty years reached a peak under the presidency of José López Portillo (1976–82). He made Mexico itself the subject of an "underdog" story as defined by Tobias—a story of the triumph of the weak over the powerful and arrogant. López Portillo had published a novel in 1965 entitled *Quetzalcóatl*. Quetzalcóatl was an Aztec god, who, like Christ, was expected to make a reappearance at a time of great transformation. The novel was reissued in 1975, on the eve of López Portillo's election campaign, and it became a story for Mexico's future greatness, itself regenerated from the ancient Aztec tale. The presidential jets were named *Quetzalcóatl* and *Quetzalcóatl II*. The story was all the more convincing because of two fortuitous events: the discovery of major new oil reserves in Mexico and the second (1979) oil crisis, which dramatically pushed up the price of oil.

While oil was already known in Mexico, the biggest discoveries came in the states of Campeche, Chiapas, and Tabasco in the early 1970s, just before López Portillo's presidency. As a succession of wells was drilled, proven reserves steadily rose. Expectations ran wild. Some even claimed that Mexico would eventually be second only to Saudi Arabia, with no fewer than 200 billion barrels of proven reserves. Moreover, with the second oil crisis, the price of oil reached a peak in 1980 that was more than double its level in the early 1970s.

The idea of undreamt-of Mexican wealth took hold of people's imaginations. Starting with his state of the union address in 1976, López Portillo stressed the importance of oil: "in the current era, countries can be divided into those who do and those who do not have oil."[9] And he began to act like the president of a wealthy country. He offered a Mexican proposal, a Global Energy Plan, to the international community, just when the world was worried about high oil prices and the possibility that they might climb even higher. Mexico joined with Venezuela in 1980 in the Pact of San José, to sell oil at preferential rates to the nations of Central America and the Caribbean. It was offering foreign aid. In 1979 Pope John Paul visited Mexico, and the visit was widely interpreted as a sign. Mexico had become rich and important.

The confidence that López Portillo fostered led to economic prosperity. Mexican real GDP rose 55% over his six years as president. Unfortunately growth faltered at the end of his term. When López Portillo left office in 1982 Mexico had 100% inflation and unemployment was growing. Corruption and outright theft reached unheard-of levels.[10] In his effort to create the new Mexico, López Portillo had borrowed heavily against the oil still in the ground, driven the country deeply into debt, and brought about a severe economic crisis after oil prices fell in the mid-1980s.[11] Yet he lived the story while it lasted. That meant a boom for his years in power and then a bust for the next president. The assumptions that López Portillo encouraged turned out to be illusory. In particular the extent of the country's oil wealth was exaggerated. In fact Mexico today has only 12.9 billion barrels of proven reserves, about 1% of the world total. Even now, upon learning the facts many are surprised at how small the reserves are—for the vestiges of the story still stick in our memories.

## Stories Relevant to Whole Economies

It is generally considered unprofessional for economists to base their analyses on stories. On the contrary, we are supposed to stick to the quantitative facts and theory—a theory that is based on optimization, especially optimization of economic variables. Just the facts, ma'am. There is good reason to be careful about the use of stories. The news media are, after all, in the business of creating stories that people would like to hear. Thus there is a tendency toward overexplanation of economic events. Just look at the theories offered by pundit after pundit on a slow news day when stocks have moved by a fair amount. Thus economists are rightly wary of stories and of the reality they seek to define.

But what if the stories themselves move markets? What if these stories of overexplanation have real effects? What if they themselves are a real part of how the economy functions? Then economists have gone overboard. The stories no longer merely *explain* the facts; they *are* the facts. To really explain Mexico in the 1970s, and indeed the ups and downs of most economies, one must look at the driving stories.

## Stories and Confidence

The confidence of a nation, or of any large group, tends to revolve around stories. Of particular relevance are *new era* stories, those that purport to describe historic changes that will propel the economy into a brand new era. Shiller's *Irrational Exuberance* detailed the importance of the story of the invention and exploitation of the Internet (which first became available to the public in 1994) in producing the stock market boom that lasted from the mid-1990s to 2000, which in turn led to an economic boom.[12] The Internet was indeed an important new technology. This new technology was especially salient because of its presence in our daily lives. All of us use the Internet. It is on our desktops, at our fingertips. The stories of young people making fortunes were a contemporary reenactment of the nineteenth-century Gold Rush. The steady progress of technology, which has dominated economic growth for centuries—consisting of millions of incremental advances in areas like materials science, chemistry, mechanical engineering, and agricultural science—has never attracted the public's interest. These stories are not popular. There are few statistics in *People* magazine. But with the Internet, the economy literally got carried away with the story.

Confidence is not just the emotional state of an individual. It is a view of other people's confidence, and of other people's perceptions of other people's confidence. It is also a view of the world—a popular model of current events, a public understanding of the mechanism of economic change as informed by the news media and by popular discussions. High confidence tends to be associated with inspirational stories, stories about new business initiatives, tales of how others are getting rich. New era stories have tended to accompany the major booms in stock markets around the world.[13] The economic confidence of times past cannot be understood without reference to the details of these stories. As years go by we forget these stories of the past, and thus we tend to be mystified by the causes of past stock market moves and macroeconomic fluctuations.

The complexity of the different new era stories through time suggests that differences in confidence have had many effects on the economy beyond an impact on consumption and investment. Changes in these stories will affect the expectations for personal success in business, for the success of entrepreneurial ventures, and for payoffs to human capital investments.

## Epidemics of Stories and Their Impact on Confidence

We might model the spread of a story in terms of an epidemic. Stories are like viruses. Their spread by word of mouth involves a sort of contagion. Epidemiologists have developed mathematical models of epidemics, which can be applied to the spread of stories and confidence as well.[14] For these models the essential parameters are the infection rate (a measure of the ability of the disease to be communicated from one individual to another) and the removal rate (a measure of the speed at which people lose their contagion). The essential initial conditions are the number of people who have the disease and the number of people who are susceptible to the disease. Given these, a mathematical model of epidemics can predict the whole course of the epidemic. But there is always uncertainty, as various factors, such as mutations of the virus, can change the contagion rate over time.

Just as diseases spread through contagion, so does confidence, or lack of confidence. Indeed confidence, or the lack thereof, may be as contagious as any disease. Epidemics of confidence or epidemics of pessimism may arise mysteriously simply because there was a change in the contagion rate of certain modes of thinking.

## The Next Part of This Book

We now turn to the second part of this book, where we look at eight questions that are central to our understanding of the stability and functioning of the economy. These are questions that already have traditional answers, pat answers—answers that we think are in many respects wrong. The traditional answers arise in response to a demand for explanations, but they are misleading because they do not recognize the variety of fundamental forces that operate in the economy, many of which are related to animal spirits in one way or another. In the process of answering these questions, we will develop our own theory of economic instability, of economic problems and of our suggested strategies for solving them, and also offer our prescription for how to deal with the current economic and financial crisis.

*Part Two*

---

# Eight Questions and Their Answers

# SIX

# Why Do Economies
# Fall into Depression?

WE BEGIN OUR series of chapters dealing with eight key questions with a consideration of depressions. Depressions are the extreme versions of recessions, and studying them will place the origins of economic slowdowns in sharper focus. The question of their origin is especially salient at the time of this writing, during the financial crisis of 2008.

In this chapter we will consider the two worst depressions in U.S. history, the depression of the 1890s and the Great Depression that occurred mostly in the 1930s. These two case studies will show how animal spirits can bring about depressions.

## *The Depression of the 1890s*

All of the elements of our theory of animal spirits are essential to understanding the depression of the 1890s: a crash of *confidence* associated with remembered *stories* of economic failure, including stories of a growth of *corruption* in the years that preceded the depression; a heightened sense of the *unfairness* of economic policy; and *money illusion* in the failure to comprehend the consequences of the drop in consumer prices. Thus each of the chapters in Part One is relevant to understanding this depression.

The depression followed a boom in the U.S. stock market. The real Standard & Poor's Composite Stock Price Index rose 36% in just seventeen months, from December 1890 to May 1892, and then the market fell 27% in the fourteen months to July 1893.[1] From the perspective of the heady days before the peak in the market, the economic catastrophe was a total surprise, with no logical cause.

The early years of the depression of the 1890s saw a sharp drop in wholesale prices. The Warren-Pearson wholesale price index fell 18% from February 1893 to December 1894. After that prices remained more or less stable for the rest of the depression. Upon discovering the price drops, employers began telling their workers that wage cuts were necessary, and despite great acrimony there were in fact a great many such cuts.[2] Some workers, however, responded with fierce resistance, reflecting money illusion and a sense of the fairness of their old money wages. For example, one newspaper account from 1894 reads as follows: "The spinners in the Sanford Spinning Mill were notified today that they would be asked to choose between a cutdown or a shutdown Monday morning. They prefer a shutdown and will not work under a cutdown."[3] These people actively and angrily chose unemployment rather than a nominal wage cut. Judgments about fairness were often made by comparison with the wages paid to workers at other establishments, who had not yet had a wage cut. According to the standard historical data (due to Stanley Lebergott), U.S. unemployment rose to 11.7% in 1893, peaked at 18.4% in 1894, and did not fall below 10% until 1899.[4] According to the revised data of Christina Romer, U.S. unemployment rose to 12.3% by 1894, peaked at 12.4% in 1897, and did not fall below 10% until 1899.[5] By either measure, this was an intense and protracted depression indeed. Although there was associated weakness in other countries, it is possible to analyze it mostly from a U.S. standpoint. This depression was primarily a U.S. phenomenon.

In the United States the obvious "trigger" for the depression was the financial panic of 1893. The sudden crash in confidence took the form of a run on the banks: people were showing up in droves to withdraw their money, and the banks did not have enough reserves to pay their depositors. Banks were forced to scramble for cash and to call loans that they had made to businesses, so short-term interest rates skyrocketed and a wide range of businesses began to fail.[6] At the time the United States did not have a central bank, which would have served as a lender of last resort.

But why was there a run on the banks? It is hard to make sense of this event. In history books the bank panic is attributed to passage of the Silver Purchase Act of 1890, which was a plan for gradual expansion of the legal tender paper money issued by the government to be backed by silver as well as gold. Since the U.S. government was allowing redemption of legal tender paper money in either gold or silver, and people were rationally choosing gold, the government's gold reserves were falling. But this was the *government's* reserves backing the government's legal tender paper money, not the *banks'* reserves backing deposits and banknotes. Alfred Noyes, then a writer for the *New York Times* and later financial editor there, observed that

> Panic is in its nature unreasoning; therefore, although the financial fright of 1893 arose from fear of depreciation of the legal tenders, the first act of frightened bank depositors was to withdraw these very legal tenders from their banks. But the real motive lay back of any question between the various forms of currency. Experience had taught depositors that in a general collapse of credit the banks would probably be the first marks of disaster. Many of such depositors had lost their savings through bank failures in the panics of 1873 and 1884. Instinct led them, therefore, when the same financial weather-signs were visible in 1893, to get their money out of the banks and into their own possession with the least possible delay, and as a rule the legal tenders were the only form of money which they were in the habit of using. But when the depositors of interior banks demanded cash, and such banks had in immediate reserve a cash fund amounting to only six per cent. of their deposits, it followed that the Eastern "reserve agents" would be drawn upon in enormous sums.[7]

It is significant that Noyes speaks of "instinct" as driving the panic. The U.S. government had no logical reason to expect the Silver Purchase Act to lead to a banking panic. Nor was there any logical reason it should have. But as government gold reserves fell some people got a feeling that something did not look right, and their confidence likewise fell. The growth of this feeling took the form of increasing talk about, and thus social memory of, the stories of the panics of 1873 and 1884. These were stories that almost anyone at that time could easily recite, but in 1893 they suddenly came back into the public imagination. The banking panic then exploded as a social epidemic, as people reacted to the observation of long lines at banks—responding to the fears of others by retelling the stories of past banking panics.

The run on the banks led to chaos, which was the immediate precursor of the economic depression. A number of scholars—notably the contemporary observer William Jett Lauck in 1897 and Milton Friedman and Anna Schwartz in their *Monetary History of the United States* in 1963—interpret the banking panic as the cause of the whole extended depression.

But beyond the fact that the bank panic of 1893 was generally considered an important trigger for it, there has been little agreement about the reasons for the severity and length of this depression. Douglas Steeples and David Whitten report extensive disagreement among economic observers about the best way to think about this depression.[8] The depression of the 1890s has been variously considered an agricultural depression (Harold Underwood Faulkner), a consequence of the exhaustion of the safety valve of unexploited lands to the west (Frederic Jackson Turner), and the result of the essential completion of the nation's network of railroads, depriving the economy of an investment opportunity (Joseph Schumpeter).[9] Steeples and Whitten do not offer any way to resolve the confusing list of contributory factors; instead they stress the ongoing class war between populist and business interests. This war culminated in the presidential election of 1896, in the very middle of the depression, which became an intense battle over the desirability of inflation. Democratic candidate William Jennings Bryan advocated free coinage of silver, which would have caused inflation, to the benefit of farmers and others with large debts. Republican candidate William McKinley advocated a strict gold standard, to the benefit of business interests. The candidates were debating nothing less than a huge redistribution of wealth between classes in the United States.

Money illusion played an important role in the changing thinking of that time. Bryan came close to winning the election of 1896 by arguing that expansion of the money supply, thus causing inflation, would benefit everyone—as if debtors could be helped by inflation without harming creditors. The outcry of deception that greeted Bryan led to economists' first recognition of the phenomenon of money illusion. In 1895, in the middle of the depression, Columbia University economist John Bates Clark wrote an article that coined the term *real interest rate,* meaning the interest rate corrected for inflation—a term that has entered economists' everyday vocabulary and that has ever since been a cornerstone of economic theorizing.[10] Clark explained with some urgency the inflation confusions of the time, and he dismissed the entire bimetallism debate as built on this confusion. The world of economic theory has never been quite the same since Clark's article, and even though most people today may not remember that depression of the 1890s, our thinking about inflation has been forever changed by it.

The intensity of the bimetallism debate, not just during the election but over the whole decade, meant, according to Steeples and Whitten, that a "pervasive sense of crisis and despondency cast doubt on faith in human perfectibility."[11] This deep sense of crisis sprang from a sense of unprincipled self-interest and corrupt and unfair politics, built on deception.

When the depression began, newspapers were reporting a huge increase in corruption. A January 1, 1895, article in the *Chicago Daily Tribune* reported the largest number of embezzlement schemes in 1894 since 1878, which had also been a year of serious depression:

> In order to understand this it is necessary to bear in mind that the ordinary embezzlement is sudden only in its finality. It is a gradual process till near the end, like the wearing away of land that forms the bank of a river. It begins with the abstraction of a little by a man who would be horror-struck at the thought of not putting back what he is taking. He ventures that usually in some kind of speculation akin to gambling or in an out-and-out gambling operation—and loses. He takes more in the hope of being able to recover the first sum, loses again, and plunges deeper and deeper. At last he becomes reckless under the dissipation which almost always accompanies the embezzling process. He still would like to retain the good opinion of the world, but the time arrives when he has gone so far that it is a question of restitution or exposure, the restitution cannot be made without another abstraction, and the loss of that brings the collapse. The business conditions of last year favored a great deal of that kind of outcome to speculations previously begun.[12]

As the social historian Carl Degler has documented, the social atmosphere in the United States in the 1890s led to extraordinary discord between labor and management. This was manifested in the newfound prominence, if not success, of labor unions, and in an unprecedented number of strikes. In 1892 a dispute over wages at the Carnegie Steel Company in Homestead, Pennsylvania, led to a twelve-hour battle between the strikers and an army of three hundred Pinkerton guards hired by the company. Nine strikers and seven Pinkerton guards died. Labor unrest accelerated, reaching a peak in 1894, when there were 1,400 industrial strikes involving 500,000 workers, the highest number in the nineteenth century. In 1894 a strike at the Pullman Palace Car Company near Chicago resulted in a battle between strikers and soldiers brought in to break the strike. Twenty people died and two thousand railway cars were destroyed.[13]

The sense of unfairness, of rapacity, of selfishness, and of uncertainty about the future still echoes today. The feelings of the time were reflected in the 1900 children's novel *The Wizard of Oz* by L. Frank Baum. The yellow brick road and Dorothy's magical silver slippers (replaced for the 1939 movie with ruby slippers since these showed up more dramatically on color film) were metaphors for the intense conflict over the gold standard and the proposed free coinage of silver. The little people, the munchkins, represented the poor working class. The wicked witch stood for the selfish business interests. The wizard himself was the great deceiver, the U.S. president.[14] These and other images stay with us as symbolic testimony to the importance of some of the elements of our theory of animal spirits.

## The Overheated Economy of the 1920s Leads to the Depression of the 1930s

After the depression of the 1890s there was much discussion of what had happened, and eventually corrections were made that were supposed to prevent a recurrence. Notably the Federal Reserve System was created by an act of Congress in 1913 to prevent the kind of bank run that had started the depression. The act was hailed as a "fireproof credit structure"[15] and a "safeguard against business depressions." President Woodrow Wilson, upon signing the Federal Reserve Act on December 14, 1913, was almost euphoric about its ability to stabilize the economy, and he even called the act "the constitution of peace."[16]

But in fact the new system did not function as well as had been hoped. The first thing to go wrong was a huge economic boom the new Federal Reserve apparently did not understand and did not try adequately to correct. It was not that the central bankers did not appreciate that this was their appointed task. Roy A. Young, chairman of the Federal Reserve Board, in a 1928 address before the American Bankers Association, said that central bankers should "contribute to a smoother and more even working of the mechanism to prevent overheated parts and possible explosions" and that they should be concerned about "excessive growth in any line of credit."[17] Yet the Federal Reserve did not effectively rein in the unprecedented growth of stock market margin credit, which accompanied the biggest stock market boom ever, and did not take significant steps against the boom itself until mid-1928. By that time it had been in progress for over six years.

Part of the reason for the bankers' failure to appreciate the significance of the overheating of the economy is that such overheating was less prominent before the depression of the 1890s. Thus they did fully appreciate its dangers. But their failure to act had other explanations.

Businesspeople and economists have always had trouble understanding the idea of an overheated economy, because it relies essentially on animal spirits—a concept that is not always congenial to them. In the popular press the term *overheated economy* is widely used, and it seems to be pregnant with meaning.[18] Yet professional economists rarely use it, and when they do so it is most typically to disparage popular economics.[19] Occasionally they will speak of an *inflationary economy* as *overheated*. The term *overheated economy*, as we shall use it, refers to a situation in which confidence has gone beyond normal bounds, in which an increasing fraction of people have lost their normal skepticism about the economic outlook and are ready to believe stories about a new economic boom. It is a time when careless spending by consumers is the norm and when bad real investments are made, with the initiators of those investments merely hoping that others will buy them out, not feeling independently confident that the underlying real investment is sound. It is a time when corruption and bad faith run high, since they rely on trusting behavior on the part of the public and of apathetic government regulators. This corruption, however, is mostly recognized publicly only after the fact, when the euphoria has ended. It is often also a time when people feel social pressure to consume at a high level because they see everyone else doing so, do not want to be seen as laggards, and do not worry about such high levels of consumption because they feel that others don't either.

Most economists are uncomfortable with such notions. Our case that such things in fact happen is based primarily on the psychological research summarized in Part One, coupled with direct evidence regarding the nature of economic fluctuations.

Most academic economists, if asked to define the term *overheated*, would say that it describes a period in which inflation, as measured by the consumer price index, has been increasing. It may mean that, but it generally means more than that.

Inflation itself, particularly when it is increasing, can ultimately create a negative effect on the atmosphere of an economy, akin to the effect of broken windows and graffiti on a city. These lead to a breakdown in the sense of civil society, in the sense that all is right with the world.[20] But inflation is not synonymous with overheating. Indeed the

1920s, while a period of significant stock market inflation and also land bubbles, were not a period of significant consumer price inflation.

The 1920s, the Roaring Twenties, were a time of peace and prosperity, of good fun, social activity, and solid economic growth. There was a spectacular boom in stock prices around the world, peaking in the worldwide stock market crash in 1929. Thereafter the world was plunged into the Depression of the 1930s. In understanding these events, we must again turn to our theory of animal spirits, and its key elements.

Why was there such a stock market boom? Why did it have to happen? It is not enough to say that the 1920s was a period of rapidly growing corporate earnings, for the rapidly growing earnings were in an important sense the *consequence* of the boom, through the encouragement they gave to spending and the economy

In *Irrational Exuberance* it was shown that person-to-person contagion of thought spurred by an initial stock market price increase can lead to the amplification of optimistic new era stories. The investor excitement itself propagates such stories.[21]

That is what appeared to happen in the 1920s. Many people really believed that investing genius was behind their success, even though it should have been plain that "the market did it." Stories of brilliant investors were readily believed. Samuel Insull was a legendary investor of the time. His bookkeeper later recalled: "The bankers would call us the way the grocer used to call mamma, and try to push their money at us. We have some nice lettuce today, Mrs. McEnroe; we have some nice fresh green money today, Mr. Insull. Isn't there something you could maybe use $10,000,000 for?"[22] Insull achieved his apparent success through highly leveraged investments, which collapsed in the Depression and left him ruined.

Edgar Lawrence Smith's 1925 book *Common Stocks as Long-Term Investments* promoted the story that stocks had always had excellent long-term performance, and that this was a sort of inside secret among wise and farsighted investors.[23] People began to think of themselves as just such long-term investors, but in reality their enthusiasm for stocks lasted only so long as the market kept going up. Noyes wrote of this time:

> The speculative mania seemed by 1929 to have neither geographical nor social bounds. There were occasions, even in social conversation, when expression of disapproval or skepticism would provoke the same resentment as if the controversy had to do with politics or

religion. . . . It was not in all respects an agreeable task to point out in the *Times* what seemed to me the very visible signs of danger. Expression of such comment had to meet the denunciatory comment that the writer was trying to discredit or stop American prosperity.[24]

When the market collapsed after 1929 the stories changed completely. The economies of major countries around the world fell into deep depression, and the stories turned to unfairness, corruption, and deception.

## The Great Depression

In contrast to the U.S. depression of the 1890s, the Great Depression of the 1930s raged on both sides of the Atlantic Ocean. In the United States unemployment rose above 10% in November 1930 and peaked at 25.6% in May 1933. In the United Kingdom the unemployment rate rose above 10% in the month of the stock market crash of 1929, peaked at 26.6% in January 1931, and did not fall below 10% until April 1937. In Germany the unemployment rate rose above 10% in October 1929, peaked at 33.7% in December 1930, and did not fall below 10% until June 1935. Nor was the Depression confined to North America and Europe. For example, in Australia the unemployment rate surpassed 10% in December 1928, reached its highest point at 28.3% in September 1931, and did not drop below 10% until January 1937.

Why did the Great Depression happen? As with the depression of the 1890s, that of the 1930s seems to be associated with a financial trigger: a worldwide stock market crash in 1929, in particular a huge drop on October 28–29, 1929, and related banking crises. Yet once again the real significance of the economic decline cannot be understood only in terms of this trigger.

As has become clear from work by Barry Eichengreen and Jeffrey Sachs, in the early 1930s the Depression spread from one country to the next through the collapse of the gold standard.[25] With a worldwide loss of confidence in the currency, central banks could defend the gold standard only by greatly raising interest rates, thereby squelching their own economies. Eichengreen and Sachs found that countries that adhered longer to the gold standard suffered more. Countries that devalued earlier saw earlier recovery, not only because of the lower interest rates but also because of the competitive advantage afforded by lower international prices. And yet many countries (most notably France) held out against devaluation of the currency in a futile attempt to defend the gold standard, whose time had passed. This behavior by central banks helped turn the initial trigger, the stock market crash, into a prolonged depression.

But the Great Depression cannot be summarized in just these technical terms. Animal spirits were of fundamental importance. Consider fairness. As in the 1890s, the Depression of the 1930s led to an intense feeling of unfairness in employment relations and to a surge of labor disputes worldwide. Communism emerged into its heyday, as intellectuals around the world began to see it as the solution to the exploitation of working people and the failures of the macroeconomy. A sense of instability in business institutions developed, with fears that the social contract would be changed unpredictably.

The early years of the Great Depression were marked by a sharp deflation. The U.S. Consumer Price Index fell 27% from the month of the stock market crash, October 1929, until it hit bottom in March 1933.[26] (For the rest of the Depression, consumer prices generally slowly increased.) The deflation in the early 1930s meant that profits were squeezed: firms' revenues from sales were declining sharply and yet their payments to workers would remain the same if wages were not reduced.

Economist Anthony O'Brien found that nominal wages changed very little in the first two years of the Great Depression. He provides data showing that nominal manufacturing wages fell by only about 2% by January 1931, when consumer prices had already fallen 8.1%, and that manufacturing wages fell by only a total of 3.5% by August 1931, when consumer prices had already fallen by 12.7%.[27] There were more substantial wage cuts in 1932 and 1933, when the Depression became even more serious, but, even so, as the 1930s wore on real wages continued to rise, exceeding trend wage growth by 20% by the end of the decade.

The need for wage cuts was articulated by many. For example, at an open meeting of 150 voters at a Hartford, Connecticut, public school on February 18, 1932, one participant asked: "If food and clothing have been reduced 28%, wherein will it hurt if any government employee receives a 25% pay cut?"[28] Obviously that is the correct view, and, just as obviously, if the city were to raise taxes to pay a higher real wage, it would represent a redistribution from taxpayers to government employees.

However, the public never fully accepted the argument for nominal wage cuts. Thanks to money illusion, people who experienced nominal (if not real) wage cuts felt hurt, and so the public looked for reasons to resist such cuts. Labor union leaders did not endorse real wage cuts because such an admission would not have served their interests. The idea that high nominal wages were the route to prosperity had already become conventional wisdom by the 1920s, and now it assumed even more prominence.[29] The American Federation of Labor issued a statement declaring that "Our object from now on should be to raise wages, not to reduce them. Only thus can we build up buying power and keep business rising."[30]

The rationale that real wages needed to be increased to build up buying power was widely used. President Herbert Hoover embraced it, as did industry leaders. It served as a justification for political support for labor unions in fighting for higher wages. Once deflation had ended, the argument for nominal wage cuts lost its force, and a desire to garner public support for increased wages took hold. These feelings led to a political atmosphere that produced the National Labor Relations Act of 1935 (the Wagner Act), a strongly pro-labor measure.

Other government actions in the United States were also undertaken in response to public perceptions of fairness. In accordance with its view that falling prices were a cause of the economic problems, in 1933 the Roosevelt administration successfully pressed for enactment of the National Industrial Recovery Act (NIRA). This legislation created "rules of fair competition," which had the effect of raising prices and the wages of the employed.[31]

But the theory behind these measures was fundamentally flawed, as Keynes later argued in his *General Theory* in 1936. Economic policy focused on the level of nominal wages because the public was preoccupied with money illusion. They were completely distracted from good economic policy by their deep money illusion.

The policy lost sight of the real problem: In the Depression, confidence was so shattered that banks were holding vast unlent sums, and businesses did not want to invest in new capital even though interest rates were at abnormally low levels. In such a situation, no policy regarding nominal wages-either to increase them or to decrease them-would address this fundamental problem.[32] The general loss in confidence was the main cause of the low demand, and thus the low level of employment. Real fears about the future of capitalism itself were one component of this loss of confidence, which prolonged the Depression.

Economic historian Robert Higgs concludes that in the United States, "Taken together, the many menacing New Deal measures, especially those from 1935 onward, gave businesspeople and investors good reason to fear that the market economy might not survive in anything like its traditional form and that even more drastic developments, perhaps even some kind of collectivist dictatorship, could not be ruled out entirely."[33] Such worries drove business investment to very low levels and brought corporate plans for expansion to a standstill.

Public opinion polls confirm the worries of businesspeople, even into the 1940s. In November 1941, just before the United States entered World War II, a *Fortune* poll of U.S. business executives asked: "Which of the following comes closest to being your prediction of the kind of economic structure with which this country will emerge after the war?" The options (with the percentage response for each in brackets) were as follows: "1. A system of free enterprise restored very much along prewar lines, with modifications to take care of conditions then current [7.2%]. 2. An economic system in which government will take over many public services formerly under private management but still leave many opportunities for private enterprise [52.4%]. 3. A semi-socialized society in which there will be very little room for the profit system to operate [36.7%]. . . . 4. A complete economic dictatorship along fascist or communist lines [3.7%]."[34] Over 90% of executives expected some kind of radical restructuring of the nation's economy that would decrease their expected returns from investing in their businesses. Certainly this is a plausible explanation for why they had been investing so little during the Depression.

But the real amplitude and persistence of the Depression appear to depend on even more than government regulations and actions and the resulting lack of confidence on the part of the business community. As the 1930s wore on, deep economic malaise set in. Many observers of the period noted this malaise, but their observations tend to be ignored by modern economists, who generally see no advantage in contemporary assessments of market psychology that cannot be scientifically confirmed today, and who would rather focus on things they can measure.

An editorial by "Callisthenes" in the *Times* of London in 1931 was titled "The Duty of Confidence." It made a moral and patriotic appeal to citizens to try to resist the malaise in their thoughts and actions:

> The decline of confidence is a grave national weakness. We would call it a danger and a disaster if it were not that these words have become hackneyed by exaggerated and insincere use. For it would be almost impossible to over-state the loss which the nation inflicts upon itself by this lack of confidence. The numbers of unemployed swell weekly partly because the lack of confidence prevents the originating or developing of enterprises which might provide work. The country loses more foreign markets because too often its manufacturers have not confidence enough to go in for the large-scale production which is necessary to hold them. Confidence, confidence, more confidence is what is necessary to raise the businesses which are up to the axles in the slough of despond—the confidence of the public which may penetrate and energize these businesses into a new confidence in themselves. It is plain here that confidence ceases to be merely the optional reward of good service and becomes the plain and insistent duty of every citizen.[35]

We have no way of measuring to what extent such patriotic appeals for the willful reassertion of confidence helped ameliorate the Depression. We do know that when the British economy began to recover, the improved situation was attributed to such efforts. According to the venerable businessman and civil servant Lord Meston, "The real secret of our emergence from the trough of depression was that men and women in business had made up their mind to mind their own affairs and to make the best of them. This had kept trade and commerce honest and clean and had maintained a buttress of British credit and probity."[36]

The United States was slower to recover from the Depression. Commenting in 1938, the chairman of General Motors, Alfred P. Sloan Jr., remarked on the weakness that was still very evident:

> Why has it happened? Simply because of fear as to the future of American enterprise and the rules upon which it is to be conducted. In other words, our difficulties are political economic rather than purely economic. It seems to me that there is one remedy, and only one. Confidence must be reestablished on a firm foundation by demon-

strated fact and understanding as to objectives and methods before American business can go forward with confidence. Panaceas will accentuate the lack of confidence that is already existing.[37]

Lamont DuPont, president of the chemical company that bears his name, made a similar point, as summarized by *Washington Post* writer Anna P. Youngman:

At present, Mr. Dupont notes, there is uncertainty about the future burden of taxation, the cost of labor, the spending policies of the Government, the legal restrictions applicable to industry—all matters affecting computations of profit and loss. It is this uncertainty rather than any deep-seated antagonism to governmental policies that explains the momentary paralysis of industry. It is that which causes some people to question whether the recuperative powers of industry will work as effectively to bring recovery from the current depression as they have heretofore.[38]

The drop in confidence during the Great Depression was so fundamental that it continued for a decade. Confidence—and the economy itself—was not restored until World War II completely changed the dominant story of people's lives, transforming the economy.[39]

## Summing Up Depression History

We have seen that the two most significant depressions in U.S. history were characterized by fundamental changes in confidence in the economy, in the willingness to press pursuit of profit to antisocial limits, in money illusion, and in changes in the perception of economic fairness. The depressions were intimately linked with these hard-to-measure variables.

These two epochs may seem remote in history, and we may think that our economic institutions have improved enough to prevent such events from ever being repeated. Both depressions involved bank runs, and such runs now appear to be a thing of a past because of the establishment, in the 1930s, of comprehensive deposit insurance. The first of these depressions also preceded the founding of the U.S. central bank, the Federal Reserve System; and there has been considerable development in the theory of central banking since the second depression.

On the other hand, the subprime crisis may be directly traced to a shortcoming of modern deposit insurance. A shadow banking sector, unprotected by deposit insurance, grew up after the early 1990s in the United States, in the form of subprime lenders who supported their lending activities by issuing short-term commercial paper. Moreover, even the Federal Reserve System as it existed at the beginning of 2007 was apparently not up to the task of preventing behavior that looked very much *like* bank runs, as one financial institution after another failed. In response the Fed had to reinvent itself, with new lending facilities that went far beyond its original turf of depository institutions. The increasing complexity of our financial system makes it hard for economic institutions like deposit insurers or central banks to stay ahead of financial innovation.

Central banks today are concerned about deflation, and they are unlikely to let it happen. But they are not necessarily going to stop it entirely—witness the deflation in Japan in the late 1990s and early 2000s.[40] If there were deflation today, would we be more enlightened about nominal wage cuts than we were in the 1930s? It is hard to say that we would. Simple economic truths can get lost in the heat of emotion.

Many of these past events are rooted in human nature, which remains as powerful a force as ever. People are still every bit as concerned about fairness, still vulnerable to the temptations of corruption, still repulsed when others are revealed in their evil deeds, still confused by inflation, still dominated in their thinking by empty stories rather than economic reasoning. Events like the two depressions we have just described cannot be counted as things of the past.

# SEVEN

# Why Do Central Bankers Have Power over the Economy (Insofar as They Do)?

WE NOW COME to what may be our central chapter—at least regarding the world economy at this writing. "Why do central bankers (in the United States, at the Fed) have power over the economy?" we ask. We add the qualifier "insofar as they do" because there are times when normal policy has very limited effectiveness. Unfortunately those are exactly the times when such control is most urgently needed: when we are in a severe recession.

Our analysis to this point has stressed major human foibles that can contribute to economic contractions, including fragile confidence, a tendency toward rigidity and a resentment of unfairness, and corruption. Yet we tend to rely on the central bank's ability to set things right. It might not seem that a central bank has much power to control anything as big as the macroeconomy.

Indeed the central bank is viewed by many as just the guardian of the money supply. But the money supply is in fact very small: in 2008 in the United States the M1 measure of the money supply, consisting of cash and demand deposits (that is, checking accounts), amounted to only $1.4 trillion, of which $800 billion was currency.[1] And most of the currency is stashed away by a relatively small number of hoarders, often in foreign countries; most of us have only a few bills in our purses or wallets at any given time. How then can the amount of this currency matter so much? The other component of the money supply, the demand deposits and other checkable deposits, amounted to only about $600 billion in 2008, about 1% of national wealth. How can it be that by managing the quantity of demand deposits the Fed can fix all of the problems that we have so far detailed in this book?

It can't. There are limits to the effectiveness of such standard monetary policy when there is a loss in confidence, and businesses and consumers are loath to spend.

## The Standard Story about the Power
## of the Central Bank

Let us begin by considering the standard story about how a central bank influences an economy through its control of the money supply. Make no mistake: we introduce this story as a half-truth. We actually like it—sort of. And yet we will also, later, offer an alternative story of how a central bank can exert influence—one that we feel is more relevant in times of crisis, as now, when the power of the central bank is most clearly needed.

There are two major ways in which the central bank (we will use the example of the Fed) uses its control over reserves to affect the amount of money and the macroeconomy. The standard story emphasizes so-called *open market operations*. The Fed has a large portfolio (approximately $500 billion) of government bonds.[2] In an open market operation it either buys or sells bonds from this portfolio. If it buys bonds it makes a payment from its reserve account. It thus expands or contracts the money supply by pouring it into or out of general markets—thereby affecting interest rates but not focusing on any one part of the economy. Interest rates are the "price of time," and theorists have found it attractive to build their models around this seemingly fundamental parameter.[3]

There is a second way in which the Fed affects the economy. It can expand credit by lending directly to troubled banks, receiving collateral in return. And, of course, it can contract credit by accepting the repayment of these loans. This second method of operation is called *rediscounting* or *lending at the discount window*. It will also affect the volume of reserves and the amount of money in the economy. In normal times rediscounting is a mere sideshow. The Fed typically charges a slight penalty for such borrowing, so banks use the discount window sparingly. The big difference between open market operations and rediscounting is that in the latter case the money is being put out to those institutions that really need it, not spit out to the economy at large.

In normal times open market operations are the Fed's principal method for influencing the economy. But we will argue later that it is the other method, rediscounting, that matters most. Rediscounting has been designed to deal with systemic crises by funneling money directly to troubled institutions.

According to conventional economic thinking—what we mainly see in academic economics—the Fed plays its major role through open market operations. In this story open market operations work through the money supply and the interest rates that pervade the economy. Economists' stories usually involve supply and demand—key concepts for economic theory. In this case we are talking about the supply of and demand for checking account balances. The supply will change proportionally with changes in the reserves held at the Federal Reserve Banks. The demand for checking accounts derives from their usefulness in transactions. Economists picture these transactions as being proportional to income. This explains why the demand for checking accounts depends on income. In both the short run and the long run people need to make transactions. And, according to the conventional wisdom, those transactions are roughly proportional to income. Thus demand deposits will in turn be roughly proportional to income.

Like the demand for any other commodity, this demand should not depend only on income, but also on the price of the commodity, or its cost. In this case that would be the "price of holding those checking accounts." According to this favorite story of economists, people periodically ask themselves whether they have too much or too little money in their bank accounts. If they feel they have too much money, they buy securities, or perhaps something else, and reduce their bank accounts. And if they have too little in their bank accounts, they must borrow money, or refrain from spending, to raise their balances. The frequency of this monitoring depends on the cost of holding money. What is that cost? It is what they could earn elsewhere if they held something other than money in the bank. And that is the rate of interest—the opportunity cost of holding money. The rate of interest is the "price" of holding money.

This is a very elegant story indeed, and it is the basis for the standard theory of the determination of the interest rate. The demand for money is considered to depend on the level of income and also on the rate of interest. Now, especially in the short run, the demand for it is quite insensitive to the rate of interest. (Economists would say that this demand is price inelastic.) Why would that be? Because holding some money in one's checking account is necessary to engage in transactions, but the total cost of holding it is typically not a large part of people's budgets. People may even be unconscious of the cost. It does not matter much to them whether they monitor their bank accounts more or less diligently since it does not make very much difference to their budgets (unless of course interest rates are very high). So it is natural to think that in the short run the amounts people hold in their checking accounts will be fairly insensitive to the rate of interest.[4]

The parable here is that checking account balances are like salt. People need salt. But its cost is only a small part of their budgets. Similarly people need money in their checking accounts because it is essential if they are to carry out transactions. But, as in the case of salt, it is but a small part of their total budgets. So people pay relatively little attention to the price, which in this case is the rate of interest. There is a low elasticity of demand with respect to the rate of interest.

According to this favorite story of economists, small changes in the *quantity* of salt supplied will significantly change the *price* of it. It takes a very large change in price to get people either to increase or to decrease their use of it. Similarly, small changes in the quantity of demand deposits will change the price, the opportunity cost of holding them, the interest rate, by a large amount. Why? Because, especially in the short run, most people will go about their regular business and will not change the way in which they monitor their bank accounts, even if there have been significant changes in the rate of interest. It takes large changes in this particular "price" to get people to change their level of demand by even small amounts.

The standard economists' story about the reason for central bank power is almost complete. We have shown how that small and seemingly inconsequential quantity of salt called the money supply can have big effects on the price of salt, that is, on interest rates. But we need to explain why this price matters so much. Nobody except salt producers much cares if the price of salt rises or falls. The price of salt is more or less irrelevant to the economy.

Economists finish the story by noting that the price of holding demand deposits, which is the interest rate, matters a great deal—not necessarily to the depositors per se, but to the rest of the economy. The current value of assets is sensitive to the rate of interest, which is used to discount future earnings. Small changes in checking account balances then are said to cause very large changes in the rate of interest, and therefore significant changes in the value of *all* assets. And there are trillions and trillions of dollars of those other assets. In the U.S. economy there are about $50 trillion of them. Changes in the price of assets have major repercussions.

This then is the standard economists' story, as we interpret it. Changes in the supply of demand deposits cause changes in interest rates, which cause changes in the value of other assets, which cause changes in income. There are many ways in which high asset values spur income. Take a walk around your own neighborhood. If your neighborhood is like ours in Berkeley and in New Haven, we suspect that, until a year or so ago, that lot that you thought would be vacant for your entire lifetime was sprouting a new building, and houses and buildings in serious disrepair were suddenly, surprisingly, being renovated. This is just the most mundane manifestation of the way in which high asset prices pervasively spur construction and the economy as a whole.

## Problems with the Standard View

The preceding story about how the Fed affects the economy through the demand for and supply of money is economists' usual tale. Yet there are a handful of economists, including us, who disagree with it—at least a bit. We think that it fails to see that when people's checking accounts are low, they will find ingenious ways to make their payments other than just out of those accounts. (One could always use a credit card, or some other form of trade credit. In this case payments from the checking accounts may not be quite proportional to income, as supposed.) But even if one takes such an alternative view of how the Fed affects the economy—the loanable funds theory—there is little change in the conclusion that the actions of the Fed can strongly affect the economy in normal times, because money is like salt.[5]

In this alternative view people are quite flexible about how they make payments, and the money in their checking accounts is not much of a constraint on their purchases or sales. But, from the perspective of loanable funds, when the Fed, for example, does decide to buy bonds, the banks will have more reserves, and that will empower them to make more loans. The ratio between deposits and the reserves required at the Federal Reserve Banks is typically 10%.[6] This means that an increase in loan reserves of $30 billion—which is a proverbial drop in the bucket relative to the size of the whole U.S. economy—would permit a $300 billion expansion in demand deposits, or roughly 2% of GDP. And the banks get to increase their portfolios of nonreserve assets by 90% of that amount. This availability of new funds will also bid down the rate of interest. That will directly raise spending as people get more credit for their projects from the banks and use these funds.

And there is a second channel whereby the Fed will have increased purchases and sales. The decline in interest rates caused by this purchase raises the value of people's assets. Since they are richer, they will feel entitled to spend more, both on their own consumption and also in investing for the future.

## *Limits on the Effectiveness of Open Market Operations*

We have so far described how the Fed, despite its relatively limited resources, manages to influence the economy through open market operations. The interest rate plays a key role.

The Fed usually trades only in safe, short-term bonds (Treasury bills), although it might also trade government securities with longer maturities. And its open market operations directly affect the rate of interest on what the Fed trades, that is, the short-term, risk-free interest rate. Long-term rates are fairly sensitive to these short-term rates, so they are affected as well. But when the Fed wants to reduce interest rates, as it does in a recession, there is a limit to the usefulness of open market operations. Why? Because in practical terms it cannot drive the short-term rates below zero. Obviously no one would want to hold Treasury bills if their interest rates went more than a tiny amount below zero. They could hold cash instead. As a result, once open market operations have pushed safe short-term interest rates to zero, they have no further bite. Further purchases of short-term Treasury bonds cannot reduce the rate of interest further.

When these rates have fallen to zero, conventional monetary policy has reached the limits of its effectiveness. Only other types of monetary policies can have an effect. What might those policies entail?

## *An Alternative View of Central Bank Power*

The Fed has a way other than open market operations to prevent economic crises—which is what it was set up to do long ago. We will here present an alternative view of central bank power that has more to do with systemic effects, and with animal spirits as well.

Open market operations may have become the garden-variety way in which the Fed exercises control over the economy. In fact this mechanism of control was not how the Fed was originally envisioned as affecting the economy. When the Fed was initially set up in 1913, in imitation of European central banks, direct lending by the Federal Reserve Banks in times of crisis—in times of special need for liquidity—was thought to be its major tool. The Fed was supposed to be dealing with systemic effects—the contagion of failure from one business to another.

Throughout the nineteenth century there were periodic banking panics. The depositors would literally line up in front of their bank, fearful that those ahead of them in line would be the last to make their withdrawals and that the bank would then be out of money. Such runs on banks were contagious. Word that one bank had failed its obligations led depositors at other banks to line up as well. Even banks that were solvent prior to the crisis could have a hard time meeting their obligations. Indeed when *everyone* was withdrawing their deposits out of fear, there might not be enough currency to meet their demands.

For the public, the banking panic of 1907 was the last straw. Once again the same pattern had repeated itself. The financial crisis appears to have gone out of control with the suspension of currency payments by New York's Knickerbocker Trust in October 1907. The bank run spread from there. Banks in the interior, outside New York, held deposits at large New York banks, including Knickerbocker. They counted on using these deposits when there was a demand for currency by their own depositors. After the Knickerbocker suspension, there was a run on all the banks, both in the interior, where the depositors actually lined up, and in New York, where the interior banks were trying to cash in their deposits. The resulting disruption of commerce caused a sharp reduction in the country's economic output. From 1907 to 1908 real output declined by 11%.[7]

Nelson Aldrich, the prominent Republican senator from Rhode Island and father-in-law of John D. Rockefeller Jr., was appointed chairman of a National Monetary Commission. He went to Europe for almost two years to study central banking. On his return, Aldrich sequestered himself in deep secrecy for a week with four of New York's leading bankers at the Jekyll Island Club, off the coast of Georgia. There they hatched the plan that, duly amended, became the basis for the Federal Reserve System. It was designed to cure the problem of flight from deposits into currency. The Fed was empowered to provide credit (hence the discount window) and also cash for banks that were in temporary need, especially in times of panic. When the Fed was founded in 1913, this provision of a "flexible currency" was considered its major innovation.[8] It was the lender of last resort, providing credit when no one else would.

Note that the original motivation for providing this elastic currency via the Fed was to deal with confidence and its opposite, panics. These issues were frequently discussed in connection with proposals for monetary reform after the panic of 1907. Indeed Massachusetts Senator Henry Cabot Lodge, speaking on the Senate floor in 1908, just after the panic, pointed out that "What was lacking during the panic was not currency, but confidence, which is always the condition in such cases."[9] In 1911, as Nelson Aldrich continued to press his case for a U.S. institution modeled after a central bank, a *Washington Post* editorial summed up the situation: "We need first of all some centralizing organization, so that an impending crisis may be met and repulsed with combined power—instead of every bank or every local bank association scurrying to cover for itself, thereby precipitating or intensifying the panic. This happened in 1907, when the demoralizing factor consisted precisely of the banks' lack of confidence in one another."[10] The actual implementation of the Federal Reserve System—after it had been talked about for years—took place in anticipation of yet another possible panic. Representative Carter Glass of Virginia declared early in 1913 that "There are symptoms that should not go unobserved. . . . It would be the height of folly for us to deter action until it is forced upon us by the imminence of panic."[11]

The word *panic* clearly carries hefty psychological freight. Members of the Federal Open Market Committee instinctively know this as they deliberate during any financial crisis. From its inception the Fed was seen as an agency that would take decisive action at those moments when confidence might be collapsing.

### The Changing Nature of the Problem

The Fed and subsequently the FDIC were the clever solutions to liquidity problems that could give rise to bank panics. Indeed for some time now bank panics and liquidity crises have seemed a thing of the past, so much so that most economists, until very recently, have viewed them as a solved problem.

Four lines of defense prevent the failure of normal depository institutions from causing a systemic crisis. First, they are supervised—although, as we know all too well, that supervision is not foolproof. Second, such institutions are guaranteed liquidity in the event of panic (but not in the event of insolvency) at the Fed's discount window. Third, individual depositors are insured by the FDIC for amounts up to $250,000, according to current limits. Finally, if all three of these lines of defense have failed, the FDIC has the power to take the bank into resolution. Indeed this insolvency function of the FDIC may be the most important government tool for limiting and preventing bank panic, because it can resolve the bank (that is, it can take over the bank's assets and sell them) slowly, according to its own schedule.

But not all institutions of credit are covered by this careful overlapping system of defense. Over the course of the twentieth century, and especially in recent years, a new shadow banking system has grown up. These so-called non-bank banks are the investment banks, bank holding companies, and hedge funds. Functionally these do just what a "bank" does. They take out loans with short maturities—a great deal of it typically borrowed from banks or from bank holding companies— and then they invest that money.

And there can be a "run" on these institutions just as there can be a run on traditional banks. In the same way that nineteenth-century bank depositors fled into currency in times of panic, every short-term lender may want to be the first in line not to renew its loans to investment banks, bank holding companies, and hedge funds.

Furthermore such a flight to safety can occur systemically, as everyone rushes for the door at once. The lenders' apprehension of a demand by their own depositors may make them especially skittish. This reduces the funds available to the non-bank banks. It also raises the rates that they must pay for the funds they are able to borrow. They may have been fully solvent before the flight to liquidity began, but in a liquidity crisis they may not be able to afford the higher rates required for continued borrowing.[12]

## Bear Stearns and Long Term Capital Management

The interactions between the Fed and Bear Stearns in 2008, and between the Fed and Long Term Capital Management in 1998, are illustrative of the Fed's concern about the shadow banking system and the possibility that failures there would lead to a financial panic.

On a Monday morning in March 2008 the public was stunned to discover that over the weekend Bear Stearns, a leading investment bank, had been merged with JPMorgan Chase at the bargain-basement price of $2 per share. In the words of one prominent Wall Street lawyer: "This is like waking up in summer with snow on the ground."[13] The Fed had acted as the midwife to the deal; it gave JPMorgan a $30 billion line of credit, backed by the collateral from Bear Stearns.[14] Commentators seemed as surprised by the role played by the Fed as by the collapse of Bear Stearns.

In 2008 Ben Bernanke related to the Senate Committee on Banking, Housing, and Urban Affairs his fears of the potential consequences of a failure of Bear Stearns.

> Our financial system is extremely complex and interconnected, and Bear Stearns participated extensively in a range of critical markets. The sudden failure of Bear Stearns likely would have led to a chaotic unwinding of positions in those markets and could have severely shaken confidence. The company's failure could also have cast doubt on the financial positions of some of Bear Stearns' thousands of counterparties and perhaps of companies with similar businesses. Given the exceptional pressures on the global economy and the financial system, the damage caused by a default by Bear Stearns could have been severe and extremely difficult to contain.[15]

But the history of the Federal Reserve and the original intent of the discount window suggest exactly why the Fed helped broker such a deal. Federal Reserve Chairman Ben Bernanke, one of the leading historians of monetary crises and the role the Fed has played in them, understood the original intent of the founders of the Fed. He had been worried that the collapse of Bear Stearns would create a liquidity crisis. If the creditworthiness of Bear Stearns was in doubt, who in turn would loan to their creditors? That is exactly what had happened a century earlier with the failure of Knickerbocker Trust. When it failed, who was to trust that its creditors—especially all of those interior banks, with their deposits—would be paid off? A chain reaction set in.

We have but to look back ten years to find another similar event. Here again, in the nick of time, the Fed came to the rescue. The institution at risk was not an investment bank but rather a hedge fund. In 1994 an offshoot financial group from Salomon Brothers opened a hedge fund, which they called Long Term Capital Management (LTCM). They would arbitrage risks according to the financial theories of Myron Scholes and Robert Merton—who would, three years later, share the Nobel Prize in economics for "a new method to determine the value of derivatives." Because of the impeccable reputation of its advisers, not only was LTCM able to assemble $1.25 billion in capital, it was also given, unthinkingly, carte blanche to borrow from Wall Street's leading banking houses.

The partners in LTCM were at first just as successful as their initial prospectus suggested they would be. They had a fairly simple basic strategy—largely based on regression analysis and options theory—of how to make money on Wall Street. Past behavior indicated how options behaved. On a large variety of comparable trades, spreads would regress toward their historical means. If these spreads were large they would decline. If they were small they would rise. It was almost a sure thing to make such bets. And that is exactly what happened in the first years of LTCM. One of us remembers meeting one of the partners at a cocktail party in Washington at the time. Asked how he was doing, he grinned and answered that the pay was better than in the government, where he had worked previously. By 1997 LTCM's capital had grown through profits and new subscriptions to $7 billion. Its profits were $2.1 billion.

But pride goeth before a fall. In 1998 a problem developed with the LTCM strategy. Whereas in previous years markets had obligingly agreed with prior econometric estimations, and spreads had almost universally regressed toward their means, 1998 saw the Russian and Asian currency crises. Rather than converging, market spreads diverged. And LTCM began to lose its shirt. All that leverage from Wall Street's borrowed money, instead of being an asset, was now a liability. By August it seemed possible that the fund might go under. By mid-September it seemed all but certain that LTCM—with more than $100 billion of borrowed money, and bets on derivatives with a face value far in excess of that—would go bankrupt. No one really knew what would ensue in the event of a bankruptcy. What would happen if there was a gap in the chain of payments, while bankruptcy courts sorted out who would owe what to whom?

The Fed intervened. An emergency meeting of the titans of Wall Street was convened in the boardroom of the Federal Reserve Bank of New York. An agreement was hammered out, whereby the leading lenders would contribute a pool of $3.65 billion to LTCM. They would also take 90% of the partners' shares.[16]

In the cases of both Bear Stearns and LTCM, the role of the Fed was to be the banker of last resort. It was to counter systemic risk in a liquidity crisis. In both cases it acted heroically, and a liquidity crisis was avoided. But these proved to be just the early warning signs of what was to come.

Then on September 15, 2008, Lehman Brothers filed for Chapter 11 bankruptcy. The Federal Reserve and the federal government began a new mode regarding intervention in the economy. It is no longer a question of using the powers of the Fed and the Treasury to rescue a single institution, to keep the first domino from falling. Central banks and governments all over the world are trying to rescue their own economies, and the world economy more generally.

Our view of animal spirits, and our discussion in this chapter about the powers of central banks, especially in a crisis, inform our interpretation of why the current crisis has occurred. They also suggest to us what now must be done, and it is to those prescriptions that we turn in the postscript to this chapter that follows.

# The Current Financial Crisis: What Is to Be Done?

OUR THEORY—and especially the theory presented in the previous chapter on monetary policy and the powers of the central bank—has implications for the current economic crisis. The prescription for most economic recessions—the equivalent of "take two aspirin and get some rest"—is a reduction in interest rates (that is, reliance on standard monetary policy) and fiscal expansion, in the form of either additional spending or, more probably, politically popular tax cuts. But this time we need to do more.

This recession is different. It is not just due to low demand. Nor is it primarily due to high energy prices, although oil prices were especially high in the summer of 2008. The overwhelming threat to the current economy is the credit crunch. It will be difficult and perhaps even impossible to achieve the goal of full employment if credit falls considerably below its normal levels.[1]

Problems in the financial sector have occurred before. For example, as we saw in Chapter 3, there was massive failure of savings and loan associations in the United States in the 1980s. Their resolution cost $140 billion, which was a lot of money, especially to be wasted. But it was still only about 2% of GDP at the time.[2] The failures did not have a major macroeconomic impact.

In contrast, the current crisis is pervasive. It involves the economy as a whole. It is not just about those who bought houses they could not afford. It is about the state of California, which says that it can no longer borrow; about the demise of investment houses around the world, which seemed like they would last forever; about consumers who do not want to buy a car, and who could not obtain the credit to buy one if they wanted to. It is even about our mailboxes. We have noticed recently that we are receiving fewer offerings of credit cards with that very special deal just for us.

Lest there be statistical doubt that the credit crunch is just one more story, every economist has his or her favorite statistical indicator of it. Ours is commercial paper outstanding. From the third quarter of 2007 to the third quarter of 2008 nominal (not inflation-corrected) GDP grew by 3.4%. In the normal course of events the amount of commercial paper outstanding would also have risen—at least a little. But that is not what happened. According to official Federal Reserve statistics, commercial paper outstanding fell by more than 25% (from $2.19 trillion to $1.58 trillion).[3] Asset-backed commercial paper has been especially hard hit; it has fallen more than 40% (from a high of $1.21 trillion to $725 billion).[4] Commercial paper is our favorite indicator because it is commonly perceived as a major vehicle whereby businesses finance their working capital. This is the money they need to meet their payrolls and to pay their suppliers. It is not the only source of such current finance, but if it falls by as much as 25% while business has stayed pretty much constant, that means that something is wrong. There really must be a credit crunch.

Previous chapters have explained why this credit crunch has occurred. The old system of finance changed. In the old days, for the most part, those who originated loans kept them in their own portfolios. But then the proponents of the "new finance" discovered all kinds of ways to package these loans (to "securitize" them) and to divide up those securities. And then exotic financial derivatives further spiced up the stew. These financial products did not even need to be backed by underlying assets: they were promises to pay if some future event took place. Relying on a curious financial alchemy, investors combined these products in clever ways, thinking that they were thus able to exorcise the underlying risk. In the spring of 2007—just before the financial markets began to notice that, maybe, something was wrong—risk premiums were at all-time lows.

The story of the go-go years was that all of these securitizations and derivatives were about "risk management." Indeed both securitization and some futures contracts do play this role. But then the story changed. The new story, as we recounted it previously, suggested that securitization and the exotic derivatives could be nothing more than a new way of selling snake oil. And as this new story about the nature of Wall Street and its products replaced the old story, the life drained out of the financial markets. The demand for the exotic products collapsed, and the credit crunch began.

The credit crunch began for three separate reasons. First, and most obviously, a standard mode of financing had collapsed. Those who originated loans (mortgages, for instance) could no longer expect to be able to package them and pass them on easily to unsuspecting third parties. Now if they were going to originate those loans either they would have to keep them ultra-safe before they passed them on, or they would have to keep them themselves.[5]

The second reason for the credit crunch involves the relation between capital loss and leverage. Many of the institutions that held the loans or that originated them—depository banks, investment banks, and bank holding companies—had themselves invested in the new financial products. They had also been highly leveraged. And now, with the change in the story and the collapse of trust, their assets had fallen in value. For every dollar they lost on these assets, the institutions would lose a dollar's worth of capital. Not only did this edge them toward bankruptcy, it also increased their leverage.[6] Institutions had to choose among a three-way trade-off between an increase in leverage, a curtailment of loans, and taking out new capital. The credit crunch came as they chose to curtail their loans and other securities. The leverage problem was further compounded by the fact that the nondepository institutions were borrowing short but lending long. The bank holding companies, the hedge funds, and the investment banks were banks in fact but not in name: they were the shadow banking system.

The use of already-promised credit lines gives a third reason for the credit crunch. While the good times rolled, banks had granted lines of credit to their customers. Now, facing a shortage of credit, these customers cashed in, in unexpected numbers, on the promises they had found relatively easy to extract in better times. Meeting these promises put the banks in a further squeeze in terms of their ability to make new loans.

## A Credit Target

The preceding summary of what has happened is in no way original. A careful reading of the *Financial Times* or the *Wall Street Journal* on even a single day would, implicitly or explicitly, reveal this interpretation of events. It is now the standard story.

But it has implications for macroeconomic policy. The usual macroeconomic models, used to make forecasts, do not contain the financial detail that would describe the credit crunch and why it has occurred. It is fairly easy now to project the fiscal and monetary stimulus necessary for aggregate demand to be at full employment—*if* financial markets are freely flowing. Such estimates should be used to determine the size of the needed fiscal stimulus. The Federal Reserve, the Congress, and the Council of Economic Advisers are all experienced in making such predictions.

But, with the loss of confidence in the financial sector, macroeconomic planners must also have a *second* target. In such abnormal times, the traditional ways of determining the needed stimulus are misleading. The planners must also make a plan—we might call it a target or an intermediate target—for the amount of credit of different sorts that is to be granted.[7] This target should correspond to the credit that would normally be given if the economy were at full employment. The target should not be merely a mechanical credit aggregate, but should reflect the more general condition that credit be available for those who, under normal conditions, would be deserving of it. The idea of targeting credit goes at least as far back as an article written by current Fed Chair Ben Bernanke and former Fed Vice-Chair Alan Blinder in 1988.[8] (It should not be confused with economists' discussions of targeting monetary policy, mainly by targeting the rate of inflation.[9] That literature does not concern itself with how to countervail a credit crunch.)

Achieving the credit target is urgent for several reasons. Most notably, firms that count on outside finance will go bankrupt if they cannot obtain credit. If the credit crunch continues and many firms go bankrupt, it would take an impossibly large fiscal and monetary policy stimulus to achieve full employment.

There is the further problem that, as long as credit markets are frozen, the need for fiscal and monetary stimulation will continue. Using the appropriate fiscal and monetary stimulus, in sufficient amount, could possibly keep us at full employment. But to do so without relieving the credit crunch would be like propping a sick man up in bed so that he looks all right. He will collapse again just as soon as you remove the prop. Japan during the 1990s is illustrative. After its own stock market and real estate debacle in the early 1990s, Japan was frequently in deficit for a span of over fifteen years. Eventually the government debt rose to 1.71 times annual GDP.

Furthermore, as long as the credit crunch continues, multipliers will be smaller than they would otherwise be. For example, a person who cannot borrow is unlikely to buy a car—even if a generous fiscal policy has provided him with the needed down payment.

## *Implications for the Future*

The nursery rhyme about Humpty Dumpty originated before children's illustrated storybooks were common. It was a riddle. Who was Humpty Dumpty? He was an egg. So when he fell, all the king's horses and all the king's men could not put him back together again.

And that tale well describes the current financial crisis. The segment of the financial system that initiated loans, and then passed them on, was fragile. It fell. In terms of our animal spirits, confidence disappeared. People became suspicious of transactions that they had previously undertaken to the tune of trillions of dollars. And the story changed. It was now about snake oil. There was no going back.

Yet the sophisticated financing involving securitized debt and the derivatives (like credit default swaps and other financial futures) that seemed to be insurance for those debt packages had been serving a purpose. Over the years it had replaced a great deal of the old system of (more or less) direct lending.

The public now looks to the still-existing financial structure of depository banks, bank holding companies, insurance companies, retirement funds, hedge funds, investment banks, and others to fill in the void that has been left by Humpty Dumpty's sudden fall. It is our belief—echoing Keynes' view of the role of macro policy—that if there is a macroeconomic void the government must fill it. It must once again set the stage for a healthy capitalism. This had been the vision in previous generations of those who established central banks: the role of central banks is to insure the credit conditions that enable full employment.

## *The Policy Response*

Since the beginning of the credit crunch in August 2007 the U.S. government has used three types of instruments to expand credit.

*Method 1: The Discount Window.* The Federal Reserve has greatly expanded its discount operations, especially by the creation of different special loan facilities.[10] The first of these was the Term Auction Facility

(TAF), which enables banks to obtain Federal Reserve loans by competitive auction. The two auctions in October 2008, following the fall of Lehman Brothers, illustrate its use: the first auction furnished $138 billion for credit of 85 days and the second, $113 billion of credit for 28 days.[11]

The Fed and the Treasury Department have also discovered an ingenious way to jumpstart failing credit markets. In November 2008 the Fed set up the Term Asset-Backed Securities Loan Facility (TALF). The loans in the TALF are nonrecourse, i.e., the banks can walk away from them. In addition the Fed offers them with only a small "haircut" on the collateral. (For example, the Fed might require collateral of $105 million against a $100 million loan. The haircut in this case is 5%.)

These provisions have two effects. Because the loans in the TALF are nonrecourse, banks' potential losses are limited. As a result, banks should not require very high returns on loans to offset the risk—even now, in the midst of the crisis. They cannot lose more than the haircut. But at the same time, because the banks would be losing the haircut if the loans went sour, they also have an incentive to initiate good loans in the first place.

Another provision of the TALF, in turn, limits the Fed's liability. The losses on the collateral are shared between the Treasury Department and the Fed, so that Treasury is the junior creditor and the Fed is the senior creditor. The very first announced offering on TALF illustrates how it will work—and why it is so powerful and ingenious. In this first offering, the Fed is granting $200 billion of loans of one-year maturity against pools of collateral consisting of new or recent car loans, student loans, credit card loans, and small business loans. The collateral must be rated AAA by at least two rating houses. Treasury is using money it received under the $700 billion Troubled Assets Relief Program (TARP) to contribute a $20 billion junior tranche of the $200 billion. So the first $20 billion of loss will be taken by Treasury, not the Fed. This provision (plus the initial haircut taken by the banks) makes the Fed's interest relatively safe—enough so that it is legally empowered to make loans against it.[12]

This scheme simultaneously accomplishes three goals. First, it gives powerful incentives for banks to make new loans. The most they have to lose is the haircut. Current spreads between Treasury bills and the types of loans that would go into the collateral pool should more than compensate for losses due to small haircuts. Second, TALF renders the Fed's portion of the collateral sufficiently safe. Third, Treasury's money can go much farther than if it were buying troubled assets outright. For example, if Treasury takes up 10% of the collateral as junior partner (as in the initial offering), a $300 billion contribution could support $3 trillion worth of new credit. That is the order of magnitude of impact on credit that would be needed to replace the fallen Humpty Dumpty. Of course future TALF offerings may vary in many respects: they are now contemplated for commercial paper, loans against commercial property, and other types of collateral. Such offerings can also have different loan maturities, different required ratings on the loans, and different pricing schemes.

More generally, TALF shows us that there are two sides to creative finance: It may have gotten us into this crisis. But its genius may also get us out of it. Most important of all, TALF holds out the hope that Treasury money of the very large order of magnitude initially authorized by TARP can enhance credit flows by the yet larger order of magnitude necessary to have a serious impact on the credit crunch.

*Method 2: Direct Injections of Capital.* A second method of expanding credit, to replace the fallen Humpty Dumpty, is direct injection of capital into banks. The Treasury Department has already allocated approximately $250 billion from TARP for this purpose. Approximately half of this was given to the seven biggest banks: Bank of America, Bank of New York Mellon, Citigroup, Goldman Sachs, JPMorgan Chase, Morgan Stanley, and Wells Fargo. Additional bank capital is especially valuable insofar as banks' lending is limited by their capital constraints.

*Method 3: Direct Credit from Government-Sponsored Enterprises.* There is yet a third approach. The federal government can use government-sponsored enterprises (GSEs) directly to increase lending. In February 2008, as part of the government's stimulus package, the maximum size of mortgage that could be purchased by two such enterprises, Fannie Mae and Freddie Mac, was increased. Previously there had been a flat limit of $417,000; the limit was now 125% of median regional home prices, up to a maximum as high as $729,750 for the most expensive regions. Moreover, the government directed Fannie and Freddie to continue to increase their portfolios of mortgage securities from 2008 to the end of 2009.[13]

The federal government was thus instructing Fannie Mae and Freddie Mac to place massive support behind mortgages. Their combined book of business at the end of 2007, just before the crisis, was $4.9 trillion—a significant fraction of the entire publicly held U.S. national debt. Had these institutions not been taken into conservatorship and given this directive, their failure would have caused a deadly drop in mortgage financing, and possible immense downward overshooting in the housing market. But the government's near-guarantee of Fannie Mae and Freddie Mac (which had been only implicit prior to their takeover in September 2008) now meant that bonds issued by the two agencies were safe.[14] The Federal Reserve also announced, on November 25, 2008, that it would be buying up to $500 billion of the mortgage-backed securities issued by the GSEs, and up to $100 billion of their direct obligations, further helping support the market for mortgages. Fannie and Freddie were thus free to replace a considerable share of the failing mortgage market.

It is only because of such dramatic action that the mortgage market in the United States has not already fallen apart. But this action was easily justified politically only because these were GSEs, initially created by the U.S. government.

In addition to TALF and other discount window–based operations, prudence suggests that we simultaneously prepare alternative approaches to deal with the credit crunch. A plan for recovery should include the possibility that relatively well-run banks that fall into the lap of the FDIC be incorporated into a new GSE. This corporation could be used directly to support lending activities beyond the conventional mortgages represented by Fannie Mae and Freddie Mac. This would require new legislation, setting up a corporation similar to the Resolution Trust Corporation, which resolved the S&L crisis. But here the mandate would be different: rather than focusing on expeditious resolution of assets, the banks in this new corporation would, with suitable supervision, be directed to make loans with the specific purpose of relieving the credit crunch. In the Swedish financial crisis of the early 1990s, a variety of methods, including state ownership of banks, insured that credit did not come to a standstill.[15]

# Advantages and Disadvantages
## of Methods 1, 2, and 3

The actual mix of methods 1, 2, and 3 that should be used to achieve the credit target depends on their respective advantages and disadvantages.

*Method 1: Expansionary Discount Window.* Although the TALF would seem to be the method of relief involving the least expenditure of federal money and also the least direct intervention in the operation of credit markets, it is only experimental. Currently the Fed is basing its collateral only on AAA-rated securities. There may be many difficulties in extending use of the TALF to credit of lower grades. Furthermore, those who offer assets through the facility will surely try to game the system to dispose of their less well-performing assets. This potential problem of "lemons" in the collateral pool makes it difficult to extend operation of the TALF to securities that are not highly rated.

*Method 2: Direct Investment in Banks.* Direct investment in banks has its own issues, among which the problem of legitimacy and acceptance is especially salient. The public and the press do not like the idea of "bailing the banks out." It offends their—and our—sense of fairness. The public also fears—surely rightly so—that highly compensated bankers will somehow appropriate the funds from the bailout to increase their own bonuses. The *New York Times'* Gretchen Morgenson reflects such a political reaction when she describes how an "irreverent friend" thought TARP referred to "The Act Rewarding Plutocrats."[16]

It may also be difficult to make injections of the necessary magnitude. The public may believe that injections of capital into the banks are necessary to make *them* solvent. But this fails to perceive the Humpty Dumpty problem. To relieve the credit crunch it is necessary to make the banks so super-solvent that they will replace *those parts of the credit system that have failed.* When it was announced that the Fed would inject $250 billion of capital into U.S. banks, the *Financial Times* ran a headline that suggested that even this amount was of the wrong order of magnitude to solve the credit crisis. Its banner headline compared the $250 billion being allocated by the United States to "Europe's $2,546bn Move."[17]

There is also the lead-the-horse-to-water-but-not-make-it-drink problem. The injections may make the banks richer, and therefore less likely to become insolvent, but they will not necessarily lend more money. They may already feel constrained by the extra loans they have extended in making good on their promised lines of credit.

But injections of capital into banks have two potential advantages. Such injections involve minimal interference with private systems of credit. They may also be a relatively cheap way to meet the credit target—provided that the banks' refusal to lend really depends on capital constraints. A $250 billion injection of capital will permit an extra $3.125 trillion worth of loans, if there is an 8% capital requirement. Furthermore there is an interaction with schemes such as TALF. Relatively small injections are likely to greatly enhance the ability of banks that would otherwise be on the brink of insolvency to take advantage of TALF.

*Method 3: Use of Government-Sponsored Enterprises.* There are, of course, problems with government-run enterprises. A GSE will have difficulty in choosing to give loans to some citizens while denying others. Typically the resolution of such problems within public institutions involves cumbersome bureaucracies. In a credit crunch, when swift action is needed, this can prove a particular disadvantage. Yet many government operations function well. And many private companies function poorly; they too may be bureaucratic and inefficient. On the other hand, GSEs also solve the lead-the-horse-to-water problem. Government directives, as in the case of Fannie and Freddie, can compel the horse to drink.

## The Role of Financial Market Targets

The aim of replacing the falling Humpty Dumpty financial sector is obvious to almost all policy macroeconomists. Our broad interpretation of Federal Reserve policy since the beginning of the credit crunch in August 2007, and also of fiscal policy during that period, is that the major goals have been to keep as close to the two full-employment targets as possible.

The two-target notion is useful as a vehicle for summarizing current economic policy. But its usefulness goes beyond that, and the experience of the Great Depression explains why. Both Hoover and Roosevelt moved in the right direction in terms of running budget deficits and also in their creation of new agencies to replace the then-failing financial system. Both presidents are heroes of ours, although we are not blind to the great deficiencies in their plans. Their economic policies sometimes worked in the right (Keynesian expansionary) direction, but often they themselves were misinformed, as when they both tried to balance their budgets. In the absence of a Keynesian model to gauge the size of the deficits necessary to target full employment, neither Hoover nor Roosevelt had either the inclination or the political legitimacy to go far enough. Their deficit spending was orders of magnitude short.

The two targets provide such a gauge. Standard macro models are fairly accurate regarding the monetary-fiscal stimulus necessary to achieve full employment. But financial markets must also be targeted. The financial system is not the same as it was just a few months ago, before the fall of Humpty Dumpty. Only a portion of its prior self is now operating. The aggregate demand target will indicate, on the one hand, the fiscal stimulus and interest rate policy needed for full employment. The credit target will show what judicious application of methods 1, 2, and 3 must achieve: together they must create the financial flows—the issuance of commercial paper, bonds, and other instruments—that are also associated with full employment.

The targets are needed not just to devise a plan that stands a good chance of getting us back to recovery. They are also necessary because such a plan will involve a huge sticker shock. When Treasury Secretary Henry Paulson initially suggested his $700 billion bailout plan, the Congress balked. Paulson's description of how that money was to be spent was lacking in detail. But even after the Congress had fleshed out the plan, $700 billion still seemed like just too much money. Indeed the House of Representatives initially vetoed the modified bill.

A study of animal spirits tells us why we need the two targets. These two targets, and the reasoning behind them, are needed to give policy makers not only the confidence but also the legitimacy to undertake a plan that is sufficiently bold. Our theory of confidence, snake oil, and stories shows why it is essential to do more than just keep the existing financial system solvent. Any plan that has a real possibility of ending the crisis must be of sufficient magnitude to replace the fallen Humpty Dumpty.

Of course the two-target approach and Humpty Dumpty do not apply only to the United States but internationally as well.

# EIGHT

# Why Are There People
# Who Cannot Find a Job?

THE DEPRESSIONS we studied in Chapter 6 proved that high unemployment can last for years and years.[1] We discussed the causes of the depressions, but we need now to focus on the failure of labor markets to clear properly—which is the hallmark of unemployment. Even if confidence faltered in these depressions, even if there was a general perception of unfairness and attention to stories of corruption and doubts about the future, how can the wage rate fail to adjust to clear the labor market?

In this chapter we focus on one aspect of our theory of animal spirits, the human demand for fairness, to help us understand unemployment. This explanation in turn will help us understand how high levels of unemployment could happen again, and that economic policy must be carefully directed to ensure against such a recurrence.

## Involuntary Unemployment

We know a distinguished economist who was proud of his powers of will. When he decided to sell his house and the expected buyers did not show up at his door, he told his colleagues he *could not* sell it. His colleagues were not surprised that the house had not sold, but they were surprised at his assertion: it violated the basic principles of supply and demand from Economics 1. They were certain that the absence of bidders had a very simple explanation: the house was overpriced. Eventually it did sell—but, as predicted, only after the price had been considerably reduced.

Involuntary unemployment does not conform to many economists' view of economic theory, precisely because they ask about the unemployed the same question they asked about our colleague's house. If the unemployed are unable to get jobs (which means that they are unable to sell their labor), why do they not simply ask for a lower wage?

Or, if that is not possible, why do they not seek jobs with fewer qualifications? Why is the labor market different from stock markets or commodity markets, where people can make a sale (indeed, all but instantly) by reducing their asking price just a little bit?

There is an answer to these questions. It is called the efficiency wage theory, so named because it posits the idea that the efficiency or effectiveness of labor depends on the wage employees are paid.[2] In the housing market, the stock market, and the wheat market, transactions between buyers and sellers end with the exchange of their goods for the agreed-upon price. A lower price unambiguously benefits the buyer. But that is not the case in the purchase of labor. The transaction between the buyer and the seller of labor only *begins* when the labor is employed and the wage is agreed upon. No doubt most employers would welcome a lower wage, if there were no further repercussions. But in the labor market a lower wage usually *will* engender further repercussions. Why? Because the individual worker, and also the employer's other workers, must not only appear for the appointed number of hours. He or she must be motivated. It does not do the employer much good to hire a worker at a low wage if this causes the worker to be angry or resentful and thus to screw up the employer's operations. There are few employees who are so carefully monitored that they lack any opportunity to figuratively spit in the soup.

We can represent the effects of such concerns even with the simplest economic tool, the supply and demand curves that are the staple of elementary economics. In this representation the employer sets the wage, and only one of his interests in that wage is the dollars of payment. The other interest is its effect on worker morale. Because of its effect on morale the employer may want to pay a wage that is higher than the lowest wage the worker would be willing to accept. And for all employers these fair wages that they want to pay their workers may be higher than the wages at which all the workers in the market start accepting work. In that case the supply of labor is more than the demand for it. Thus there is a gap between the supply of labor and the demand for labor. That gap consists of people who cannot find jobs.

The market for jobs is then like a game of musical chairs, with more people on the dance floor than there are chairs. When the music stops, some people cannot find a chair. We may not know who among the dancers they will be, but we do know that, for sure, some will be left out and will involuntarily have to stop dancing. Similarly when there are fewer jobs than there are people looking for them, some among them will not be able to find a job. It may be true that the more intrepid among these unemployed will be among the select who do find jobs. On average those who find jobs will have searched out more options and will be more willing to take positions they had not previously contemplated. But that does not invalidate the concept of involuntary unemployment. Involuntary unemployment will consist of the gap between the supply of and the demand for labor at the wage that firms are willing to pay.

This theory of unemployment is so simple that it can be taught easily in Econ 1. It is now presented in the more complete macroeconomic textbooks and in some of the "principles" books as well, but usually only at the end of the chapter on unemployment. An exploration of economists' reservations about the theory is useful—especially since our answers to these reservations allow an appreciation for why the theory does indeed offer both the best theoretical and the best empirical depiction of involuntary unemployment. Indeed as simple as the theory may be, because of these possible objections it was only developed in the early 1980s, and as we have seen it still has only limited popularity today.

This simplest theory of unemployment—that firms want to pay more for their workers than what is merely necessary to attract them—seems contrary to common sense. Why? Because it seems an odd notion that buyers of any good or service would ever pay more than necessary. But with efficiency wages employers are doing exactly that. They are paying more for their labor than needed merely to get their labor force to show up for work. In contrast it would make no sense to have a theory of the stock market or the wheat market in which buyers do not want to pay less for what they buy.

The efficiency wage theory further contradicts economists' theoretical intuitions because it violates their usual conceptual framework of how to set up a theoretical problem. The usual methodology of economics is to ask questions, first on the demand side of the market and then on the supply side. According to this protocol, regarding the purchase of labor one would first ask: who are the potential employers? And then, at any given wage, how much labor would they want? The answers to these queries yield the demand for labor. On the supply side, the traditional method first asks: who are the potential sellers of labor? And, at each wage, how much labor would they wish to supply? Equilibrium in this traditional view then occurs at the wage at which supply is equal to demand. There may be people who are disappointed that the wage is so low that they do not even seek employment. But in this standard view there is no such thing as involuntary unemployment. Like our friend and his house, everyone can sell their labor: they just have to be sufficiently flexible about the price they get for it, which is their wage.

But this theory does not describe the labor market as it actually exists. As we shall see, elementary statistics show precisely that most employers *do* willingly pay more for their labor than they have to. And thus the efficiency wage theory makes complete sense.

## Wages, Prices, and Efficiency Wages

Goods are much simpler commodities than labor. Unlike workers, who become unhappy if they think their wages are too low, goods are inanimate and emotionless. (And therefore there is even less reason why anyone would purchase a good above the lowest possible price than they would pay more than necessary for labor.) But when we think about it, we realize that even goods do not always sell at exactly the lowest possible price.

Indeed differences in the prices paid for the same good in the same city are often quite large. Some years ago three Harvard economists decided to see how much variation there was for thirty-nine closely specified commodities and services in the Boston area.[3] The items were as varied as a particular model of Raleigh ten-speed bicycle and a horoscope reading. There was considerable variation in the price for most of them. The bicycle had the least variation, with only an 11% difference between the maximum and the minimum price. But the median difference between maximum and minimum price for the exact same item in the Boston area for the thirty-nine commodities was 157%. The maximum price for a Denman seven-row style brush was almost seven times the minimum.[4] This study reminds us that while we often do search for the lowest price (sometimes aggressively so), we also often do not make our purchases at the cheapest store (sometimes knowingly so).

If there are significant differences in prices for the same good in the same city, it should then not come as much of a surprise that different firms pay different wages for what would seem to be exactly the same labor, even in the same city. Early evidence came from a striking table published by John Dunlop. Dunlop was one of that crusty breed of applied economists who want to know how the labor market *really* works. He was as much at home with union leaders as in the halls of Harvard (where in due course he became dean of the faculty). President Lyndon Johnson made him his secretary of labor. One of Dunlop's most influential articles showed the vast wage disparities among unionized drivers of different types of delivery trucks in the Boston area. For example, the union scale for "motor-truck drivers" in Boston in July 1951 was $1.20 per hour for those in wholesale laundry and almost double that, $2.25, for those involved in the delivery of magazines. Dunlop's table is reproduced here.

**TABLE 1**

Union Scale for Motor-Truck Drivers (Boston, July 1, 1951)[a]

| | |
|---|---|
| Magazine | $2.25 |
| Newspaper, day | $2.16 |
| Oil | $1.985 |
| Building construction | $1.85 |
| Paper handlers, newspaper | $1.832 |
| Beer, bottle and keg | $1.775 |
| Grocery, chain store | $1.679 |
| Meat packing house, 3–5 tons | $1.64 |
| Bakery, Hebrew | $1.595 |
| Wholesale | $1.57 |
| Rendering | $1.55 |
| Coal | $1.518 |
| Garbage disposal | $1.50 |
| General hauling | $1.50 |
| Food service, retail | $1.475 |
| Ice | $1.45 |
| Armored car | $1.405 |
| Carbonated beverage | $1.38 |
| Waste paper | $1.38 |
| Linen supply | $1.342 |
| Movers, piano and household | $1.30 |
| Scrap, iron and metal | $1.20 |
| Laundry, wholesale | $1.20 |

[a]From Dunlop (1957, p. 21). Original source: U.S. Bureau of Labor Statistics (1951, pp. 9–10).

These figures suggest a phenomenon that is in fact quite general: wages vary a great deal. And furthermore that variation only partly reflects differences in skill. We can begin to explore this question just by looking at how large the variation in wages actually is. A classic article on wage differentials by Chinhui Juhn, Kevin Murphy, and Brooks Pierce gives us some answers.[5] In 1988 for men age 25–65 there was more than a fourfold difference between the 90th percentile of weekly wages (10% of wages are higher) and the 10th percentile of wages (10% of wages are lower). Surprisingly few of these differences, it turns out, are explained by education and work experience, which are the leading causes of skill variation. If education and experience are held constant, there is still more than a threefold difference in pay between the 90th and the 10th percentiles of wages.[6]

These estimates of the variation in pay can be adjusted yet further to take into account differences in skill. Erica Groshen looked at wages in six different industries as workers moved from one establishment to another.[7] In that way she could discover how much of the wage could be ascribed to individual workers and how much could be ascribed to the luck of where they happened to work. She found that 50% of the variation in wages was explained not by the individual workers with their different skill levels but instead by their work establishment.[8] This finding seems to suggest robustly that indeed Dunlop's original conjecture was right: workers at the same skill level do receive very different wages.

There is a further reason, other than skill, for the observed wage variation. Firms with difficult working conditions might have to offer high wages to attract workers. One of us recently met a mining engineer at a zinc mine in Alaska above the Arctic Circle. He did not like the two-week stints that took him away from both his wife and his newborn daughter in Spokane, during which he lived in a dormitory. Nor was the winter to his liking. But he explained that the high wages at the mine made the job worthwhile. (He also reminded us that, since he had chosen to work as a mining engineer, almost any other job he might have would also be in some remote place, where conditions would be only slightly better.)

So varying skill level and work conditions are, of course, responsible for some of the wage variation we see. But they cannot be the full explanation. William Dickens and Lawrence Katz have shown that there is a high correlation between the pay in different industries by occupation. Thus, for example, those industries that pay more to the bosses also pay, on average, more to the secretaries. Similarly a study by Alan Krueger and Lawrence Summers shows that when workers move from industries with high pay to industries with low pay, they tend to take a wage cut; when they go in the opposite direction they tend to get a raise.[9] They also showed that workers seem to prefer working in the high-paying industries. They are less likely to leave such jobs voluntarily. Thus the quit rates from low-pay industries are higher than those from high-pay industries. This suggests that the wage differentials in the high-paying industries are more than what is just needed to attract workers to the jobs.

## *People Rarely Quit Their Jobs in Recessions*

We see the same behavior when we look at quits, not between different firms or industries, but over time. Krueger and Summers' workers with high-paying jobs apparently realize that they are lucky, since they are less likely to quit than workers with low-paying jobs.

We observe similar behavior over the business cycle. The efficiency wage theory of unemployment views high unemployment as due to a large gap between the wages that firms pay and the wages at which the supply and demand for labor are equal. Thus when unemployment is high the supply of labor considerably exceeds the demand for it. When unemployment is low there is only a small gap between the number of people who want jobs and those who get them. Thus we would expect that when unemployment is high relatively few people will quit their jobs. The employed deem themselves lucky.

Indeed the statistics show exactly such a relation—strongly so. Economics is full of all kinds of weak relations. The best economic models of national income or employment do only slightly better than the trivial prediction that tomorrow's income is today's income with a small adjustment for trend (that income is a "random walk" with trend). We have seen that even education and experience together explain relatively little of the variation in weekly wages. In contrast, however, when the unemployment rate rises quits invariably go down.[10] Indeed a simple relation between quits and unemployment explains three-quarters of the variation. When unemployment goes up by 1 percentage point, the monthly quit rate per hundred employees falls by 1.26.[11]

These changes in the quit rate suggest that unemployment is exactly caused by wages in excess of market clearing. That of course exactly corresponds to the predictions of efficiency wage theory. In its view, when unemployment goes up the gap between the supply of and demand for labor increases. Workers with jobs at existing wages realize that they are lucky. They see how they would fare elsewhere, and they are therefore highly reluctant to quit their jobs.

## Why Employers Really Pay More Than They Need To

There are two principal versions of the efficiency wage theory. Carl Shapiro and Joseph Stiglitz' theory of unemployment is based on the observation that firms cannot fully monitor their workers.[12] This gives workers a choice. They can work, or they can shirk. If they shirk they take a chance: if caught, they will be fired. Now Shapiro and Stiglitz have an insight: economies in which workers face such a choice will have unemployment in equilibrium. Why? If there were no unemployment and all firms paid the same wage, workers would have no incentive to put in effort. With no unemployment, a worker has nothing to lose if fired for shirking. She could, figuratively, just "walk across the street" and get a job exactly like her old one. So employers must give their workers something extra to keep them from shirking. According to Shapiro and Stiglitz that extra sweetener takes the form of extra wages, above those at which the supply of labor is just equal to the demand for it, at which every worker can instantaneously get a job. If all firms pay the extra wages, as they will in equilibrium, there will be unemployment.

This version of the efficiency wage theory is the most popular with economists. As presented by Shapiro and Stiglitz it is mathematically elegant. No one, either the firm or the workers, has any other motive than the cold economic calculus that economists think should be at the root of all economic behavior. Largely for that reason, the model also dovetails with what students of economics, especially graduate students, learn outside their macroeconomics class. This makes for a great class—as both of us know from experience. The students and the teacher end the lecture fully satisfied. The students have the epiphany that the mathematical methods they are learning with so much pain in their other courses can actually explain a real and pressing social problem. They can explain why there is unemployment.

We like this model of Shapiro and Stiglitz. There is some truth in it. After all, when unemployment falls, absenteeism (which is one form of shirking) rises.

But he who rides the tiger's back will end up inside. The appeal of this explanation for unemployment—that it depends only on cool economic motivation—is also its Achilles' heel. Why? Because economists who consider themselves yet smarter than Shapiro and Stiglitz have pointed out that if workers only care about money and how hard they work, employers could devise incentive schemes that are yet more profitable for themselves, and that do not result in wages in excess of market clearing. For example, Edward Lazear, who was a successor to Stiglitz as the chair of the Council of Economic Advisers, has shown that seniority rights give an alternative incentive to keep workers from shirking.[13] If you get caught shirking and have to find a new job, you lose all those privileges you may have earned from working at your job for so long. Perhaps yet more important, educated workers have a great deal to lose if they are fired and lose reputation. The returns from all that hard work in high school and college, not to say all that tuition money, are threatened. So while the Shapiro-Stiglitz version of efficiency wages may be popular among economists because it pictures employees and labor as having purely economic motivations, many macroeconomists are wary of it for that very same reason.

This brings us to our favorite theory of why firms pay wages so high that there is unemployment. The previous picture of the relation between employer and employee—that the worker works only for the pay, and also works as little as possible—seems to us too simple a view of the employee-employer relationship. Certainly in our view employees care about their pay. Certainly we also know that there are times when the employee would rather shirk than work. But we also view most employees as having a complicated relationship with their employers, in most cases a love-hate relationship. They wish their employers would pay them more. They wish their employers would have a higher opinion of their services. But at the same time they have some sense of duty to get the job done. That sense of duty will be modulated by the extent to which they feel they are being treated fairly by their employers. At one extreme, if they think they are being unfairly treated they will feel no sense of duty at all. They will do the least amount of work they can get away with. Yet worse, if they are angry they may even sabotage the operation. At the other extreme, if they sense they are being treated more than fairly (and their wage is the ultimate symbol of this treatment), they will fully buy into the goals of their employers.

According to tabulations from the General Social Survey the vast majority of workers indicated that they are loyal to their organizations, they share their values, they are proud to be working there, and they are satisfied with their jobs.[14] The wage then is not only an incentive. It is a symbol in the exchange between the employer and the employee.[15] The worker may decide whether to work or to shirk depending on the cost of doing so. But that decision is also based on whether or not she thinks she is being fairly treated.[16] Employers therefore have reason to pay a fair wage. And that fair wage will almost surely be so high as to provoke unemployment. The better the outside opportunities, or the lower the unemployment rate, the higher will be the fair wage that workers think their employer should pay them.

Of course most workplaces have many workers, and therefore the interaction between the worker and the employer is very complex. The employees form work groups and social groups that interact in many overlapping ways. But these complex interactions between workers, as well as between the worker and the employer, restrict still further the freedom of the employer to set wages freely and simply sit back to see who comes through the door to apply for jobs. In deciding on wages, the employer must always consider the effects of those wages on the current workforce.[17] Wages that are too low, and wages that are considered to be distributed unfairly according to the pecking orders of the workplace, undercut the willingness of employees to consider the tasks of the workplace their personal responsibilities.

This view of the labor market is at once simpler and also more complex than the traditional economic argument. It is more complex because we ascribe to the employee motives that are more realistic than those of the strictly economic model. It is simpler because we think that we can represent the wage as depending at least in part on what workers think would be fair, and those fair wages are almost always above the market clearing wage. They are also slow to change. It is an explanation for unemployment that seems to hit the sweet spot. It is simple and realistic, and it also fits the facts. In particular it explains easily and naturally why quits go up as unemployment falls.

This is a fundamental building block of the economy. If jobs are really what people care about, then a theory of the macroeconomy must begin by explaining the reason for the perennial job shortage. This theory gives us exactly that.

# NINE

# Why Is There a Trade-off between Inflation and Unemployment in the Long Run?

WE HAVE ALREADY SEEN that animal spirits are necessary to understand why the economy fluctuates so much, how the Fed controls the economy (insofar as it does), and why there is involuntary unemployment.[1] This chapter recounts a further instance in which the presence of animal spirits—and in particular the interaction between money illusion and fairness—makes a difference.

In Chapter 4, on money illusion, we discussed how Milton Friedman undermined one of the essential tenets of macroeconomics as it existed at the time. The earlier macroeconomists had believed that in normal times central banks could bring about higher employment and output if only they were willing to tolerate higher inflation. In contrast Friedman maintained that there was only one sustainable level of unemployment—he called it the natural rate—that would lead to neither accelerating inflation nor decelerating deflation. Natural rate theory is now economists' conventional wisdom. It is accepted by the vast majority of economists—but, as we shall see, we do not believe it to be true. And it has also been the justification for economic policy of great foolishness.

## Inflation Responds to Unemployment

Looking back, the 1950s and the 1960s before the Vietnam escalation were simpler times. The counterpart of *Leave It to Beaver* for the field of economics was Paul Samuelson's textbook, *Economics*.[2] Samuelson was far and away the leading economist of his time. He was not only the author of the leading textbook but also the leading academic economist and the *eminence grise* behind the economic policies of the Kennedy administration. He believed that economic science had solved the great problems of recession and depression. Monetary policy might be ineffective in getting us out of a slump, if it was a really bad one. But then fiscal policy could get us out of almost any hole. And, as an added dividend, both monetary and fiscal policy could even be fine-tuned to engineer permanently low unemployment and permanently high output. There was a cost for lower unemployment, and up to a point it was well worth paying. Employment should be expanded until its costs, in terms of added inflation, just balanced the benefits. Since the trade-off between inflation and unemployment—the Phillips curve—showed inflation as escalating to high levels only at very low levels of unemployment, that meant that employment could be permanently high.

These views were eventually challenged, especially by Milton Friedman, who argued that they were based on a view of the Phillips curve that was flawed by money illusion. In a proper Phillips curve, said Friedman, wages will shift with the expected rate of inflation. At a given level of unemployment, if both employers and employees expect inflation to be 3%, for example, rather than zero, wage increases will be exactly 3% higher. A Phillips curve that incorporates this reaction of inflation to expectations does not give a long-run trade-off between the level of inflation and the level of unemployment. Unemployment lower than the natural rate does not yield steady inflation. Instead it yields accelerating inflation. And unemployment above the natural rate yields accelerating deflation.

## Going Too Far

Friedman and Samuelson were rivals. Samuelson acknowledged that Friedman often did have a point, but he felt that he took such points too far. He remarked that Friedman was like the boy who knew how to spell *banana* but did not know when to stop. Of course, regarding the role of inflationary expectations Friedman was partially right. It is only common sense, especially when inflation is very high, that both wage bargains and price setting will incorporate inflationary expectations. He was teaching us how to spell *banana*.

But Samuelson was also right. Friedman did not know when to stop. In the absence of any money illusion at all, natural rate theory will hold. But, just as we think it was naïve to believe that wage bargains and price setting take no account of inflationary expectations, we also think it is naïve to presume that there is no money illusion at all. It seems unlikely to us that there is not some money illusion, somewhere in the economy. And if there is, will this money illusion not induce some long-run trade-off between inflation and unemployment, even if it is a diminished one? That is the subject of this chapter.

## Money Illusion Affects Wages

Natural rate theory is appealing because it seems so general. It has only one key assumption—that people do not have money illusion. This assumption seems highly reasonable, at least as long as we do not think about it too carefully. But we do not need to look very long to find an obvious example of money illusion, and therefore an obvious violation of the basic, fundamental, supposedly universal assumption of natural rate theory. People think money wage cuts are unfair. And therefore wages are downwardly rigid.

We probably all have our own example of such resistance to money wage cuts, which brings the reality home to us personally. But there is also statistical evidence. Downward money wage rigidity can be easily detected from data on wage changes. All one needs to do is look at how often wage changes of different magnitudes occur. Suppose we see that wage changes bunch at exactly zero, and there are many more wage changes just above zero than just below zero. Then we can conclude that employers stop to think before they give their workers wage cuts. And that is exactly what we see. Careful studies have documented such wage stickiness in Australia, Canada, Germany, Japan, Mexico, New Zealand, Switzerland, the United States, and the United Kingdom.[3] Union wage contracts rarely provide for wage cuts. In the United States (except in the recession year of 1982) unions have rarely accepted wage cuts. Some Canadian data are especially dramatic: in the severe Canadian recession of 1992–94, Canadian inflation fell to 1.2% and unemployment rose to an average of 11.0%. Yet 47% of union contracts without inflation adjustments had first-year wage freezes. And only 5.7% had wage cuts.[4]

Yale's Truman Bewley gives qualitative evidence on money wage stickiness. He conducted an intensive interview study of New Englanders involved in the wage setting process.[5] He asked why money wages had not declined in the New England recession of 1991–92. With the high unemployment of the time, any worker who might quit in response to a wage cut could have been replaced easily and rapidly. But Bewley found that employers were loath to reduce wages during the recession. In the employers' opinions workers would view such wage cuts as unfair. They would reduce their commitment to their jobs. Furthermore, when the economy revived they would still be angry and thus more likely to quit. Bewley found a few firms that made such cuts, but only after considerable agonizing and also after continued losses.[6] In these rare instances workers accepted wage cuts as fair. They were a last resort, necessary to save their jobs.[7]

In the face of the irrefutable evidence, macroeconomists have agreed —although often reluctantly—that yes, maybe there is such a thing as money wage rigidity. But for the most part they have also viewed it as too minor a factor to affect seriously the conclusions of natural rate theory. One of us (Akerlof) has studied, with William Dickens and George Perry, how large that impact would be. We performed simulations, with realistically chosen parameters, of the impact on unemployment of going from 2% to zero inflation. In the benchmark simulation a permanent reduction of inflation from 2% to zero increases the unemployment rate permanently by 1.5%.[8] We obtained roughly similar results from econometric estimations and in hundreds of other simulations, in which the parameters were chosen randomly over a reasonable range.

A back-of-the-envelope calculation shows why these results occurred, and so robustly. If workers resist wage cuts, when inflation is lower their wages will be higher (as long as unemployment remains the same). In our benchmark simulation they would be higher by about 0.75% if inflation were zero rather than 2%. Other methods of calculation yield similar results.[9] The 0.75% impact on wages translates into an increase in unemployment of 1.5 percentage points. How do we know? There is a rule of thumb that comes from the estimation of Phillips curves: it takes a 2-percentage-point increase in unemployment to reduce inflation by 1%. Therefore to neutralize the 0.75% cost increase to the firms, unemployment must rise by 1.5 percentage points.[10]

## The Long Term

If correct, natural rate theory has major consequences for monetary policy. If it is correct, there is little loss from very low inflation targets. Long-term price stability, with an inflation target of zero, can be achieved with no permanent ill consequences. On the average, over a long period of time unemployment will be unaffected by the choice of inflation target.

If, on the other hand, natural rate theory is not true, so that there is a long-term trade-off between inflation and unemployment, a zero inflation target is poor economic policy. The calculated increase in the unemployment rate of 1.5% would make a significant difference. In human terms, for the United States such an increase would render jobless 2.3 million people—more than all the men, women, and children within the city boundaries of Boston, Detroit, and San Francisco combined. It would entail a loss of GDP of more than $400 billion per year.[11]

## *Money Wages as a Telltale*

It is not just these simulations and calculations that make sticky money wages a Pandora's box for natural rate theorists. Natural rate theory rests on an a priori, almost philosophical argument—that people do not have money illusion. That argument would seem to be a much better one if it were not so easy to point to the money wage stickiness counterexample. As Bewley's interviews indicate, money wage rigidity occurs fundamentally because workers, and also employers, think that money wage cuts are unfair. If money illusion enters considerations of fairness in one form (employers should not give wage cuts), it should not come as a great surprise if it enters in other ways as well.

One of us (Shiller) has carried out interview studies regarding how economists and the general public variously view inflation. The two groups answer questions about inflation very differently. Four of the many questions asked in the interviews are particularly illustrative of their sharp differences.

The answers given by the economists can all be explained easily by natural rate theory, as we described, with the added assumption that the inflation is generated by a central bank that is steadily increasing its money supply. In this case inflation will have little effect on the economy, and there will be little effect on the buying power of wages. Thus only 12% of economists, in contrast to 77% of the public, say that their greatest gripe about inflation is that it makes them poorer. Economists endorse strongly the notion that "competition among employers will cause my pay to be bid up. I could get outside offers from other employers, and so, to keep me my employer will have to raise my pay too." Of economists 60%, compared to only 11% of the public, think that describes "how general inflation on wages and salary relates to [my own situation]."

Economists and the general public also differ markedly on how much they worry about inflation. Only 20% of economists, in contrast to 86% of the general public, agree with the following statement: "When I see projections about how many times more a college education will cost or how many times more the cost of living will be in coming decades I feel a sense of uneasiness: these inflation projections really make me worry that my own income will not rise as much as such costs will." The public and economists also have different reactions to the statement "I think that if my pay went up I would feel more satisfaction in my job, more sense of fulfillment, even if prices went up as much." Fully 90% of economists, in contrast to 41% of the public, disagree with this statement.[12]

While the economists' reactions can be explained in terms of natural rate theory, the public's reaction also seems to have a simple, easy interpretation. They view wage increases as occurring because their boss has wanted to reward them. They do not understand that their wage increases at least partly reflect the pass-through that occurs because of inflation. This easily explains why they think inflation will make them poorer, why they do not think that competition or the boss's sense of fairness will result in an inflation adjustment, why they are worried about how they will pay for their children's college education in the future, and also why they should be satisfied if their wage increases do manage to keep up with inflation.

## A Further Reason for a Trade-off

To confirm that workers have such money illusion, we can look at how the relation between inflation and unemployment changes through time. This evidence suggests another reason (other than aversion to wage cuts) for a trade-off between inflation and unemployment. If workers genuinely think that they should get extra satisfaction if their wages keep up with inflation, then at higher levels of inflation employers will need to pay their workers less in terms of buying power to keep them equally satisfied.[13] With such a favorable shock to employers, firms should be able to save on labor costs. As inflation rises the sustainable level of unemployment should go down.

There is some evidence that wage bargains do have such money illusion at low levels of inflation, but then as inflation increases they increasingly take into account inflationary expectations.[14] It seems that when expected inflation is close to zero it is not added into wage increases. But when inflation is high, expected inflation is added one-for-one into wage increases.[15] This is consistent with a view that when inflation is low, employees do not think their employer must add in an inflation adjustment to be fair. But when inflation becomes higher, they think their employer should do so.[16]

We should admit that it is hard to estimate the way Phillips curves depend on inflationary expectations. But economic policy must be made in an environment in which there are doubts. Our problem with natural rate theory is not with the theory itself. We think that it does offer a correct insight: that wage and price setting will both be affected by inflationary expectations. But we are highly skeptical that these inflationary expectations always, exactly, and invariably affect wage setting and price setting one for one. Our simulations and estimations indicate that, especially at low inflation, there should be great skepticism.

Indeed this takes one of the authors (Akerlof) back to a memory from more than four decades ago. He was taking a class on monetary theory given by Paul Samuelson at MIT in the spring of 1964. Samuelson related that a member of President Dwight Eisenhower's Council of Economic Advisers, Raymond Saulnier, had proposed the following idea. It might be possible to attain low unemployment in the short run, at the cost of high inflation. But as that inflation occurred, expectations about inflation would increase, so that maintenance of the low level of unemployment would entail higher inflation. That argument should sound familiar—although in this class it was related by Paul Samuelson, not Milton Friedman.

But the ending of the argument does not remind us of Milton Friedman. Samuelson concluded that although this was an intriguing idea, it might not be indicative of the way the world worked. And if the monetary and fiscal authorities acted on it, and it was not true, we would have permanently higher unemployment. He was thinking of the extra unemployment—comparable in size to the combined populations of Boston, Detroit, and San Francisco—of which we spoke earlier. We find that reasoning just as compelling today as we did over forty years ago.

There are many reasons why natural rate theory may not hold. Wage setting and price setting involve all kinds of considerations of money illusion and fairness. These considerations are contrary to the assumptions of natural rate theory. We should not accept it uncritically.

## Going North

We need only go north to Canada to see a case in which Samuelson's fears came true. Canada provides an instance in which denial of a trade-off between inflation and unemployment not only mattered but mattered greatly. The U.S. economy was roaring in the 1990s. But up north our neighbors were experiencing the "Great Canadian Slump," as it was named by the distinguished Canadian economist Pierre Fortin.[17] In 1996 Fortin compared this slump to that seen in the Great Depression of the 1930s. His measure of the two recessions was the cumulative decline from peak of the employed fraction of the working-age population. As of 1996 the Canadian economy had already suffered 30% of the cumulative decline seen in the Great Depression.[18] The Depression was not all that much worse, said Fortin in 1996. It had been deeper, and it had lasted longer. He could not have known then that it would take four more years for the economy to recover.

Where does Fortin place the blame? He makes a long list of all the possible causes of the recession, such as trade, fiscal policy, minimum wages, and restrictive monetary policy. He rapidly dismisses all of these but one: the restrictive monetary policy of the Bank of Canada. In 1987 the Canadians chose a new governor of their central bank, John Crow. Crow, born in London, had graduated from Oxford, worked at the International Monetary Fund for twelve years, and then transferred to the research department of the Bank of Canada. There he rose through the ranks: deputy chief of the research department, chief of the research department, adviser to the governor, and deputy governor. When Crow took over as governor, inflation was 4.8%. He took the bank's mandate to maintain price stability seriously. Crow was a firm believer in both natural rate theory and the ability of the central bank to bring inflation down. And he was successful in this task. In 1993 inflation fell to 1.8%—but at a terrible cost.[19] Unemployment reached levels not seen since the Great Depression. In 1992 it stood at 11.3%.[20]

Yet Crow was proud of what he had accomplished. In his view the costs of lowering inflation were temporary, but the benefits, because of the changed expectations, would be permanent. Crow defended his policies vigorously, to the point that the Canadian press described him as "combative" and "abrasive."[21] In 1994 he was replaced by Gordon Thiessen, who, in contrast, was unfailingly polite. But—true to his spots as a central banker who had learned his trade in the same Bank of Canada shop as Crow—Thiessen continued the very low inflation targets of the previous regime, for seven more years.

This story should serve as a warning. Too much faith is placed today in natural rate theory. For the past quarter century the United States has had a sensible monetary policy, which carefully balances the twin goals of price stability and full employment. But we are in great fear of ideologues on a future Federal Reserve Board who will take natural rate theory as more than a useful parable, consider it their duty to define price stability as zero inflation, and see no great cost in achieving it. It would take only a handful of believers in this theory—which is only partially right—to bring about the "Great United States Slump."

Indeed our concern regarding this future possibility was one of the primary motivations for writing this book. If and when such an ideological takeover occurs, it is our hope that the chair of the Fed and her board will be more like Crow than like his successor, Thiessen. Let's hope that she is not unfailingly polite.

# TEN

# Why Is Saving for the Future So Arbitrary?

WE CAN SEE how much the all-important decision on how much to save for the future is affected by animal spirits if we have a discussion with students in one of our classes on how much they plan to save over their lives.

One of us (Shiller) has been asking them: "Why not save 30% or more of your income?" This would seem to be a shocking question, given that the average person in the United States saves just about 0% of personal income. But surprisingly there is little reaction to the question, and our students generally reflect that such savings would not entail much sacrifice. They observe that their consumption would correspond to their total earnings had they graduated just fifteen or twenty years ago, since real income has been growing at about 2% a year, and they see people pretty much as well off then as now.

The bottom line is that they really just don't seem to care how much they save, over a wide range. This leaves a huge scope for animal spirits to intervene to determine the level of saving. And determining the level of saving is fundamental for the economy. In the short run, an exogenous increase in the desired saving rate of just a couple of percentage points may be enough to tip the economy into recession, as indeed seems to be happening in the current financial crisis. In the long run it could make a huge difference in the level of accumulated wealth. In that sense the effect of animal spirits on saving is the place to look to understand our economic fluctuations and prospects for growth.

## Long-Term Consequences and the Power of Compound Interest

There are many ways to become rich. Invent the fax machine. Gain a near-monopoly on the operating system for most of the world's computers. Buy a gold mine that has just gone out of production because its operating costs were too high, then wait until the price of gold has reached $1,000 an ounce. Be the nation's best surgeon. Become a trial lawyer and win a huge class action suit. Inherit a fortune. Some people do these things. But for most people these routes to a fortune, or others like them, are flukes of luck.

But there has been one way, at least in the past, in which almost everyone could become at least moderately rich. Save a lot of money. Invest it for the long term in the stock market, where the rate of return after adjustment for inflation has been 7% per year.

Consider the saving program of Christina and David, who are each laying away a nest egg of $10,000 a year for ten years, while they are still in their twenties. They put it into the stock market for their retirement years. Even if they do not lay away a single additional dime for the remainder of their working careers, they will still be comfortable in retirement. If the stock market behaves as it has on average for the past century, at age 65 they will have more than $3 million. Of course if they keep their savings up beyond the age of 30, they will be much richer.

The thought experiment that we performed about Christina and David underlies the key to the economics of the great conservative economist Martin Feldstein. Feldstein's personal cause is to get individuals, and whole countries, to save more. Thanks to the wonders of compound interest, even moderate sacrifices, in the form of increased savings, especially when one is young, will make a great difference when one retires.

Indeed one of the authors is a direct beneficiary of Feldstein's wisdom. Back in the 1970s, when assistant professors arrived at Harvard the university immediately began contributions to their retirement accounts. But no interest accrued in these accounts until the beneficiaries filled out the forms that declared how this money should be invested. This was a minor task that took about half an hour. But Feldstein observed that most assistant professors filled out their forms only five or six years later, when they were leaving Harvard (only a few assistant professors get tenure). Akerlof's wife, Janet Yellen, was an assistant professor at Harvard in the 1970s. As a result of just the accrual of interest over those years, because she heeded Feldstein's advice, we are now $15,000 richer. That is not a bad return for half an hour's work. It also provides a lesson in the power of compound interest.

But when we discuss the power of compound interest with our young students, their eyes glaze over. They see that they might live a much better retirement, but they find it hard to imagine what the difference in retirement would be. They cannot visualize their older selves well enough to know what they will want to spend.

If they saved a great deal, they could bequeath a fortune to their grandchildren, but they wonder aloud what they would do with all that money. Would their grandchildren have great opportunity from such wealth, or would they find themselves spoiled and deprived of purpose by such saving? Would their grandchildren view them as heroes or not think about them at all?

Our students seem never to have thought about the long-term possibilities that the power of compound interest creates for them, and when we confront them with the facts, they are unable to latch onto this question and come up with a definitive answer about how much they would save. It is as if they cannot attach any clear meaning to the ultimate purpose of saving, of providing for the future. Actually engaging young people in such discussions shows the absurdity of modeling their behavior as calculatingly balancing the benefits of current versus future spending, as economic theorists say they do.

If they are having a hard time focusing on these fundamental economic costs and benefits of saving, they will look elsewhere for indications of how much they should save—to their animal spirits. These indications may be tied up with such elements of our theory of animal spirits as confidence, trust, various alarms and fears, and the stories people tell about our lives today and in the future.

## The Role of Psychological Framing

It should be no surprise then that the rate of saving is highly variable across countries. Some countries have net saving of a third of their national incomes; some have negative net saving. The personal saving rate in the United States was about 10% in the early 1980s. Recently it has been negative. Consumer bankruptcy filings have soared in the United States just as the saving rate has plunged, and in apparent connection with the declining saving rate. The rate of saving also varies across individuals. There are vast individual differences in retirement wealth, substantially caused by enormous differences in the propensity to save.[1]

This variation in saving is a puzzle for the current standard economic theory of saving. According to this theory people trade off savings and consumption to achieve an exact balance. At each time in their lives they balance the benefit from spending an extra dollar today with the benefit of deferring that expenditure. In that case they receive the expected extra benefit of spending that money with accrued interest in the future. We shall see that such a theory is useful in some contexts, as it does reflect some of the real motivations for saving. But we shall also see that this theory flies in the face of many facts about saving. In particular it completely sidesteps the variability puzzle. Why is saving so sensitive to small cues and to small institutional changes? To understand that we must add considerably to the existing theory.

In our view saving is partially a result of standard fundamental economic motivations. People want a nest egg for retirement. They want to leave a bequest to their children, or perhaps even to their church or to their alma mater. But the standard theory does not explain many of the detailed facts about saving. To comprehend these detailed observations, we must understand that saving depends upon the stories we tell about our lives and our future, that is, on how the decision to consume or to save is framed. That framing determines how people answer the question "Should I be saving this extra dollar (or this extra yuan or this extra dinar), or should I be consuming it?" The stories and their framing keep changing, bringing an element of animal spirits into the saving decision.

This framing has its effect at many different levels. We see it at the shopping mall, where people draw out their credit cards and unthinkingly make purchases that on closer reflection they would have rejected or deferred. We see it in economic experiments, specially constructed to reveal exactly how changing mental frames affect people's decisions to spend or to save. We see it in the differences in spending across countries, for example, between the United States and China. We see it as well in the trend toward ever more personal bankruptcies in the United States, which are less and less framed as personal failures.[2]

The importance of this framing seems to have a common explanation. People have a hard time knowing what to save. They have a hard time envisioning themselves in a distant future and envisioning how much they will or will not need to consume. They may even think that such thoughts are inappropriate given who they are. Thus they are very susceptible to different cues in making their saving decisions—to cues that tell them how much they should be consuming and how much they should be saving. These cues come from the behavior and the views of others. For example, such behaviors may indicate how much I should spend or how much I should save as a patriotic American, or as a patriotic Chinese. These cues also come from perceptions of how people of their age and environment should be thinking. For example, in America saving is supposed to be mainly for retirement, and it is considered odd if a young person should even be thinking about that distant future. Or the cues may be more immediate, such as on the one hand credit cards, which seem to say "Spend me! Spend me!", or on the other hand the default contribution or allocation provisions for retirement programs, which seem to be indications of the recommended amount to save and how to save it.

It is this deer-in-the-headlights aspect to people's approach to the saving decision, coupled with their susceptibility to cues, that causes the variability in saving. Small wonder that many policy recommendations —which are based on the standard theory of saving, which is in turn based on the economic fundamentals, and therefore has nothing to say about these cues—are very often simply wrong.

An experiment by economists Hersh Shefrin and Richard Thaler demonstrates just such a tendency to grasp at straws. They asked experimental subjects how much they would likely spend out of an unexpected, one-time-only windfall of $2,400 in each of three possible situational framings.

In the first framing the additional income is a new bonus at work that will be paid out at a rate of $200 a month over the next year. The median subject said that $100 a month would be consumed, for a total of $1,200. The second framing was additional income received as a single lump sum of $2,400 this month. The median respondent said that $400 would be spent immediately, and then $35 a month for the next eleven months, so only a total of $785 would be spent. The third framing was an inheritance of $2,400 to be placed in an interest-bearing account for five years; at the end of that period the subject would receive the $2,400 plus all the interest (so that the present value of the inheritance remains $2,400). Subjects' median response was that *none* of the inheritance would be spent this year.[3]

Rational economic theory would imply that the subjects would spend the same portion of the extra money in all three framings. Shefrin and Thaler interpreted these results as confirming that people behave as if they put different kinds of income or wealth into different "mental accounts"—in this case current income, asset, and future income accounts—and view these accounts with such sharply different psychology that they spend very differently from each of them. How much they wish to spend depends crucially on how they frame the question "How much should I save?"

Generalizing from these results, it is clear that context and point of view are crucially important in determining saving. Indeed thinking about mental frames allows us to guess what is on the minds of both our students and the Harvard assistant professors. The reaction of both to saving reflects their current views regarding who they think they should be. Consider the newly arrived Harvard assistant professor. She is rightly proud of (at last!) finishing her Ph.D. And here she is at Harvard no less—the pinnacle of world universities. Her mind will be foremost on living up to the expectations that have brought her to Harvard—not on filling out a form that relates, of all things, to her retirement, far in the future. Our students have similar thoughts in the backs of their minds. Their thoughts are on glamorous ways they can make their way in the world. In their current frame of mind there is something wrong with thinking about their rate of saving. It is inappropriate for them to be contemplating retirement before their careers have even begun.

Other findings confirm the fickleness of saving decisions, and also their sensitivity to any cue regarding how much income should be saved. Thaler and Shlomo Benartzi have devised a saving plan, which they call Save More Tomorrow, to overcome workers' tendency to procrastinate. They have even put it into practice. Employees were invited to join a savings plan. They could elect in advance a fraction of their current wages and salaries, and also a potentially different fraction of all future wage and salary increases, to be set aside for savings. Thaler and Benartzi analyzed in detail the effects of the program at a midsize manufacturing firm. Even this minimal prodding resulted in large changes in savings. Workers chose relatively modest rates of saving out of current income. But they committed to save large fractions of future wage and salary increases. Within a short period of time the average saving rate had doubled.[4]

Another observation indicates yet again the relation between contributions and the framing of the saving decision. Largely at the behest of behavioral economists, the regulations regarding tax-advantaged 401(k) savings plans were changed in 1998. At that time the U.S. Congress permitted firms to automatically enroll employees in these savings plans at a default level, which the workers could override by filling out a form. Since then U.S. companies have increasingly adopted the practice for their employees. With such automatic enrollment, workers are much quicker to enroll, so that plan participation increases from around 75% of eligible employees to between 85% and 95%.[5] Most notably, most workers maintain their contributions exactly at the default level.[6] It is as if they do not know how much they should be saving. They let the default option determine what they should do.

Anna Maria Lusardi and Olivia Mitchell did a study that indicates how little overt planning goes into the saving decision. Since so little planning is involved, it should not be surprising that saving will be so very sensitive to indications of what people should or should not do. Lusardi and Mitchell added a module on retirement planning to the U.S. Health and Retirement Survey, which randomly samples Americans over the age of 50. Remarkably, considering that all these folks were already that old—indeed most of them were already retired—only 31% said that they or their spouse had ever tried to make such a plan.[7] And of that 31%, only 58% said they had developed one.[8] We find it truly remarkable that so few people—especially older ones—had taken the time and trouble to spend the hour or so needed to make a plan for how they would be supported for a good portion of their adult lives. After all, retirement typically lasts a long time. According to current life tables, a man age 50 has a 48% chance of living to be 80. A 50-year-old woman has a 62% chance of living another thirty years. It is fairly common for women to live to be 90 (26% do so).[9]

## *Why Conventional Theories of Saving Have It Wrong*

All of these facts—the seemingly haphazard nature of saving, the failure to save, the sensitivity of saving to framing—are remarkable for their deviation from what economists currently say about the saving decision.

Keynes thought that most people put little thought into how much they will save. In his view they merely react automatically to the changes in their incomes: "men are disposed, as a rule and on the average, to increase their consumption as their income increases, but not by as much as the increase in their incomes."[10] There is no contradiction between this view of consumption and the variability puzzle, which is the focus of this chapter. Indeed Keynes' careful insertion of the phrase "as a rule and on the average" seems to be exactly acknowledging the lack of precision we ascribe to the saving decision. But after Keynes, economists' views of consumption began to harden, and the assumption that savings is the result of rational optimizing decisions gradually crept back into economics. Economists were looking for a more precise model upon which to base their econometric work. From the emerging theory of optimal control and dynamic programming, they developed the notion that individuals exactly balance the extra benefits from spending at different dates. This is now the fundamental paradigm of research, not only in macroeconomics but in many other branches of economics as well.[11]

Of course saving does occur because people have economic motivation for it. A theory that takes account of such motivation, and nothing else, does in fact—correctly and for the right reasons—predict one of the most easily observed aspects of consumption. This is its behavior over the life cycle.[12] This theory correctly predicts that most people in the United States and elsewhere on average tend to save when they are young, build up a nest egg, and then dissipate it when they grow older. Even for the sloppy planners who are the subject of this chapter this is not a surprising finding. Even savers who are sloppy in their planning have *some* rationality behind what they do, and that should be sufficient to explain these patterns. But the standard theory seems to say almost nothing about why saving is so variable. In some important way it must be either incomplete or imprecise.

Remarkably too—because the standard economic framework assumes that saving decisions are optimal—it cannot be used to analyze some of the questions that most concern us about saving. If, by assumption, people's decisions regarding saving are optimal, then whatever happens, they must be saving exactly the right amount. But that, of course, has assumed away the problem. According to the picture that we have painted, people do not think carefully about their saving behavior. Instead saving is largely cued by different institutional and mental frames. And on average, as a result, most people undersave. That makes them vulnerable in old age.

Undersaving is, of course, the popular conception in most advanced countries. In one U.S. survey 76% of respondents reported that they themselves undersave. Another survey asked two questions: "How much do you save?" and "How much do you think you should save?" The approximately 10% difference (relative to income) in the replies to these two questions indicates that people think they should be saving a great deal more.[13] To compensate for this failure, the governments of most developed countries heavily support the elderly in retirement. In addition a large number of employers require and subsidize the pension contributions of their employees. Many forms of saving receive tax advantages. Yet even with these legs up the common wisdom is that the financial assets of most households still fall considerably short of what they need to maintain their consumption in retirement.[14]

Indeed these questions are often at the core of national politics. The Bush administration did not encounter much resistance to its significant proposals until it tried to privatize Social Security. Here, for the first time, the public resisted. Josepha Q. Public may not be a good financial planner, but she is at least generally aware of how dependent she will be on Social Security in her old age. The Brookings Institution's Gary Burtless made a study of exactly how dependent she will be.[15] He divided the population age 65 and over into quintiles (twenty percentile groups) by income. In each of the bottom four quintiles (from the 0th to the 80th percentile) more than half of nonwage income came from Social Security, and overwhelmingly so in the bottom three quintiles. This dependence of the vast majority of the population on Social Security explains popular reaction to the administration's proposals for privatization, and also the popularity of Social Security as a program. People depend on it because their own retirement savings are so scant.

One of the authors (Akerlof) adds a personal footnote. He was on a panel of economic advisers (a minor one) to the Kerry campaign in 2004. Up until the elections we had a conference call every two weeks. From the very first to the very last of these calls, Akerlof asserted that Kerry should affirm his support for maintaining Social Security in its current form. Toward the end, Austan Goolsbee (who is now a leading adviser to President Barack Obama) would joke, "And now we will hear from George, who will say that Kerry should demagogue the Social Security issue." Kerry held his fire in denouncing Bush's privatization proposal because he could not devise a plan that would preserve current benefit formulas without any outside infusion of funds. We understood that problem then, but we thought that it was a minor one. Estimates from the Brookings Institution say that preservation of Social Security at current levels would entail expenditure of about 2% of taxable earnings.[16] We thought then, and we still think now, that Kerry's mistake cost him the election.

## Saving and the Wealth of Nations

We have been talking so far about personal decisions to save, why saving varies, and how important it is to people's welfare in retirement. But there has long been another theme regarding savings. There are vast differences in the wealth of nations. In per capita terms there is more than a 200-fold difference between per capita income from the richest countries to the poorest. Indeed if we include Luxembourg and Burundi it is closer to a 1,000-fold difference.[17] Income and wealth depend upon countries' freedom to trade, the skills of their people, their geography, their current and past history of wars, their political and legal institutions. Most recently economists have emphasized the role of technical change as the major determinant of economic growth. But the classical economists, such as Adam Smith, emphasized the capital accumulation that comes from saving.

Even today some countries, particularly in East Asia, have taken Smith seriously. They have adopted the strategy of saving their way out of poverty.[18] The most prominent of these is Singapore. In 1955 it started the Central Provident Fund (CPF). Like the Save More Tomorrow program of Thaler and Benartzi—but in this case with the choices made by the government. Initially it required employees and employers each to contribute 5% of employees' wage income to the fund, but then contribution rates were rapidly increased. They were steadily raised until 1983, when employer and employee were required to give 25% each (a total of 50%!). The contribution rates follow a complicated schedule, but even today high-wage employees age 25–50 pay 34.5% and their employers pay 20%.[19] The system has not been "pay-as-you-go," and the sums collected have been really invested. Largely because of the CPF, the gross national saving rate of Singapore has been in the vicinity of 50% for decades.[20]

The author of the plan, Lee Kuan Yew, the longtime prime minister of Singapore, may be one of the most important economic thinkers of the twentieth century. His high-saving economy became a model for China, which has copied Singapore's saving achievement and has now been achieving significant economic growth for decades. The differences in savings between China and the United States, which are at opposite ends of the saving spectrum, will illustrate why there is so much variation across countries in saving behavior. Not surprisingly, savers in the two countries have very different attitudes toward spending and saving.

China's rate of saving is one of the highest in the world, surpassed recently only by Singapore and Malaysia. China owes much of its miraculous economic success since the early 1980s to this high saving.[21] Chinese total gross (inclusive of depreciation) saving, including personal saving (saving by individuals), corporate saving (saving by companies), and government saving (saving by the government in the form of a surplus of taxes over expenditures), together, has in recent years approached half of GDP. Chinese gross *personal* saving was over 20% of GDP in the 1990s, and is nearly as high today.

The governments of both the United States and China have wanted to promote personal saving for many decades. Since the early 1950s the United States has promoted saving with special tax incentives, such as individual retirement accounts, 401(k) and 403(b) plans, and savings bonds campaigns.

In Communist China, where there was no income tax, efforts to spur saving took the form of propaganda campaigns. Today people collect the old propaganda posters. A 1953 poster shows a group of happy, smiling workers turning in cash for government bonds at the People's Bank of China. A 1990 poster shows a smiling Lei Feng, a young, handsome, traditional hero, writing the word *save* on a money box. In the 1990s big red banners were hung in the streets: "Saving is glorious." These campaigns, which made saving everyone's patriotic duty, set the stage for today's high saving rates.

The modern economic history of China begins in 1978, two years after the death of Chairman Mao Zedong. In a celebrated speech at the third plenum of the Eleventh Party Congress, Vice Premier Deng Xiaoping made it clear that the government would support private investment in China. The Chinese economic miracle had begun.

Some small Chinese villages, such as Huaxi and Liutuan, made spectacularly successful investments in village enterprises starting in the late 1970s. Renowned for their success, they became models throughout China. In these villages saving, in the form of labor or money contributed to the village enterprise, was practically demanded by the village elders.

We sent one of our students, Andy Di Wu, to the village of Liutuan to interview the mayor, Shao Changzue.[22] We wanted to know how the leaders encouraged people to make such sacrifices to promote the village business. Shao had led the village for decades, through its transition from a poor socialist community to a model of parsimony and entrepreneurship for all of China.

Shao had initially provided the model for Liutuan by starting his own illegal metal molding shop there in 1972. After the reforms had made it legal, he gave it to the village in 1982. The villagers became shareholders in the enterprise. Andy asked him why he gave the already highly valuable enterprise to the village. The mayor answered: "There are several reasons for that. The most important reason is that I don't want to appear conspicuous in front of the villagers. I will feel bad if they are so poor while I have a lot of things. I am the kind of person who wants to appear good in front of the villagers. I just can't have a better living when everyone else is poor."

Andy had noticed that there was a BMW 765 parked outside his house, and he asked the mayor to explain how the car was consistent with this view. He replied: "The fact is I got that car for my son. In addition, we can say that many of the villagers can afford cars like that BMW. They just didn't buy it. We old people don't really like to buy fancy stuff and it's the young generation like you who want fancy cars and fancy clothes. We are still influenced by the old Lei Feng example of frugality and struggle against harsh conditions."

Andy asked him if he had made any appeal to patriotism or collectivism to get the villagers to contribute to the enterprise, and the mayor answered: "Yes indeed. I basically used three kinds of arguments. First, the country has been changing. Deng Xiaoping has opened the country up and what we would be doing would change the country and make it a better place. Secondly, I told them that the village business is good for the village itself and was good for everybody. Thirdly, I told them that I managed this business secretly for ten years and I knew how it worked, so my managerial skills could be trusted." "Did they trust you?" "They did. I was very grateful that they were trusting. The people of Liutuan are good people. They love their country and their village and are willing to do anything to make it a better place."

From these beginnings, and from the inspiration of villages like Liutuan, a national story began to grip the imagination of the people of China, a story of individual effort and sacrifice. This effort and sacrifice were born of personal initiative, but they were also motivated by a common patriotic vision for the future of China. There was a sense of a major new historic epoch beginning, which would eventually propel China once again to the pinnacle of human achievement. China would return to its place in centuries past. Each individual would gain in self-esteem by making her own contribution. For the time being, there is no shame in being poor in China, since that is viewed as a transitional state. Stories of struggle and sacrifice will one day be told with pleasure to grandchildren.

## The Shopping Mall and the Credit Card

In the United States, we see something quite different. The American icons of the shopping mall and the credit card are suggestive of our lax attitudes toward saving—the exact opposite of what we saw in China. The love affair between Americans and their credit cards is expressed in a single statistic: U.S. citizens hold more than 1.3 billion of them. That is not just a large number: it means that there are more than four credit cards for every man, woman, and child in the United States. In contrast the Chinese have only a total of 5 million credit cards, for all 1.2 billion of them.

Some economists believe that credit card spending has played a significant role in the decline in U.S. savings. Consider some experimental evidence. Richard Feinberg, a professor of consumer sciences and retailing at Purdue, asked subjects whether they would spend if they were cued by the presence of a credit card (not their own). They chose to spend considerably more when they were cued, and they also decided to spend more quickly. Feinberg concluded that people have become conditioned so that "credit card stimuli become associated with spending."[23] In another experiment Drazen Prelec and Duncan Simester auctioned off tickets to local sporting events in Boston to MBA students. In one experimental condition payment was by credit card, in the other by cash. The experiment was designed so that the two methods of payment involved only negligible difference in convenience. The MBA students bid 60–110% more when payment was by credit card.[24]

These experimental findings are highly suggestive. But it is hard to verify statistically whether the rise in credit cards that we have seen historically is responsible for the decline in savings. The decline in savings does not exactly match the rise in credit card use. But in the aggregate economy many other things that would be expected to affect spending have occurred as credit card use has risen. For example, the massive rise in the value of stocks and in homeowner equity during the 1990s and early 2000s would be expected to depress saving. Furthermore much of the rise in credit card debt is explained by a decline in installment credit. So we might never know to what extent credit cards are directly responsible for the low U.S. saving rate, or for its decline.

But even if credit cards are not directly responsible, they do reflect aspects of American identity that must also be a major factor in the low and declining saving rate. Our devotion to the credit card and the shopping mall is symptomatic of broader views of who Americans think they are and how they think they should behave.[25]

The U.S. national identity takes great pride in America as the most capitalist country in the world. In Chapter 3 we reflected on the dual nature of capitalism. Capitalism makes it profitable for producers to sell what consumers want to buy; but it also makes it profitable to cause consumers to want to buy what producers have to sell. In identifying with capitalism, the American feels that it is fully appropriate to partake of the goods that capitalism provides and makes him want to buy. He should have a credit card. If he sees something at the mall that strikes his fancy, it is appropriate not to resist it. That is what the story of capitalism is all about. That is what it means to be a good American. With such values, it is not surprising that the U.S. citizen has so many credit cards or that U.S. savings rates are so low, irrespective of whether the credit cards themselves are the direct stimulus to consumption.

A remarkable fact seems to support this view. Indeed once again the exception may prove the rule. Only a minority of Americans now do not have credit cards. And on average those who do not are also considerably poorer than the average American. That might suggest that their financial assets will be much lower relative to their income, since richer Americans save higher fractions of their income. But that is not what we see. On the contrary: non-cardholders have considerably higher financial assets relative to income. Those who are resisting the American dream by not holding a credit card also seem to be affirming their rebellion in another way—by saving more.[26]

## Implications for Nations

A nation's policy on saving can have many consequences. Above all it determines whether people will enjoy happy retirements or instead have to battle poverty. Proper policy toward social security must reflect people's aversion to financial planning. In the absence of such planning, their decisions to save come from cues from the environment. In the absence of social security people would grossly undersave. Saving policy has an important role in correcting for their failures. The current social security systems in most Western countries are highly popular because they serve such a need. People are, with justification, afraid that left to their own devices they would not save enough for their old age. In the United States it would be a disaster to privatize Social Security and leave people's retirements to their own individual planning. They will not do it. At the same time the government should encourage cues that enhance saving, as it should discourage cues that cause people to spend.

But the United States, and to a lesser extent Western Europe, is only one among many cultures, one in which the common view is that people should spend their money. Countries in East Asia—for example, Singapore and China—have harnessed different cultural understandings of how one should behave toward consumption and saving. Indeed both of these countries have made very high levels of saving a major vehicle in achieving spectacular economic growth. As we have seen, saving policy can also be one of the keys to a nation's economic growth.

Animal spirits explain the puzzle of the arbitrariness and variability of saving. And understanding these animal spirits is in turn critical to the design of national policies on saving.

# ELEVEN

# Why Are Financial Prices and Corporate Investments So Volatile?

NO ONE HAS EVER MADE rational sense of the wild gyrations in financial prices, such as stock prices. These fluctuations are as old as the financial markets themselves.[1] And yet these prices are essential factors in investment decisions, which are fundamental to the economy. Corporate investment is much more volatile than aggregate GDP, and it appears to be an important driver of economic fluctuations. If we recognize these facts, we are left once again with more evidence that animal spirits are central to the ups and downs of the economy.

The real value of the U.S. stock market rose over fivefold between 1920 and 1929. It then came all the way back down between 1929 and 1932. The real value of the stock market doubled between 1954 and 1973. Then the market came all the way back down. It then lost half of its real value between 1973 and 1974. The real value of the stock market rose almost eightfold between 1982 and 2000. Then it lost half of its value between 2000 and 2008.[2]

The question is not just how to forecast these events before they occur. The problem is deeper than that. No one can even explain why these events rationally ought to have happened even *after* they have happened.

One might think, from the self-assurance that economists often display when extolling the efficiency of the markets, that they have reliable explanations of what has driven aggregate stock markets, which they are just keeping to themselves. They *can* of course give examples that justify the stock price changes of some individual firms. But they cannot do this for the aggregate stock market.[3]

Over the years economists have *tried* to give a convincing explanation for aggregate stock price movements in terms of economic fundamentals. But no one has ever succeeded. They do not appear to be explicable by changes in interest rates, by subsequent dividends or earnings, or by anything else.[4]

"The fundamentals of the economy remain strong." That cliché is repeated by authorities as they try to restore public confidence after every major stock market decline. They have the opportunity to say this because just about every major stock market decline appears inexplicable if one looks only at the factors that logically *ought* to influence stock markets. It is practically always the stock market that has changed; indeed the fundamentals haven't.

How do we know that these changes could not be generated by fundamentals? If prices reflect fundamentals, they do so because those fundamentals are useful in forecasting future stock payoffs. In theory the stock prices are the predictors of the discounted value of those future income streams, in the form of future dividends or future earnings. But stock prices are much too variable. They are even much more variable than those discounted streams of dividends (or earnings) that they are trying to predict.[5]

To pretend that stock prices reflect people's use of information about those future payoffs is like hiring a weather forecaster who has gone berserk. He lives in a town where temperatures are fairly stable, but he predicts that one day they will be 150° and on another they will be −100°. Even if the forecaster has the mean of those temperatures right, and even if his exaggerated estimates are at least accurate in calling the relatively hot days and the relatively cold days, he should still be fired. He would make more accurate forecasts on average if he did not predict that there would be any variation in temperature at all. For the same reason, one should reject the notion that stock prices reflect predictions, based on economic fundamentals, about future earnings. Why? The prices are much too variable.

Even this fact, blatant as it is, has not convinced efficient-markets advocates that their theory is wrong. They point out that the movements in stock prices *could* still be rational. They say that they could be reflecting new information about some possible major event affecting fundamentals that by chance did not happen in the past century, or the century before that either. In this view the stock market is still the best predictor of those future payoffs. Its gyrations are occurring because something might have happened to fundamentals. They maintain that the mere fact that the major event did not happen cannot be taken to mean that the market was irrational. Maybe they are right. One cannot decisively *prove* that the stock market has been irrational. But in all of this debate no one has offered any real evidence to think that the volatility *is* rational.[6]

The price changes appear instead to be correlated with social changes of various kinds. Andrei Shleifer and Sendhil Mullainathan have observed the changes in Merrill Lynch advertisements. Prior to the stock market bubble, in the early 1990s, Merrill Lynch was running advertisements showing a grandfather fishing with his grandson. The ad was captioned: "Maybe you should plan to grow rich slowly." By the time the market had peaked around 2000, when investors were obviously very pleased with recent results, Merrill's ads had changed dramatically. There was a picture of a computer chip shaped like a bull. The caption read: "Be Wired . . . Be Bullish." After the subsequent market correction, Merrill went back to the grandfather and the grandson. They were again patiently fishing. The caption advertised "Income for a lifetime."[7] Of course the marketing professionals who concoct these ads believe they are closely tracking public thinking as it changes dramatically over time. Why should we regard *their* professional opinion as less worth listening to than the professional opinion of finance professors and efficient-markets advocates?

## *The Beauty Contest and Delicious Apple Metaphors*

In his 1936 book Keynes compared the equilibrium in the stock market to that of a popular newspaper competition of his time. Competitors were asked to pick the six prettiest faces from a hundred photographs. The prize was awarded to the competitor whose choices came closest to the average preferences of all of the competitors as a group. Of course, to win such a competition one should not pick the faces one thinks are prettiest. Instead one should pick the faces that one thinks others are likely to think the prettiest. But even that strategy is not the best, for certainly others are employing it too. It would be better yet to pick the faces that one thinks others are most likely to think that others think are the prettiest. Or maybe one should even go a step or two further in this thinking.[8] Investing in stocks is often like that: just as in the beauty contest, in the short run one does not win by picking the company most likely to succeed in the long run, but by picking the company most likely to have high market value in the short run.

The Delicious Apple offers another metaphor for much the same theory. Hardly anyone today really likes the taste of the varietal now called Delicious. And yet these apples are ubiquitous. They are often the only choice in cafeterias, on lunch counters, and in gift baskets. Delicious Apples used to taste better, back in the nineteenth century when an entirely different apple was marketed under this name. The Delicious varietal had become overwhelmingly the best-selling apple in the United States by the 1980s. When apple connoisseurs began shifting to other varietals, apple growers tried to salvage their profits. They moved the Delicious Apple into another market niche. It became the inexpensive apple that people think other people like, or that people think other people think other people like. Most growers gave up on good taste. They cheapened the apple by switching to strains with higher yield and better shelf life. They cheapened it by clear-picking an entire orchard at once, no longer choosing the apples as they ripened individually. Since Delicious Apples are not selling based on taste, why pay extra for taste? The general public cannot imagine that an apple could be so cheapened. Nor does it imagine the real reason these apples are so ubiquitous despite their generally poor taste.[9]

The same kind of phenomenon occurs with speculative investments. Many people do not appreciate how much a company with a given name can change through time, or how many ways there are to debase its value. Stocks that nobody really believes in but that retain value are the Delicious Apples of the investment world.

## *Epidemics and the Confidence Multiplier in Speculative Markets*

Obviously investors are interested in getting rich quickly when the market is soaring. They want to protect value when the market is sagging. This is a psychological reaction to the market's behavior. If people tend to buy in reaction to stock price increases or sell in reaction to price decreases, then their reaction to past price changes has the potential to feed back into more price changes in the same direction, a phenomenon known as price-to-price feedback.[10] A vicious circle can develop, causing a continuation of the cycle, at least for a while. Eventually an upward price movement, a bubble, must burst, since price is supported only by expectations of further price increases. They cannot go on forever.

Price-to-price feedback itself may not be strong enough to create the major asset price bubbles we have seen. But, as we shall see, there are other forms of feedback besides that between prices. In particular there are feedbacks between the asset prices in the bubble and the real economy. This additional feedback increases the length of the cycle and amplifies the price-to-price effects.

We could dismiss these speculative movements in asset prices if they were only curiosities. But they are not irrelevant. As they feed back into the real economy, they affect not only those who play the game but also those who never played at all. The average American—for example, the foreman at the Caterpillar tractor plant in Peoria who is unemployed in a bust—has never directly owned a share of stock. Holdings of stocks versus other investments are heavily determined by the social groups to which individuals belong, rather than the dictates of economic optimization.[11] Even within social groups, holdings change dramatically in response to price changes.

There are at least three different sources of feedback from asset markets to the real economy. When stock prices and housing prices go up, people have less reason to save. They will spend more because they feel wealthier. They may also count their stock market gains or their housing appreciation as part of their current savings. The effect of asset prices on consumption is called the wealth effect on consumption.

Asset values also play an important role in determining investment. When the stock market drops in value, companies decrease their expenditures on new plant and equipment. As we shall discuss in the next chapter, when the market for single-family homes drops in value, construction companies drop their plans to build new homes.

Both of these forms of expenditure, in business investment and in housing, can be greatly influenced by bankruptcies. When assets fall in value, debtors will not pay their debts. That in turn compromises the financial institutions that are the normal sources of debt financing. When these institutions reduce their willingness to make further loans —either because they themselves have gone bankrupt, because they are having a hard time raising funds, or because the market correction has caused them to take a more conservative approach to lending—that causes further drops in the price of the assets.

One way or another, asset price movements feed into public confidence and into the economy. There is thus a price-to-earnings-to-price feedback. When stock prices are on the upswing, that feedback boosts confidence. It encourages people to buy more. So corporate profits go up. That in turn encourages stock prices to go up. These positive feedbacks can occur, mutually reinforcing one another, but only for a while.

On the downswing the feedback—and the economy—both go in the opposite direction.

The feedback is also enhanced by a leverage feedback and a leverage cycle.[12] The collateral ratio is the amount lenders lend to investors as a percentage of the value of the assets posted as collateral. On the upswing of the cycle collateral ratios rise. For example, in the market for single-family homes, in the upswing of the cycle the amount of money banks are willing to lend to home buyers as a fraction of the value of their homes rises. The rise in leverage feeds back into asset price increases, encouraging more and more leverage. The same process works in reverse in the downward direction as asset prices fall.

The leverage cycle operates in part because of bank capital requirements. As asset prices rise, leveraged financial institutions' capital rises relative to their regulatory requirements, and so they may buy more assets. If many financial institutions respond in this way, they may take on so many more positions in the assets they hold that they bid the prices up, thereby freeing up yet more capital. A feedback loop thus arises, propelling prices higher and higher. Moreover, if asset prices fall, leveraged financial institutions may be forced to sell to meet their capital requirements, and the systemic effect of this selling may be to lower asset prices, thus lowering the institutions' capital ratios. So they are forced to sell more assets, and a downward feedback may occur.[13] In extreme cases the feedback may cause very low or "fire sale" prices.[14] There seemed to be relatively little appreciation of the possibility of such systemic feedback in the Basel I (1988) and Basel II (2004) accords, which determined the international standards for bank capital requirements.[15] But this sort of feedback, and the need to try to reduce it with what is now often called macroprudential regulation, has come under increasing scrutiny lately.[16]

Most people have trouble thinking about broader feedbacks. For them the rise in real earnings that accompanies a stock market boom (as for example in the 1990s) is "proof" that the boom is rational. They rarely consider the possibility that the earnings rise is just another temporary manifestation of the stock market rise. If there is a rise in rents during a home-price boom (there was a slight rise in real rents in the U.S. housing boom of the early 2000s), they will think that the rental increases are a justification for home-price increases. They will not think of the possibility that the rent increases are just a temporary manifestation of the home-price rise.

## Feedback and Animal Spirits

Consider an example that illustrates the kinds of feedback that drive stock prices, one that indicates even more broadly how animal spirits become part of the feedback. The example shows how multifaceted this feedback really is. It involves many elements of our theory of animal spirits—not just confidence but also issues of fairness and the emergence of stories that inspire or discourage.

Let us compare the history of the Toyota Motor Company in Japan, founded in 1933, and Industrias Kaiser Argentina S.A. (IKA) in Argentina, founded in 1955. The stocks represented by these two automobile companies have had very different histories. Toyota's common stock as of this writing has a market capitalization of $157 billion, and Toyota was recently ranked by *Forbes* (in terms of a composite of sales, profits, assets, and market value) as the eighth largest company in the world. In contrast IKA, after years of failure, was sold in 1970 to the French automaker Renault and no longer exists.

But why, ultimately, should the outcomes for these two firms be so different? What created so much stock market value in Japan, and what went so wrong in Argentina? Analysts may focus on many different proximate causes, but the ultimate cause is a feedback mechanism, involving animal spirits, that went in different directions in the different countries.

Toyota was founded by a family that was in the business of operating mechanical looms.[17] At its very start it must have appeared to be an instance not just of confidence but of pathological *overconfidence*. By the 1920s automobile producers in Europe and the United States had been producing cars for decades. They already had assembly plants in Japan. Furthermore Japan had no industries to support the manufacture of a car from scratch. For example, there was no producer of stamping machines to shape sheet metal. Even worse, there was not even a manufacturer of the sheet metal itself. Such industries had to be developed in Japan along with the automobile industry itself. The creation of Toyota was a clear example of the triumph of individual bravado over conventional common sense. In some ways it mirrored the optimism and patriotism that perversely led Japan to undertake its march into Manchuria in 1931.

But that kind of overconfidence had been visible in Japanese culture for some time. It was part of a national philosophy, notably developed by Yukichi Fukuzawa, who is widely regarded as one of the founders of modern Japan.[18] He encouraged a story of self-reliance and willingness to learn from foreigners, arguing that there should be no shame in energetically imitating their successes. He made such imitation of others into a symbol of Japanese ingenuity and intelligence.

In contrast, when IKA was founded in 1955, with strong government assistance, there was no well-articulated philosophy in Argentina that would lead to such strong individual initiative and confidence in ultimate success, as in Japan. There was no Argentine Fukuzawa. Indeed the managers of IKA were not Argentine; they were imported from the United States. The enterprise came about because the Argentine government wished to create an automobile industry. It offered Henry Kaiser—who had already failed as an automobile producer in the United States—strong tariff protection. The province of Cordoba granted him ten-year protection from taxes.[19]

Born as it was as a government project, IKA survived as a product of economic protection, and everyone knew it. The auto workers themselves had a sense of neither shared trust nor shared mission. In 1963, when IKA announced a one-week layoff for its 9,000 employees, issues of fairness became deadly for the enterprise. Workers "promptly rioted, seized the plant and herded 150 supervisors and foremen into the paint shop. Brandishing cans of sloshing gasoline, they vowed to set fire to the shop unless officials rescinded the shutdown order. Fearing for the safety of the management hostages, Kaiser Argentina president James F. McCloud finally capitulated." In 1969 and 1972 there were other violent and destructive strikes at IKA. In 1972 the government went so far as to call out the army to protect the plants from the strikers.

Under such conditions it is not surprising that investors were unenthusiastic about committing further funds. "'From an economic viewpoint, manufacturing automobiles in Latin America is sheer nonsense,' says the treasurer of one big firm. 'If it were not for the duties, you could import cars here for just a couple of hundred dollars more than what they cost in the United States or Europe.'"[20] That view became a widely shared story that depressed not only the stock price but also the workforce at IKA. The only hope was that continuing government subsidies would sustain the business.

Of course in Japan the auto industry also received government subsidies. The Automobile Manufacturing Business Act of 1936 gave it preferential tax and tariff treatment. But the formation of both Toyota and Nissan Motor Company preceded this act by years. In contrast to IKA, the founding and progress of Toyota were about self-esteem and confidence. The Japanese, individually and collectively, had ambitions: somehow, they felt, an auto industry just had to be in the future of that great country. In her studies of the emergence of modern Japanese culture, Eiko Ikegami traces the evolution of a unique social order in Japan that seems outwardly polite and formal.[21] But this same culture is unusually conducive to allowing people to collaborate on ambitious aesthetic ventures without crossing boundaries in a way that would challenge personal egos or suggest unfairness. These projects bring together a broad array of people, with only weak ties to one another. Before haiku poetry emerged in the form we know today, she reports, there was a Japanese movement toward writing so-called linked verse. These were long poems by many poets, each contributing a small component that could stand as a haiku by itself, but which was valued only as part of the whole. Metaphorically, the great firms of Japan are such linked haikus.

The concept of a labor union was hardly recognized in Japan before the end of World War II.[22] The labor organizations that did exist did not generally go on strike or bargain collectively with management.[23] After the war, under the influence of the U.S. Occupation, genuine unions, and even a Japanese national autoworkers union, Zenji, were established in the late 1940s. But the Japanese national character still found the concept of a union, and in particular a strike, difficult to grasp. The Zenji organization found itself with some communist leaders, who were opposed by significant elements of Japanese society. Given the widespread public opposition to labor unions, and especially fear of communism, the Japanese government took a strong anti-union stand after a 1953 strike at Nissan. In effect it busted the existing union. It subsidized the creation of a new company union that was founded with the cooperation of Nissan. Shortly thereafter, Nissan offered lifetime employment to its employees.

In contrast, the labor movement in Argentina had been very strong and combative at least since the railroad strike of 1910. There were riots in Buenos Aires, which precipitated such a forceful response from the government that the city was turned into a "military encampment."[24] Labor-management conflict was prominent in Argentine national politics from then on. In 1946 the labor-oriented government of Juan Perón was elected and wrote a new constitution that guaranteed the rights of labor. It is no surprise then that hostile labor-management relations took their toll on IKA. The company was hit by a long series of strikes, which not only made production increasingly costly but also limited production to seventy vehicles a day.[25]

Why would labor unions be so accommodating in Japan and not in Argentina? A key underlying factor was a different sense of identity. In Japan automobile workers thought of themselves as part of the organization, and so they did not interpret every action by the company in terms of its fairness. They tended to consider the company's success to be their own success. The policy of lifetime employment allowed workers to identify with the corporation. Nissan wanted to promote a shared sense of confidence and trust. Its tactic succeeded.

The contrast in confidence and perceptions of fairness between Japan and Argentina that we have presented here might be construed as entirely a matter of differences in national culture. In fact, however, there is every reason to believe that these factors change through time, even within a given firm, as well as across countries, as the success of the enterprise is realized and as the price of its stock changes. If then we are living with a system of feedback from price to animal spirits to price, we are in a world that is very difficult to predict. Companies and people in today's Japan or Argentina may be rather different from those we have described from the past—and they will change again in the future, as part of an endless economic feedback.

Most economists don't like these stories of psychological feedback. They consider them offensive to their core concept of human rationality. And they are dismissive for another reason: there are no standard ways to quantify the psychology of people.[26] Most economists view the attempts that have been made thus far to quantify the feedbacks and incorporate them into macro models as too arbitrary, and thus they remain unconvinced.

## Animal Spirits and Oil Price Movements

Like the price of stocks, the price of oil undergoes great fluctuations. These were especially dramatic in the oil-crisis years from 1973 to 1986. The first oil crisis hit the economy from 1972 to 1974, when the oil-producing nations of the Organization of Petroleum Exporting Countries (OPEC) restricted production. The price of crude oil more than doubled, from $3.56 per barrel in 1972 to $10.29 per barrel in 1974.[27]

Ostensibly the OPEC ministers were retaliating for the Arab defeat in the 1973 Yom Kippur War. But there is another less well-known explanation for when and why they acted as they did. Prior to 1973 the anachronistically titled Texas Railroad Commission regulated the fraction of time that oil producers in the state of Texas were allowed to pump. By restricting pumping it raised the price of oil and benefited Texas producers. Little notice was taken by the public in late 1972 when the commission raised the quota to 100%, effectively eliminating it altogether.[28] But that action meant that from then on OPEC would have free rein. They could restrict their output, to push up prices, and no one in the United States could countervail their actions.

This was the first time oil prices had risen this dramatically, but then in 1979 they shot up again. The Iran-Iraq War disrupted the supply of Persian Gulf oil, and oil prices doubled once more. They remained high until 1986. Then, in the wake of the terrible recession of the early 1980s, the OPEC cartel collapsed and oil prices fell by half.

This brief summary of the oil market in these crucial years seems to suggest that oil prices were determined by fundamentals—if not economic fundamentals, then political and military fundamentals, like war and peace. Indeed these probably were the dominant factors in the oil market in these years, and they have been since. Even so, we also see feedbacks among confidence, production, and prices operating in the oil market (although in attenuated form) that are strikingly similar to those we saw in the stock market.

The rise in oil prices of the 1970s was accompanied by a crescendo of rhetoric about the human population explosion and the commodity shortages it would engender. When the oil crisis ended a decade later this rhetoric did not disappear, but it died down considerably. Just eighteen months prior to OPEC's production restriction, a team of researchers at the Massachusetts Institute of Technology, under the direction of Jay Forrester, issued an alarming study. Forrester was famous as the computer scientist who had designed the magnetically based memory system of the first widely used computer, the IBM 650, some two decades earlier. His group's report concluded that the world was running out of natural resources.

The study, titled *The Limits to Growth: A Report for the Club of Rome's Project on the Predicament of Mankind,* predicted disastrous worldwide economic problems. In one scenario these would result, late in the twenty-first century, in the death of a quarter to a half of the world's population. Severe shortages of natural resources, reflected in huge price increases, would eventually mean that "the death rate [would be] driven upward by lack of food and health services."[29] Forrester's prestige lent popular credibility to the report, though critics argued that it was based on questionable assumptions. Yet *The Limits to Growth* was symptomatic of the popular thinking of its time. And those views were fodder for the OPEC ministers setting up their cartel. By reducing their oil production now, they would not only be rewarded by immediately higher prices. They would also be saving their remaining oil for a yet rainier day, when its price would be higher still. And of course the decision by OPEC also gave heart to those who placed stock in the Club of Rome's findings. What more dramatic proof of their theory could they imagine than a tripling of the price of oil before their very eyes?

But then the unthinkable happened. In the wake of the serious recession of the early 1980s the price of oil fell. And, at least for a time, the stories about running out of resources abated. A ProQuest search of the *New York Times, Los Angeles Times,* and *Washington Post* for articles containing both *proven reserves* and *oil* confirmed the pattern. There were only 18 articles with these words in the five-year period 1965–69; there were 60 articles during the period 1970–74, 115 articles 1975–79, 137 articles 1980–84, and then only 73 articles 1985–89. A similar pattern appears in a search for articles containing the phrase *nonrenewable resources.*

Certainly economic and political considerations played the major role in the boom and bust of OPEC and the oil industry as a whole during these years. And—as suggested by the fact that oil prices rose to a peak of $145.31 a barrel on July 2, 2008, before collapsing again—there are indeed limits to our resources. Global warming is a looming threat. But amid these long-term prospects—for the earth and for the production of oil—the price of oil, and the stories about it, are remarkably like the stock market and its myths. They are too variable. Once again, whoever is forecasting the weather should be fired.

## The Markets as Drivers of Investment

A nation's investment—in new machinery and equipment, new factory buildings, new bridges and highways, new software, new communications infrastructure—ought to matter enormously for its economic prosperity. These tools convert our simple labor into modern and sophisticated output. The better our tools, the better our standard of living will be. If a country imports the most up-to-date machinery and software, or better yet builds it itself, its workers are forced into a learning experience that keeps them abreast of the latest thinking in technology. The investment produces hands-on experience with new technology. Careful studies have confirmed that countries that have made more such investments have higher standards of living.[30]

Even so, governments today (with some rare exceptions) do not decide their countries' investments. Businesspeople do. And while they are constrained by financial parameters, they also have to *believe* in their investments. Their decision process is ultimately intuitive and psychological. Thus the future of any country is in the hands of the businesspeople who decide on investments, and it is in large measure dependent on their psychology.

Business school students study the mathematics of capital budgeting and the theory of optimal investment decisions. But when companies actually decide how much to invest, the psychological factors underlying investment play a major role. The application of capital budgeting theory requires inputs: projected cash flows from investments, estimated cost of capital for the firm, estimated reactions of the stock market to the investment, and correlations with other risks. Moreover, these depend indirectly on a host of other factors: opportunities for the company to learn from the experience, opportunities to establish contacts and distribution channels, synergies with other investments, effects on corporate reputation and market niche. There is no simple recipe for how to quantify such factors and to fill in all the numbers that capital budgeting theory requires. And those in business typically work in a highly competitive atmosphere. They must make quick decisions based on the information at hand, and then move on.

We return to Jack Welch's autobiography, *Jack: Straight from the Gut,* to see this psychological view of business in action. He writes: "We wouldn't merely grow with GNP. . . . Instead, GE would be the locomotive pulling the GNP, not the caboose following it." Welch stressed his distrust of quantitative procedures: "The last thing I wanted was a series of technical questions to score a few points. We had dozens of people routinely going through what I considered 'dead books.' All my career, I never wanted to see a planning book before the person presented it. To me, the value of these sessions wasn't in the books. It was in the heads and hearts of the people who were coming to Fairfield [GE headquarters in Connecticut]. I wanted to drill down, to get beyond the binders and into the thinking that went into them. I needed to see the business leaders' body language and the passion they poured into their arguments." Welch tells of his reaction to an employee's investment analysis: "I crossed out the payback analysis on his last chart. I drew an $X$ over the transparency and scrawled the word *Infinite* to make the point that the returns on our investment would last forever."[31]

Businesspeople make decisions with fundamental uncertainty about the future. *Risk, Uncertainty and Profit,* written by Chicago's Frank Knight in 1921, is today regarded as a classic. Knight made a distinction between economists' concept of risk and the different sort of uncertainty in almost all business decisions. *Risk,* he said, refers to something that can be measured by mathematical probabilities. In contrast, *uncertainty* refers to something that cannot be measured because there are no objective standards to express probabilities. Theoretical economists have been struggling ever since to make sense of how people handle such true uncertainty.[32] As time goes by, their efforts seem to be converging more and more on behavioral economics. Jack Welch's phrase "straight from the gut" sums it up: decisions that matter for investment are intuitive rather than analytical. That intuition is a social process that follows the laws of psychology—and in particular, since group decisions are being made, social psychology.

Business—at least successful business—thrives on the excitement of *creating* the future. And successful business is what matters for the aggregate economy. The investment decisions that go into making a successful business are incidental to that vision. The story of a business is told in entirely different terms than economists' usual story of purchases of factories and equipment. Asking why capital expenditure fluctuates from year to year is a bit like asking why beer consumption fluctuates from one poker party to another. Who knows or remembers? And who would really care? The investment was only a means to an end. It seemed necessary at the time when something big was going on. Or maybe there was no investment because other problems forced the postponement of big ideas. So the possibility of investing big was never even discussed.

Given the speculative fluctuations in asset prices that we have already discussed, it would certainly seem that part of the reason for these variations has to do with changing asset prices and the associated beliefs about them. Welch observed, "The company's mood fluctuated on the bullishness of our press clippings and the price of our stock. Every positive story seemed to make the organization perk up. Every downbeat article gave the whimpering cynics hope."[33]

We should be careful about what we say, and also indicate that there is some degree of doubt about the relation between stock prices and investment. There is a simple story, called Tobin's $q$, devised by economist James Tobin and his colleague William Brainard, which says that there should be an exact correlation between the stock market and investment.[34] The quantity $q$ is the ratio of the market value of the firm— the value of its stocks plus the value of its bonds—to the value of its capital. Its capital, of course, is its machinery, equipment, land, inventories, software, and so on. If the price of a company rises far above the value of its capital, the story goes, there is then an incentive to duplicate the company. That entails buying the capital. So investment will be high if $q$ is high. And, of course, it does not have to be a new company that makes this investment. The old company might expand its size. The greater is $q$, the greater are the incentives to invest.[35]

Tobin's $q$ model may be applicable to some extent, but it turns out that the correlation between $q$ and investment is weak.[36] We see this in a plot of the relation between investment (relative to capital stock) and $q$ for the past hundred years. The 1920s and the 1930s give an excellent correlation between investment and $q$. The stock market was high in 1929. So was investment. The stock market crashed and bottomed out in the early 1930s. So did investment. The stock market then rallied to a peak in 1937, almost as high in real terms as in 1929. So too did investment. The stock market was quite volatile during the millennium boom in the 1990s. As the stock market soared, so too did investment. Then after 2000 they crashed together. But between the Depression and recent times there were two significant episodes when the stock market declined yet investment remained strong. After World War II the stock market tanked, yet the economy became strong. Indeed the economy became so strong that inflation rose to more than 14% in 1947. In this episode $q$ fell far below one, but investment was also high. Then again, after the first oil crisis the stock market fell significantly. And again investment remained strong. What was happening? Again there was inflation. In 1974 inflation exceeded 11%. Chapter 4 discussed the stock market's typical reaction to inflation. There is money illusion, and the market, irrationally, goes down.

Although the data do not speak with any certainty here, they seem to say that when loss of confidence causes stock markets to fall, there will be a fall in investment. But if the stock market is falling because of inflation, while the economy remains otherwise strong, then most likely investment will also remain strong.[37] The data may not be speaking loud and clear, but this interpretation of the past century of U.S. history seems to us highly consistent with our theory and our fine-grained reading of business behavior over the course of the business cycle.

## Taming the Beast: Making Financial Markets Work for Us

This chapter has discussed why asset markets move too much, the psychology that affects them, and the feedbacks between them and the real economy. But what does this mean for economic policy? Throughout the chapter one theme has been recurring: the theories economists typically put forth about how the whole economy works are too simplistic. That means we should fire the weather forecaster.

So what does it mean in practical terms to fire the forecaster? The weather forecaster for the U.S. economy has been the pundits and politicians who have increasingly been singing the praises—and nothing else—of free markets. This view of the wonders of free markets is just one of those stories that have fueled the booms and busts in stock markets and in real markets. Earlier in this book we sang our own praises of the wonders of capitalism in a major key—but not without some notes in a minor key. Capitalism fills the supermarkets with thousands of items that meet our fancy. But if our fancy is for snake oil, it will produce that too.

In the encomia that capitalism has been receiving in the past decade or two this theme in the minor key has been forgotten. Yes, capitalism is good. But yes, it also has its excesses. And it must be watched. And financial markets should be watched with special care. We saw in the previous chapter how Josepha Q. Public hated to think about her finances. Indeed in the absence of Social Security she would be broke in retirement. Her inability to approach these problems means that financial markets must be especially closely regulated. Why? Because it is here more than anywhere else that Josepha is especially at risk of purchasing snake oil. One of the manifestations of this snake oil is the excessive boom and bust in asset markets. Josepha buys. But she does not know what she is buying. As the pundits and the politicians—and also the economists—have adopted an increasingly uncritical view of capitalism, a whole industry has arisen to produce and sell questionable financial products. For the most part, Josepha herself has not bought these. Instead she has empowered those who control her pension funds, her 401(k) account, her money market fund, or, if she is very rich, her hedge fund managers to buy these products. There has been financial gain for those who trade on behalf of these funds—often very significant gain. But poor Josepha has been left holding the bag.

Our worry, however, is not just for Josepha. This is a book about macroeconomics. Our worry is that when Josepha is left holding the bag, there is a loss of confidence in markets more generally, and a serious recession will follow.

So firing the forecaster means giving up the myth that capitalism is purely good. It means also taking on the other side of capitalism, which is that if you do not watch what you buy, someone will sell you a lemon. The time has come to appreciate that what allows capitalism to function is the regulations which assure Josepha that when she puts her money into the market, when she takes out a mortgage, or when she buys a car, she is getting a product with some guarantees. In the 1930s, in the wake of a catastrophe of unimaginable size and consequences, the Roosevelt administration took this message seriously. It set up safeguards to protect the public from the excesses of capitalism. These especially concerned financial and banking regulation, and they included the Securities and Exchange Commission, the FDIC, and many others. For over seventy years we have benefited from the safeguards that were set up at that time. They, in addition to wise fiscal and monetary policy, have kept us out of severe recession.

But the financial markets have changed. They have become ever more complex. In the United States this complexity has been a way to evade the regulation by the alphabet agencies set up by Roosevelt and his followers. Firing the weather forecaster now means that we need a new story of what goes on in markets—a story that does not always predict capitalist sunshine. We then need to take stock. We need to realize that the stories people tell themselves about the economy exaggerate. There is a new need to protect them from these exaggerations. It requires a renewal of the view that financial markets require regulation. And sometimes, when these regulations fail, because of all the feedbacks between financial markets and the real economy, there is also room for thoughtful, careful policies of financial insurance. Rededication to protecting the financial consumer must be one of our highest economic priorities.

In an emergency, as a backup, when we do get into recession, there is monetary and fiscal policy. But we know that there are limits to such policy and to its effectiveness. It is now time to redesign financial regulations to take account of the animal spirits that often drive the markets, to make the markets work more effectively, and to minimize the extent to which we will need after-the-fact bailouts to get us out of the hole.

# TWELVE

# Why Do Real Estate Markets
# Go through Cycles?

REAL ESTATE MARKETS are almost as volatile as stock markets. Prices of agricultural land, of commercial real estate, and of homes and condominiums have gone through a series of huge bubbles, as if people never learn from the previous one.[1] We shall argue in this chapter that such events—in particular the recent enormous bubble in the prices of homes in the early twenty-first century—are driven by the same animal spirits that we have seen at work elsewhere in the economy. And most of the now-familiar elements of animal spirits—confidence, corruption, money illusion, and storytelling—play a central role in real estate markets as well.

For some reason, in the late 1990s and early 2000s the idea that homes and apartments were spectacular investments gained a stronghold on the public imagination, in the United States and in many other countries as well. Not only did prices go up, but there was palpable excitement about real estate investments. One could see the animal spirits in action everywhere.

It was the biggest home-price boom in U.S. history. It extended over nearly a decade, beginning in the late 1990s. Prices nearly doubled before the bust began in 2006.[2] While it lasted, this spectacular boom, mirrored in other countries as well, helped drive the entire world economy and its stock markets. In its wake it has left the biggest real estate crisis since the 1930s, the so-called subprime crisis, as well as a global financial crisis whose full dimensions have yet to be grasped.

But what caused such a boom-and-bust event? What really drove people's thinking?

A good place to start is *How a Second Home Can Be Your Best Investment* by Tom Kelly (a radio show host) and John Tuccillo (former chief economist of the National Association of Realtors). It was published in 2004, when home prices were rising the fastest. The book explained: "Look at it this way: If you think a house is good enough to live in, someone else will too, and they'll pay you for the privilege. The ownership of a real estate investment, particularly property that you can personally enjoy—a vacation home, your retirement residence—is the most profitable investment within the reach of the average American."[3] Other than the rationale in this sentence, the book is singularly devoid of arguments as to why real estate would be the best investment.

Kelly and Tuccillo pointed out that real estate investments are typically leveraged investments. But that is not an argument for high returns; leveraged investments can turn spectacularly bad if prices go down, as homeowners have been discovering in the current financial crisis. The possibility of a national home-price decline was not even mentioned. This kind of thinking is of course characteristic of speculative bubbles. There was no rational argument about investment possibilities.

Instead the book was filled with stories. For example, Ken and Nedda Hamilton had lived in Pennsylvania all their lives. They had dreamed about a home in Florida for years, but they took action only after their grown son Fred laid out a case for such an investment and offered to be a co-investor with them. A real estate agent allowed them to spend nights in each of several homes near Naples, Florida. They got hooked on one, bought it, and were very happy. A sequence of stories like this allows the reader to choose the story that is most congenial to him and that best serves as a model for his own behavior.

Obviously the authors felt no need to explain why homes were the best investment. But why were investors so convinced even *before* they read the book?

## *Naïve or Intuitive Beliefs about Real Estate*

It appears that people had acquired a strong intuitive feeling that home prices everywhere can only go up. They seemed really sure of this, so much so that they were ready to dismiss any economist who said otherwise. If pressed for an explanation, they typically said that, because there is only so much land, real estate prices have always gone up. Population pressures and economic growth should inevitably push real estate prices strongly upward. Those arguments are demonstrably false. But no matter.

People do not always express such opinions, particularly if home prices have not increased for years or decades. It appears that the fixed land–population growth–economic growth story has perennial appeal. But it is compelling only when home prices are going up rapidly.

The appeal of the argument means that it tends to be attached to stories about real estate booms, and it spreads by word of mouth, feeding the boom. The contagion of the argument for ever-increasing home prices during a boom is enhanced by the intuition behind it.

Yet experiments have shown that people have false intuitive models of even some of the most basic physical phenomena. A 1980 experiment by psychologist Michael McCloskey and his colleagues showed a group of undergraduates a picture of a thin curved metal tube; the investigators then asked them what would be the trajectory of a metal ball shot at high speed from it. Of the students who had studied no physics, 49% thought the ball would continue along a *curved* path suggested by the curvature of the tube. Even 19% of the students with college-level physics described a curved path for the ball.[4]

One might think that a principle of physics as elementary as the tendency of objects to move along straight paths would be learned from everyday experience. So it comes as a surprise that so many people make this error. In fact when McCloskey and his colleagues asked the students to explain their incorrect answers, their reasoning corresponded to the medieval theory of impetus as articulated by the fourteenth-century scientist John Buridan.[5] Perhaps they, in common with the medieval scientist, saw some weak parallels in ordinary experience that informed their thinking. Whatever the explanation, there must be some underlying psychological tendency to think this way, although McCloskey and his colleagues could not divine its source.

People appear to have different, but equally inexplicable, quirks in predicting the trajectory of real estate prices. The idea that they will always go up strongly, and even that real estate is the best investment of all, is somehow seductive. But it has not been uniformly prominent. Outside of booms it is hard to find statements that real estate prices will always go up. In a computer search of old newspapers, we found a newspaper article from 1887—published during a real estate boom in some U.S. cities, including New York—which used the idea to justify the boom amid a rising chorus of skeptics: "With the increase in population, the demand for land increases. As land cannot be stretched within a given area, only two ways remain to meet demands. One way is to build high in the air; the other is to raise the price of land. . . .

Because it is perfectly plain to everyone that land must always be valuable, this form of investment has become permanently strong and popular."[6] In 1952—right after the second-biggest home-price boom in U.S. history, the "baby boom" increase in home prices right after World War II —we see this argument: "Others are aware that there are few investments as stable and safe as a house or property. Although in depression years land and shelter values have dropped, an ever-increasing population has kept the long-term trend always upward."[7] Such statements during or right after a home-price boom confirm that the idea does reappear during boom times. But outside of booms such statements are rare.

That conclusion is also a non sequitur in explaining the boom. Home prices have fallen before, immediately disproving a theory that they must always go up. Notably, urban land prices have recently fallen in Japan (where land is every bit as scarce as it is in other countries). In fact they fell 68% in real terms in major Japanese cities from 1991 to 2006.[8]

Money illusion appears to explain some of the impression that homes are spectacular investments.[9] We hear quotes of purchase prices of homes from long ago. People tend to remember the purchase price of their home, even if it was fifty years ago. But they do not compare it with other prices from so long ago. One hears today statements like "I paid $12,000 for this house when I came home from World War II." This suggests enormous returns on the purchase of the house—partly because it fails to factor in the tenfold increase in consumer prices since that time. The real value of the home may have only doubled over that interval, which would mean an annual appreciation of only about 1.5% a year.

One theory of people's lack of understanding comes from the so-called present value pricing of a cash flow. Real U.S. GDP has grown 3.4% a year between 1929, when the statistics began to be kept, and 2007, so that real GDP was 13.3 times higher in 2007 than it was in 1929. Assuming that the economy continues to grow, it might seem plausible that the value of a fixed resource, land, should also grow at that rate. Suppose that is so. Does that mean that investments in land are a great deal? Not so. If the returns from land are proportional to GDP, the present value theory would predict that the price of land would also grow at 3.4% a year. But that is not itself a great return when compared, for example, with stocks, whose real return has averaged over 7% a year over the past century (2% in the form of real capital gains and 5% in terms of dividend yield). For land, the "dividend" would take the form of the value of crops that could be grown on the land, the rental value of the land, or other possible benefits that could accrue to the owner while the land was still owned. Present value theory would say that if these dividends are expected to grow at 3.4% a year, then the price of land would equilibrate at a very high level relative to these dividends, so that the total return to owning land would be no better than that of other investments.

If everything is priced in accordance with present value theory, then it makes no difference whether price is expected to grow with GDP or not. The returns are just the same as with other investments. This present value theory is taught to undergraduate finance students and those studying for MBAs. But beyond those who take these courses, few people understand it. It is also worth noting that in the United States the price of one type of land, agricultural land, has appreciated at a much slower rate than the growth of GDP over the past century. Its real value increased only by a factor of 2.3 over the whole century, or about 0.9% per year—far below GDP growth.[10] That suggests a dismal return overall for investors.

Agricultural land was in fixed supply, but prices did not keep up with real GDP growth because it was not a major factor in this GDP growth. According to the National Income and Product Accounts, agriculture, forestry, and fishing accounted for 8.3% of U.S. national income in 1948, but only 0.9% of national income in 2008. An economy increasingly dominated by the service sector has not been an intensive user of land for some time. Moreover, real home prices in the United States rose only 24% from 1900 to 2000, or 0.2% per year.[11] Apparently land hasn't been the constraint on home construction. So home prices have had negligible real appreciation from that source.

## The Confidence Multiplier in Real Estate

So there is no *rational* reason to expect real estate to be a generally good investment. It is so only at certain times and in certain places. People seem always to have a predilection to assume that since land is scarce, real estate prices should grow over time. But this predilection is not always a cause for attention and action. The magnification of this predilection in the twenty-first century is the story of the boom. And the magnification has a number of causes, both cultural and institutional.

The cycles of feedback, both price-to-price feedback and price-to-GDP-to-price feedback, discussed in the preceding chapter in reference to stocks, also operated in real estate. As home prices rose faster and faster, they reinforced the folk wisdom about increasing prices and imbued that folk wisdom with a sense of spectacular opportunity. This feedback interacted with the contagion of ideas and facts to reinforce the belief in an ever-upward trend of home prices.

The 1990s bubble in the stock market apparently set the stage for such contagion by transforming people's views of themselves, so that their self-esteem was promoted by a sense that they were smart investors. People had learned the vocabulary and habits of investors, they had increasingly begun subscribing to investment periodicals, and they watched television shows about investing. When the stock market soured, many people thought that they had to transfer their investments into another sector. Real estate looked appealing. The accounting scandals accompanying the stock market correction after 2002 caused many to mistrust Wall Street. Homes, especially their own, were something tangible that they could understand, see, and touch.

As the boom progressed after 2000, the way in which we thought about housing changed. Newspaper articles about houses as investments proliferated. Articles about houses increasingly dealt with investments in housing. Even our language changed. New phrases like "flip that house" or "property ladder" became popular. (These two were even used as the titles of popular television shows.) The old phrase "safe as houses" acquired a new currency. The phrase actually dates back to the nineteenth century, when it seems ships were compared with houses. A sailor might try to reassure a terrified passenger during a violent storm: "Don't worry, these ships are as safe as houses." But in the twenty-first century the term moved into the investment context, with the meaning "Don't worry, these investments are as safe as investments in houses." And the boom seemed to connect this phrase with the further thought ". . . and so a highly leveraged investment in houses is a *sure* winner."

Why was the home-price boom after 2000 so much bigger than any other before it? Part of the reason the housing boom reached such dimensions comes from the evolution of economic institutions related to housing.

Institutions changed because of the belief that the opportunities to take part in the housing boom were not being shared fairly among all elements of the population. Martin Luther King III, the son of the great civil rights leader, lamented in a 1999 editorial titled "Minority Housing Gap; Fannie Mae, Freddie Mac Fall Short" that minorities were being left out of the boom. He wrote: "Nearly 90 percent of all Americans, according to surveys by HUD, believe that owning a home is better than renting one."[12] Like everyone else, minorities deserved this opportunity for wealth. The allegation of unfairness in opportunities to participate in the boom led to an almost immediate, and uncritical, government reaction. Andrew Cuomo, Secretary of the Department of Housing and Urban Development, responded by aggressively increasing the mandated lending by Fannie and Freddie to underserved communities. He wanted results. The possibility of a future decline in home prices was not his concern. He was a political appointee. His charge was to secure economic justice for minorities, not to opine on the future of home prices. And so Cuomo forced Fannie Mae and Freddie Mac to make loans, even if that meant lowering credit standards and relaxing the requirements for documentation from borrowers.[13] There was never any serious examination of the premise that this policy was in the best interest of minorities.

In this atmosphere it was easy for mortgage lenders to justify loosening their own lending standards. A number of these new mortgage institutions became corrupt at the core. Some mortgage originators were willing to lend to anyone, without regard to their suitability for the loan. Corruption of this sort tends to flourish at times when people have high expectations for the future. Or maybe *corruption* is too strong a word. Is making a loan that you suspect will eventually default corrupt? After all, you didn't force the mortgager to take out the loan. You didn't force the investor to whom you were selling the securitized mortgages to buy the investment. And who really knows the future anyway? There was money to be made giving all these people what they thought they wanted. No regulator was telling you not to do it. As we have already seen, there was an economic equilibrium that linked the purchasers of snake oil houses with the purchasers of the snake oil mortgages that financed them.[14]

So the feedback that produced an epidemic of home-price increases had institutional, as well as cultural and psychological, correlates. We can see evidence of the effect of subprime lenders on the housing boom of the 2000s by noting that low-price homes appreciated faster than high-price homes. And then after 2006, when prices fell, the prices of low-price homes fell faster.[15]

Through our look at the housing market, we see once again the importance of understanding animal spirits as drivers of the economy. Residential investment (mostly construction of new homes and apartment buildings as well as improvements in existing homes) rose from 4.2% of U.S. GDP in the third quarter of 1997 to 6.3% in the fourth quarter of 2005, and it had then fallen to 3.3% by the second quarter of 2008. Thus it has been a significant factor in the recent U.S. economic boom and the bust that followed. We have seen that the reasons for this behavior had to do with all of the elements of our theory of animal spirits—with confidence, fairness, corruption, money illusion, and storytelling.

# THIRTEEN

# Why Is There Special Poverty among Minorities?

And when this happens, when we allow freedom to ring, when we let it ring from every village and every hamlet, from every state and every city, we will be able to speed up that day when all of God's children, black men and white men, Jews and Gentiles, Protestants and Catholics, will be able to join hands and sing in the words of the old Negro spiritual, "Free at last! Free at last! Thank God Almighty, we are free at last."
—Martin Luther King Jr., August 28, 1963

IN THE TWENTY-FOUR MONTHS after Martin Luther King spoke those words, white Americans would finally own up to the gap between black and white justice that had pervaded American history since the settlement of Jamestown.[1] Congress would pass a voting rights law. African Americans would be really allowed to vote in the South. Segregation in accommodations and other forms of business would be banned. Discrimination in employment because of "an individual's race, color, religion, sex, or national origin" would be declared illegal. There would even be the start of some affirmative action, whose remnants are still with us today. There was at last the promise that the divisions of race that had always been the great American Dilemma would finally be overcome.[2]

A dreamer might have hoped for, and possibly even foreseen, the changes of the months ahead. But no one could have predicted the next shoe to drop. Forty-six years have now passed. Yet the black-white difference, instead of vanishing, has metamorphosed into something different. True to King's dream, there is a large and growing black middle class. Today more than half of African Americans have incomes more than double the poverty line. By one standard, this is middle class. Amid this success, however, much black poverty remains. The African-American poverty rate, at 23.6% in 2006, is triple the white rate. Black unemployment remains double that for whites.[3]

These statistics indicate a gap between black and white America, but the reality is yet more disparate than they suggest. The problems of the poorest African Americans go beyond mere poverty. They include extraordinary rates of crime, drug and alcohol addiction, out-of-wedlock births, female-headed households, and welfare dependency. Statistics on incarceration indicate that even the worst of these problems affect a significant fraction of African Americans. Thus, for example, about 7.9% of black males age 18–64 are either in jail or in prison.[4] The black male incarceration rate exceeds the white male rate by a factor of eight to one.[5] Appallingly, the lifetime chances of a black male youth entering prison exceed 25%—and this figure excludes those who will only go to the local jail.[6] We could give comparable figures for Native Americans, who, by most measures, are yet more disadvantaged than African Americans.

We consider the solution of these problems to be America's great unfinished business. Indeed we consider them so large in scope and so important that any book on macroeconomics would be incomplete without their discussion. Also, as we shall see, two of our animal spirits, stories and fairness, play a major role in the perpetuation of these problems.

## Being Black

Significant macroeconomic events almost always lift almost all boats. For example, when the unemployment rate goes up or down by one or two points, unemployment rates for all groups—young, old, male, female, black, white, Hispanic—also go up or down significantly. If one gazes at the stock page at the end of a successful year on Wall Street, rare is the lonely stock that has gone down; and in a bad year, rare is the stock that has risen. The bifurcation of the African-American community—with a successful middle class, a U.S. president, two secretaries of state, an attorney general, and many CEOs on the one hand and more than 800,000 incarcerated on the other—is thus a singular event.[7] It requires explanation.

## Why They Were Left Behind

Social psychologists have shown in the laboratory that it is extremely easy to create group divisions, according to which subjects divide themselves between *us* and *them*. *We* show favoritism toward *us* and bias against *them*. In one of the classic experiments, subjects were divided into groups depending upon whether their birthdays fell on even or odd days of the month. Even in this division, where the groups are totally pallid and meaningless, subjects who were born on an even day of the month showed preference toward fellow evens and bias against odds, and odd subjects showed preference toward fellow odds and bias against their rival evens.[8] Even Dr. Seuss has gotten into the act. His *Butter Battle Book* depicts the Great War that ensues between those who prefer their bread butter side up and those who prefer it butter side down.[9]

If it is possible—in fact it is easy—to develop such we-they groups under the minimal conditions of the laboratory, it should then be no surprise that after four hundred years of racial division American whites and blacks have developed just such orientations. These divisions and biases are connected with two of the animal spirits we have discussed. The very existence of a *we* and a *they* is of course the result of a *story*. But then, as in the laboratory experiments, it also creates a sense of what is just and fair, with different standards for what is considered fair for us and what is considered fair for them.

These divisions are central issues for every African American: the difference between us and them in America.[10] African Americans must navigate the psychological and material difficulties of an economic system that they did not choose and that they consider unfair. Read any African American biography. These issues will invariably be at center stage.

Sociologist Michele Lamont's *The Dignity of Working Men* has shown what this means in real life.[11] Lamont interviewed both white and black working-class males. She was after just what we are after. She wanted to know their story. What motivates them to get up in the morning and go to work? Her interviewees all face the same problem. None of them is doing more than moderately well in meeting the ideals of American society. In terms of money, they are not earning much. In terms of prestige, they command little respect. To maintain their dignity, to go about their difficult and demanding jobs with so little reward, they must have a view of the world and how they fit into it.

Of course not all white and all black workers say the same thing; there is considerable variation. But nevertheless, according to Lamont, there is a modal story that seems to describe the group's view of itself. Let's first view the world according to whites. In their view the world is a tough place. It is highly competitive. But capitalism is the best of all possible systems, and they fit into it. They are proud to be independent contributors to this system. Despite all these difficulties they manage to take care of themselves and of their families, and they take great pride in that. They assume individual responsibility for their fate, and also for their relative success and failure. In addition they think they are better people, more concerned with values and less concerned with money, than those who are higher on the social scale. This is the life that they have chosen, and they are responsible for living with it. Their view of the world is, remarkably, a page out of Milton and Rose Friedman's *Free to Choose*.[12]

In contrast, the African Americans Lamont interviewed have a slightly different story. Like the whites, the working-class blacks also take pride in their self-reliance. But their self-reliance is manifested under yet more difficult circumstances than that of the whites. They did not just receive an unlucky draw from the cards of capitalism. The whites tend to believe that they live in a just society, and that their relatively low status in it is the result of mere bad luck, or perhaps of their own choices. But for African Americans their lack of success has to be viewed as the result of being *them* rather than *us*. *They* deal out the rewards in society, such as jobs and pay. *We* are the recipients. Indeed, relative to the whites, the African Americans must be especially self-reliant, since they must deal with the hostile world of *them* as well as the congenial world of *we*. This gives African Americans a view of solidarity among themselves. It also gives them a sense that there are underdogs and that those underdogs should be helped. Lack of success is not just the result of bad luck in situations in which everyone has an equal chance, or choices of a different lifestyle. That is central to their self-image of who they are and who they ought to be.

In Lamont's interviews race plays a central role for the blacks, as might have been expected, but also for the whites. The whites, priding themselves on their self-reliance, define themselves in opposition to blacks, and especially blacks who are on welfare. In contrast, blacks define themselves in contrast to whites, who they think are stingy and unfair. Each of the sides to these two stories has a script regarding who we are and how we should behave. They also have a script regarding who the others are, how they behave, and how they should behave differently.

## *Those Who Do Not Make It*

We see then that African Americans have a problem that white Americans do not. They must work in a world in which they have been dealt a bad hand in terms of the resources of their parents and the resources of their neighborhoods. They must also play this bad hand in a world that is psychologically stacked against them. The dealer cheated. It takes extra psychological work to manage in a world that cannot be seen as morally just and fair. Lamont's sample of working-class African-American males are those who, difficult as their lives may be, made it, at least to some extent. Every war has its casualties. And the fact that these working-class lives are described as so very difficult suggests that there must be others who do not make it.

In the ethnographies of those who do not make it we see the opposite side of the coin shown us by Lamont. In her view the African-American working class manage to maintain their dignity by holding their emotions at bay. Those who do not make it are unable to do this psychological work. And their emotions explode. A good place to see this is in *Tally's Corner*, Elliot Liebow's classic account of the life and times of a group of men who hang around a carry-out store in one of Washington's most blighted neighborhoods.[13] Its observations date from the early 1960s. Yet it has stood the test of time. We are quite sure that what we take from this ethnography is in no way exceptional. Any ethnography from those who have not made it in the inner city will report the same emotions.

*Tally's Corner* describes the lives of Tally, Sea Cat, Richard, Leroy, and a significant cast of supporting actors. What strikes us most about all of them is their anger. Liebow describes this anger as due to "the humiliation of it all." It comes out—it explodes—in all kinds of ways at all kinds of times. It comes out in fights between the friends, for example, in a knife fight between Richard and Tally after Richard falsely accuses Tally of taking up with his wife. It comes out in refusing opportunities, such as when Richard is offered a job to fix up a house by a real estate broker, but then does not fill out the bid. It comes out in the breakup of families, or in their refusal to make a long-term commitment. Thus Richard, for example, fights with his wife Shirley after he loses his job. Knowing that he cannot support his family as he should, he chooses to retire to "the corner" to nurse his wounds with others in the same boat. At home his family would be an ever-present reminder of his inability to provide for them. Leroy throws his wife out of the house. The anger is reflected not only in refusing jobs but in quitting them abruptly, as when Richard simply sleeps through the time when he should have been up to go to a backbreaking construction job. He feels he cannot take it any more. Or consider Sea Cat, who begins a relationship with Gloria, a 25-year-old widow who has inherited some property and also has some insurance money. He really likes her. But he cannot deal with his lack of pride, and, when he has a car accident, he gets caught with another woman. When he goes to meet Gloria, intending to reconcile, he slaps her, after which he returns to the Corner.

We could have picked any of a large number of ethnographies to describe exactly how bad jobs, poverty, and the search for self-respect all spill over into anger. This anger is then maintained, or sanctioned, by social groups, in this case the men at the Corner. The men say to themselves implicitly, if not explicitly, that, yes, this loss of self-restraint is OK.

There is, we hope, nothing new to our description. Indeed we think that it exactly corresponds to the leading conclusions in African-American studies from a long line of distinguished scholars. They include Elijah Anderson, W.E.B. Du Bois, William Henry Gates, Glenn Loury, Lee Rainwater, William Julius Wilson, and many others. Indeed we can find exact passages in the work of each of them that would summarize what we say here. We could also have told similar stories but in different contexts. We could have described the behavior of women rather than of men. We could have focused on different reasons why people do not make it—on low performance in school, involvement with gangs, alcohol and drug addictions, early pregnancies, and so on. Indeed we believe that what we have described is so general that it appears densely in all detailed descriptions of the lives of those African Americans who fall out of the middle or working class.

The interpretation we have given offers an explanation for the unexpected breakdown in the African-American family and workforce just after the era of the civil rights movement. Every African American prior to the civil rights movement knew of the injustice toward them. But, with rare exception, whites were oblivious. Like the stars in the sky, African Americans accepted the color line as unchanging and immutable. However unfair the system might be, questioning it was beyond contemplation. That would be too self-destructive.

But then the world changed. Not only African Americans but whites as well acknowledged the injustice. It even became an official part of U.S. history, celebrated with Martin Luther King Jr. Day and taught during African-American History Month. Yes, there were new opportunities. And, as we have seen, a large number of people have taken advantage of those opportunities. But it was also much more difficult to ignore—or, more accurately, to repress—the sense of unfairness. Bringing this history out into the open led to an increased sense of unfairness. So while there was new opportunity for some, many have been unable to take advantage of it.[14]

## A Remedy

Much of our description and our analysis may reflect the standard line in sociology and African-American studies. The standard view from economics is that African Americans are poorer because they have few skills and few financial assets and because they face discrimination. But we have added quite a bit to the usual description of the economics of minority poverty. The role of stories, of *us* versus *them,* of the search for self-respect, and of fairness in the lives of the poor is absent from the standard economic analysis of poverty. We call attention to the role of animal spirits here as well.

We believe that our explanation is important because it has implications for the solution to many of the problems faced by African Americans. Should we assume that African Americans are like many immigrant groups in American history, who with no special help have worked their way up the ladder of income and prestige? Or should we believe that African Americans (and also Native Americans) are special? In our telling they are special because they have a different history— a history of injustice and unfairness. Of course all immigrant groups have their own stories of discrimination, but for African Americans and for Native Americans the injustice is qualitatively different. Indeed Hispanics are very different from African Americans. Nonemployment of Hispanic males age 25–34 is about the same as for whites. Not including the incarcerated it is about 10%. In contrast, for African Americans it is about 25%.[15]

Given the role played by history, fairness, and stories, the poverty of both African Americans and Native Americans is, first of all, not just an individual choice. They are caught in a trap not merely because of their lack of resources but also because, more than other groups, there is a special division between *them* and *us*. African Americans, and Native Americans too, do have a special problem—the problem of living with a particular story, the story of their exploitation in America. And then there is the notion among both whites and blacks that there are two groups, *we* and *they*. This very notion is part of daily reality. This notion —as much as low financial assets and low skill levels—is responsible for the continued poverty of African Americans.

So what is to be done? In the 1990s there was a great debate about affirmative action. Two important books appeared at about the same time but reached radically different conclusions. Abigail and Stephan Thernstrom wrote an exhaustive history of affirmative action and how it grew out of the civil rights movement.[16] They prided themselves on both their factual history and their statistical analysis. But the Thernstroms never came to grips with what the ethnographies reveal. They never made a part of their history what happens in the inner cities to people like Sea Cat and Tally and Richard and Leroy. They could not account for the emotions that are revealed in the ethnographies. And it is these emotions, which are unavoidable, that underlie the special case for affirmative action. In contrast, in *A Country of Strangers: Blacks and Whites in America,* reporter David Shipler sought out what African Americans say about themselves and about America.[17] In his view there is a real divide. There is a *we* and a *they*. And affirmative action can play a significant role in breaking down this barrier between the two Americas.

First and foremost is its symbolism. Affirmative action indicates that whites care about blacks. Acceptance by whites of this responsibility defuses the view that America is really two countries, with the white majority uncaring about the black minority. We appreciate that there are objections: that affirmative action is difficult to administer, that it brings up important issues of fairness, and so on. But we view these issues as secondary relative to the role of affirmative action in conveying to African Americans the message "Yes, we can. Yes, we care."[18]

The naysayers, like the Thernstroms, declare that affirmative action is wrong, that there is a growing African-American middle class, that government measures are ineffective, that the problem of black-white difference should be left to the market. But the naysayers fail to understand that there are many interfaces between African Americans and federal and local governments. And in all of them there are opportunities to use resources to change the story of the two Americas.

The most obvious of these interfaces is schooling. By the time African-American children enter school they are already aware that they are black, and also that there is a difference between black and white. In addition they are more likely than whites to be poor and also to have parents and relatives who are dysfunctional. And, even where there are no problems in their own families, poor neighborhoods abound in the dysfunction of others. Witness Tally and his friends. Witness the statistics. Furthermore, the schools are middle-class institutions and they enforce middle-class values. In even the very best schools, teachers, of whatever race, are wary of the disruptions caused when their students explode with the tensions of the problems they cannot handle. And the schools themselves may be a source of such problems. A perceptive study of a middle school in Berkeley, California, showed how the teachers, afraid of the disruption caused by the poorer children from the "flats," punished them when they did not behave like the middle-class children from the "hills."[19] This differential treatment created a sense of unfairness and anger among these 12- and 13-year-olds, mirroring the feelings of Tally and his pals.

Indeed it is precisely because schools have these special problems in educating poor minorities that there is a special need for resources to deal with them. And where these resources have been available, they seem to make a significant difference. There is considerable evidence that African Americans are particularly sensitive to the quality of schooling. The size of kindergarten classes was shown to make a special difference to African-American students in a randomized experiment in Tennessee. The quality of teachers has been shown to affect African Americans' test scores in Texas.[20] Numerous experimental schools, with good teaching and just the right approach, have achieved remarkable success.[21] In these experiments trust developed between students and teachers has defused the anger that can pass from the community into the schoolyard. Given appropriate resources—and with just the right type of feeling, caring teachers who know how to handle such problems and who are not overwhelmed by their teaching loads— African-American students are remarkably responsive. There is great scope for carefully targeted, well-designed programs to help those who have been left out of the race for economic success.[22]

Such educational ventures are just one example of a program operating at the interface between the government and African Americans. Here is another. One prime way for African Americans to make it into the middle class has been through good government jobs. In the beginning these were limited to teaching school, but since the end of segregation they have included jobs in the military, in the federal government, and also at the state and local levels, including hospital work. One of the lesser-known tragedies of the Bush administration has been the systematic contracting out of low-level federal jobs. Under normal circumstances we would approve of the savings to the taxpayer. But this outsourcing has differentially led to the loss of good jobs by African Americans.[23]

There are also, of course, the areas where African Americans come into contact with the law. We are appalled at the number of African Americans in prison and in jail. A great many of these incarcerations are for the moment unavoidable. Indeed many of them may be necessary to protect the African-American community itself.[24] But we should not lose sight of the rehabilitative potential of prison and jail, of the possibilities they hold out for a second chance. We need more creative ways to divert from the general population those prisoners who are willing to learn, and also to rid them of their drug and alcohol addictions. Indeed prison may be viewed as an opportunity for renewal and for education. It should not be the place to learn how to commit more serious crimes.

## The Importance of Trying

In conclusion we see many areas where governments can use resources to defuse the story of a white *we* and a black *they,* or of a white *they* and black *we.* We have seen in this book how peoples throughout history have accomplished near-miracles, if only they have the confidence. We believe that racial division remains the great continuing American Dilemma, yet there are many ways, if only we will concentrate on them, to mute our racial differences. We must have the confidence to try.

We have, throughout this book, acknowledged the power of the market, for good or for ill. But in this case we do not agree with the naysayers, who would leave the solution of this problem only to chance, and only to the market.

# FOURTEEN

# Conclusion

OUR THEORY OF ANIMAL SPIRITS provides an answer to a conundrum: Why did most of us utterly fail to foresee the current economic crisis? How can we understand this crisis when it seems to have come out of the blue with no cause? Why have the measures to forestall it fallen short, while the economic authorities publicly express surprise at their ineffectiveness? We need to answer these questions if we are to feel any confidence in economic policy in the months to come.

The real problem, as we have repeatedly seen in these pages, is the conventional wisdom that underlies so much of current economic theory. So many members of the macroeconomics and finance profession have gone so far in the direction of "rational expectations" and "efficient markets" that they fail to consider the most important dynamics underlying economic crises. Failing to incorporate animal spirits into the model can blind us to the real sources of trouble.

The crisis was not foreseen, and is still not fully understood by the public, and also by many key decision makers, because there have been no principles in conventional economic theories regarding animal spirits. Conventional economic theories exclude the changing thought patterns and modes of doing business that bring on a crisis. They even exclude the loss of trust and confidence. They exclude the sense of fairness that inhibits the wage and price flexibility that could possibly stabilize an economy. They exclude the role of corruption and the sale of bad products in booms, and the role of their revelation when the bubbles burst. They also exclude the role of stories that interpret the economy. All of these exclusions from conventional explanations of how the economy behaves were responsible for the suspension of disbelief that led up to the current crisis. They are also responsible for our current failure in knowing how to deal with the crisis now that it has come.

The financial-markets egg has broken. If Humpty Dumpty had had the correct view of how the world works, he would not have fallen off the wall in the first place. Similarly if the purchasers of assets had realized how the economy really works, they would have been more careful in their purchase of assets, and the economy would not have taken a tumble. But even now, because of a false sense of how the world works, many policy analysts and, especially, most of the public fail to see that Humpty Dumpty cannot be *fixed* and needs to be *replaced*. That is why the measures that have been taken thus far have fallen short of maintaining the credit flows that accompany full employment.

## How Macroeconomic Theory Must Respond

It is necessary to incorporate animal spirits into macroeconomic theory in order to know how the economy really works. In this respect the macroeconomics of the past thirty years has gone in the wrong direction. In their attempts to clean up macroeconomics and make it more *scientific,* the standard macroeconomists have imposed research structure and discipline by focusing on how the economy would behave if people had only economic motives and if they were also fully rational. Picture a square divided into four boxes, denoting motives that are economic or noneconomic and responses that are rational or irrational. The current model fills only the upper left-hand box; it answers the question: How does the economy behave if people only have economic motives, and if they respond to them rationally? But that leads immediately to three more questions, corresponding to the three blank boxes: How does the economy behave with noneconomic motives and rational responses? With economic motives and irrational responses? With noneconomic motives and irrational responses?

We believe that the answers to the most important questions regarding how the macroeconomy behaves and what we ought to do when it misbehaves lie largely (though not exclusively) within those three blank boxes. The goal of this book has been to fill them in.

## A Test

Throughout this book we have been stressing that our description of the economy fits the qualitative as well as the quantitative facts, better than a macroeconomics that leaves out irrational behavior and noneconomic motives. Occasionally we have used statistics, but for the most part we have relied on history and on stories.

We believe that there is an easy and simple test to prove that what we are saying is correct—not only correct, but also more correct than the modeling that fails to deal with the three blank questions in current mainstream macroeconomics. We think that our description of how the economy operates fits almost any business cycle. If we take the most recent business cycle, starting in 2001 and continuing to the present day, we think that our description of the economy, with animal spirits at center stage, gives a remarkably good rendition of what has actually occurred.

Let's review the current U.S. economic cycle (we could do this as well for other countries) and see how the themes in this book have played themselves out. The role of animal spirits is central to our description.

The tale basically begins in 2000 and 2001. In 2000 there was a tremendous stock market crash, as the economy recoiled from the irrational exuberance of the dot-com years. The growth rate of real GDP decelerated from about 4% for 1999 and the first half of 2000 to only 0.8% for the first half of 2001.[1] The Bush administration used the downturn to argue for massive, permanent tax cuts. The first and largest of these was signed into law in June 2001.[2] The Fed also came into the act. The discount rate, which had been 6% in the last half of 2000, was brought down to only 0.75% by November 2002.[3] There is every reason to believe that both of these measures were effective. The economy rebounded.[4] The reduction in interest rates appears to have had the intended effect. The previous boom had been top-heavy in expenditures on capital equipment.[5] Investment in equipment and software had been especially high just prior to the Y2K scare. In this new boom the stimulus came from housing. In the four short years from 2001 to 2005 expenditures on housing increased by 33.1%, while GDP growth was only 11.2%.[6]

But then, as we have already recounted, odd things began to happen. These are the types of things that happen in booms as overconfidence takes hold. People began to buy housing as if this were their last chance ever to buy a house (because, they thought, prices would continue to escalate beyond their means), and speculators began to make investments in housing, as if other people were going to think that they should buy now, at almost any price, because they would not be able to afford to buy a house later. Home prices increased by almost two-thirds in the short span of time between the first quarter of 2000 and the first quarter of 2006.[7] In Los Angeles, Miami, San Francisco, and some other areas they increased considerably more.[8] Vast areas of farmland were turned into new housing developments almost overnight. It was housing speculative fever.

Even more surprisingly, it was not just home buyers who engaged in this fever. The financial markets—which are supposed to be so cautious —aided and abetted the process. Of course the real estate dealers and the mortgage brokers had no reason to dampen the fever. They were collecting transaction fees. And, with business so brisk, those fees were enormous. Most surprisingly, those on the other side of the ledger took in those mortgages and gave the home buyers the massive funds they needed for their unwise speculations.

There are many simple reasons why buyers purchased those mortgages. For one thing, the usual buyers of mortgages, the various types of banks, had discovered that they could make enormous profits from origination fees for loans, but they themselves did not have to take the mortgages onto their books. As we have seen, they could divide them up into the mortgage equivalent of chicken parts. And the buyers of these mortgages did not know what they were buying because they did not hold the mortgages themselves but rather parts of them, in vast packages, where in point of fact it was difficult or even impossible to know anything about the underlying mortgages. Besides, the securitized mortgages had been rated by the various rating houses. The rating houses based their estimates of the probability of default of mortgages such as these on recent trends in home prices—and those had always gone up. So there seemed to be little reason to fear default in this case. Even if someone in a rating agency had thought that the opposite was true—that the ratings should also incorporate the possibility that home prices might decline—anyone who actually blew the whistle would make herself immensely unpopular by casting aspersions on the whole parade of fee collectors who were getting so rich so quickly.

We have recounted in a nutshell what has happened in the current financial crisis. It corresponds to our description of what causes most of our economic ups and downs: overconfidence followed by underconfidence. The story in this case was that the price of housing had never declined (that is only a story, and it is actually untrue) and therefore that it would just continue to go up and up. There was nothing to lose.

As we write this concluding chapter we do not know the extent to which the problems of the various non-bank banks—the investment houses and the hedge funds, all but unsupervised and holding literally trillions of dollars of assets and liabilities—will contribute to this problem.[9]

This is the story of our time. It is the story of the business cycle that began in 2001. When the current downturn will end, we do not know. But the point of our book, and the test of our theory, is that we could have told this same story, or a similar story, using our description of the animal spirits and how they operate, to describe almost any other business cycle. For the United States, we could have gone back to the collapse of 1837, with its land speculation and state bank collapses, and told a similar story. Or we could have gone back to the Great Depression; or to the recession of 1991, when the challenger Bill Clinton accused the incumbent George H. W. Bush of neglecting the economy; or, we think, almost any other cyclical non-oil-related peacetime boom and bust in U.S. history.[10] We could as well have used the same theory to describe the deflationary spiral Japan suffered in the 1990s, or the current economic boom in India.

You pick the time. You pick the country. And you can be fairly well guaranteed that you will see at play in the macroeconomy the *animal spirits* that are the subject of this book.

## *What Does It All Mean?*

We have seen that our interpretation of the economy passes the test. It can be seen playing itself out almost ubiquitously, and it adds new insight to current models of the macroeconomy. But what does that mean?

To see what it all means, let's go back to the explanation of the macroeconomy that does not take account of animal spirits. To our minds, this model is severely lacking. It fails to explain the euphoria followed by pessimism.

But this view of economics is surprisingly popular, not just among professional economists and policy makers but also among the general public. In this view capitalism has brought to consumers in developed economies vast riches undreamed of in previous centuries. The average North American, European, or Japanese consumer has a higher standard of living than a medieval king. She eats better; she lives in housing that is much less roomy but much more comfortably heated; her television and radio, at the press of a button, give her better and more varied entertainment; the list goes on. In addition, as we write, other countries—Brazil, China, India, Russia—are rapidly climbing the GDP ladder.

We agree regarding the wonders of capitalism. But that does not mean that there are not different forms of capitalism, with very different properties and benefits. The debate about which form of capitalism we should have goes far back in American history and is notable for its many sharp reversals. At the beginning of the nineteenth century there was fierce debate over the role of government in the American economy. The Democrats were opposed to government intervention, while the Whigs thought that the government should provide the backdrop for a healthy capitalism. For the federal government this would mean initiation of a system of national roads. Andrew Jackson and later Martin van Buren were against the plan. In contrast, John Quincy Adams and Henry Clay were in favor of it.[11]

And this debate has gone back and forth several times since then. The last major shift occurred in the 1970s with the election of Margaret Thatcher in the United Kingdom and in the 1980s with the election of Ronald Reagan in the United States. For the previous thirty years, with the general acceptance of the New Deal, the dominant thinking of policy makers had been that government was to play a key role in providing the infrastructure for a capitalist society. This infrastructure consisted of not just physical highways, an educational system, and support for scientific research, but also regulations, especially those governing financial markets. At the end of the 1980s we had an economic system that was remarkably well adapted to weather any storm. For example, the S&Ls failed massively, but the system of government protections contained the macroeconomic damage. The failure cost taxpayers quite a bit of money, but only in rare instances did it cost them their jobs.

But then—and this is another part of our story—the economy, as it always does, changed. It adapted to the regulations that were in place. With the general acceptance after the 1980s of the belief that capitalism was a free-for-all, the playing field may have changed, but the rules of the game had not adapted. This has been nowhere more apparent than in the financial markets. The story we just told about the housing market illustrates this perfectly. In the old days there were natural limits on home mortgages. The commercial banks and savings banks had reason to be careful in their initiation of a mortgage. They themselves would be its most likely holder. But then all that changed. The banks became the initiators, but not the holders, of mortgages. But regulation did not adapt to reflect this change in the financial structure.

Public antipathy toward regulation supplied the underlying reason for this failure. The United States was deep into a new view of capitalism. We believed in the no-holds-barred interpretation of the game. We had forgotten the hard-earned lesson of the 1930s: that capitalism can give us the best of all possible worlds, but it does so only on a playing field where the government sets the rules and acts as a referee.

Yet we are currently not really in a crisis for capitalism. We must merely recognize that capitalism must live within certain rules. Indeed our whole view of the economy, with all of those animal spirits, indicates why the government must set those rules. It may be true that in the classical model there is full employment. But in our view the waves of optimism and pessimism cause large-scale changes in aggregate demand. Since wages are determined largely by considerations of fairness, these changes in demand translate not into shifts in wages and prices but into shifts in employment. When demand goes down, unemployment rises. It is the role of the government to mute those changes.

And, to emphasize what we have said previously, in our view capitalism does not just sell people what they really want; it also sells them what they *think* they want. Especially in financial markets, this leads to excesses, and to bankruptcies that cause failure in the economy more generally. All of these processes are driven by stories. The stories that people tell to themselves, about themselves, about how others behave, and even about how the economy as a whole behaves all influence what they do. These stories are not stable but vary over time.

Such a world of animal spirits gives the government an opportunity to step in. Its role is to set the conditions in which our animal spirits can be harnessed creatively to serve the greater good. Government must set the rules of the game.

There is then a fundamental reason why we differ from those who think that the economy should just be a free-for-all, that the least government is the best government, and that the government should play only the most minimal role in setting the rules. We differ because we have a different vision of the economy. Indeed if we thought that people were totally rational, and that they acted almost entirely out of economic motives, we too would believe that government should play little role in the regulation of financial markets, and perhaps even in determining the level of aggregate demand.

But, on the contrary, all of those animal spirits tend to drive the economy sometimes one way and sometimes another. Without intervention by the government the economy will suffer massive swings in employment. And financial markets will, from time to time, fall into chaos.

## *Eight Questions*

Our vision should be adopted not only because it explains macroeconomic histories. It should be adopted because it also explains the detailed operation of capitalist economies. Evidence abounds for the animal spirits discussed in the first five chapters: confidence, fairness, corruption, money illusion, and stories. These are real motivations for real people. They are ubiquitous. The *presumption* of mainstream macroeconomics that they have no important role strikes us as absurd.

This presumption strikes us as doubly absurd given that these animal spirits play a crucial role in answering the eight basic questions regarding capitalist economies that we raised in the next chapters of the book: Why do depressions occur? Why do central banks have real powers? Why do we have involuntary unemployment? Why is there a long-run trade-off between inflation and unemployment? Why is saving so variable? Why do stock markets fluctuate so wildly? Why are the cycles in the housing market so large? And why is there continued minority poverty?

These questions are easy to answer if we take into account animal spirits. They are impossible, or all but impossible, to explain with current mainstream macroeconomics.

## *What We Must Do*

This book tells how the economy works. On the personal level, an accurate view of our economy is necessary to make correct *individual* decisions, such as how much we should save, where we should invest, what house we should buy, and whether we can trust our employer (or Social Security) to pay our pension. And a correct view of how the economy works is yet more essential in making *public* decisions.

This book is being published at a time when people seem to be rethinking their views of the economy. The recent economic turmoil has brought back to the table many questions that had been considered settled. Now people are seeking new answers, urgently. We see it in the newspapers. We see it in the think tanks, and at conferences, and in the corridors of our economics departments.

From time to time it appears that democracies undergo great shifts in their stories of who people are and who they should be. Associated with these shifts are changes in the stories about how the economy works. We might view the United States as having undergone six such major shifts: at the time of the Revolution, after the elections of Andrew Jackson and later of Abraham Lincoln, at the end of Reconstruction, during the Great Depression, and after the election of Ronald Reagan. Historians may disagree with us on the details of these changes of story, but since much of history is about such shifts, they are unlikely to argue with us about their existence.

Nor are they likely to disagree with us about the most recent such shift, coinciding with the election of Ronald Reagan. At that time the explanation of how the economy worked turned to the conservative image with which we began this book, the "invisible hand." This shift was, of course, not just an American phenomenon. Britain had elected Margaret Thatcher eighteen months earlier. Other countries, from India to China to Canada, would follow, sometimes zealously so.

The story of the "invisible hand" and its consequences gives surprisingly detailed prescriptions regarding the role of government, even pertaining to questions of great specificity. But now people are asking these questions anew. Here is a small sampling: How can we allow people of varying abilities and financial sophistication to express their preferences for investments without making them vulnerable to salespeople selling "snake oil"? How can we allow people to take account of their deep intuition about investing opportunities without inviting speculative bubbles and bursts? How can we decide who should be "bailed out" and when? How shall we handle cases of individuals and institutions who have been victimized and wronged? What should be the capitalization of banks? What should be the nature and magnitudes of fiscal and monetary stimuli? Does it really matter if fiscal and monetary responses are early or late? Should they be concentrated or drawn out? What should be the design of deposit insurance? When, for example, should there be least-cost resolution of banks? When should all the depositors be paid off? What regulation should there be for hedge funds? For investment banks? For bank holding companies? How should bankruptcy law be changed to take account of systemic risk? The old answers to these questions seem not to be working. Everywhere that economists and their ilk mingle we see them reaching for new answers.

This book cannot give the *detailed* answers to these questions. It is our contention in this book that the working of the economy, and the role of government in it, cannot be described solely by considering economic motives. Such description also requires detailed understandings of confidence, of fairness, of opportunities for corruption, of money illusion, and of stories that are handed to us by history. So the answers to these questions require much more information than could be contained here. However, this book does give us the background story within which all of these answers should be worked out. And it also stresses the urgency for setting up the committees and commissions to develop the reforms in financial institutions and the regulations that are so immediately needed.

Most of all, this book tells us that the solutions to our economic problems can only be reached if we pay due respect in our thinking and in our policies to the animal spirits.

# Notes

## Preface to the Paperback Edition

1. Bagehot (1920 [1873], pp. 144, 119).
2. Nakamoto and Wighton (2007).
3. See Federal Reserve (2008a).
4. Geisel (1958).

## Preface

1. James (1983 [1904], p. 341). For Akerlof's use of this image in a different context, see Warsh (2006).
2. In 1982 Hyman Minsky wrote *Can "It" Happen Again?* Minsky's *It* was of course the Great Depression. He, like us, was especially concerned with the psychology of speculative bubbles. Our line of thinking in this book parallels that of Minsky.
3. One source estimates the death toll at 52,199,262. See http://www.historyplace.com/worldwar2/timeline/statistics.htm.
4. Friedman was quoted in the December 31, 1965, issue of *Time,* which featured Keynes on the cover. Friedman's later disclaimer is discussed at http://www.libertyhaven.com/thinkers/miltonfriedman/miltonexkeynesian.html.
5. Smith (1776).
6. See especially Levine (2006).
7. In addition to Minsky (1982, 1986), Galbraith (1997 [1955]) and Kindelberger (1978) have given seminal historical accounts of bubbles and panics. Galbraith's *The Great Crash: 1929* offers an account of the events leading up to the stock market crash of 1929 that is very much in the same spirit as the analysis in this book. Kindelberger gives a remarkable history of past manias and panics. The ubiquity with which they occur suggests—as we state explicitly here—that their origins lie in human nature, in the animal spirits.
8. In the words of Minsky (1982, p. 138), the reconstructed Keynesian theory was reduced to "banality" in that it "does not explain how an economy gets into the unemployment equilibrium. . . . [It] does not allow for disruptive internal dynamic processes."

## Introduction

1. In his book *Who's Afraid of Adam Smith?,* Peter Dougherty (2002, p. xi) writes that "Economic ideas in the tradition of Adam Smith are to democratic capi-

talism what an operating system is to a computer. The possibilities for capital-ism, as for computing, are prodigious, depending on what we make of them; but they are only as good as the instructions that drive the respective systems."

2.    Keynes (1973 [1936], pp. 149–50, 161–62).

3.    The term *animal spirits* originated in ancient times, and the works of the an-cient physician Galen (ca. 130–ca. 200) have been widely quoted ever since as a source for it. The term was commonly used in medicine through medieval times and up until Robert Burton's *The Anatomy of Melancholy* (1632) and René Descartes' *Traité de l'Homme* (1972 [1664]). There were said to be three spir-its: the *spiritus vitalis* that originated in the heart, the *spiritus naturalis* that originated in the liver, and the *spiritus animalis* that originated in the brain. The philosopher George Santayana (1955 [1923], p. 245) built a system of phi-losophy around the centrality of "animal faith," which he defined as "a pure and absolute spirit, an imperceptible cognitive energy, whose essence is intuition."

4.    The so-called IS-LM model has had an enduring influence on macroeconomic thought. Milton Friedman, who throughout his entire career was highly crit-ical of Keynesian macroeconometric models, was eventually prevailed upon, late in his academic career, to develop a model that represented his views. He came up with one that closely resembled a modern, or neo-Keynesian, Hick-sian IS-LM model (Friedman 1970). In his critique of Friedman's theoretical approach, James Tobin (1972, p. 851) said, "I have been very surprised to learn what Professor Friedman regards as his crucial theoretical differences from the neo-Keynesians." Friedman supplied a single "missing equation" on top of that model: a short-run relation between output and prices. Similarly the rational-expectations revolution in macroeconomics has often had little im-pact on macroeconometric modelers except to suggest rational-expectations "versions" of their models. Often these models were still other variations on the same IS-LM model, such as the classic Sargent-Wallace model (Sargent and Wallace 1975).

5.    Fischer (1977), Taylor (1979, 1980), and Calvo (1983).

6.    Another approach that has dominated much more recent macroeconomic thinking is that of dynamic stochastic general equilibrium (DSGE) models, in the tradition of Kydland and Prescott (1982). These are based on some im-portant insights but, in their present form, rely on a presumption that all hu-man behavior is optimizing intertemporal utility. These models allow for such things as monetary policy shocks, or productivity shocks, but no animal spir-its. In their recent paper V. V. Chari, Patrick J. Kehoe, and Ellen R. McGrattan (2008, p. 3) conclude that macroeconomics is converging on a consensus in favor of this kind of model and that "macroeconomists are also beginning to agree on the nature of the reduced-form shocks needed to be included in a model in order for it to fit the data." But, while the macroeconomists who at-tend their meetings may be nearing agreement, there is absolutely no consen-sus among economists or social scientists at large. We believe that, although the DSGE models represent an important phase in the history of economic thought, their fundamental assumptions need to be rethought.

CHAPTER ONE
CONFIDENCE AND ITS MULTIPLIERS

1. "Attitude of Waiting." See also "A Twenty-Five Million Pool."

2. Cooper and John (1988) have in particular emphasized the role of dual equilibria in macroeconomics. The view of confidence in this chapter goes beyond this interpretation. Our description of confidence corresponds to that presented in the seminal paper by Benabou (2008). To Benabou the notion of confidence corresponds to a psychological state in which people do not sufficiently utilize the information that is available to them. They are too trusting —a state of mind that leads to overinvestment. Blanchard (1993) takes a similar view on the nature of animal spirits. Concerning the Michigan Consumer Sentiment Index, he draws the distinction of whether it predicted future changes in income because it reflected consumers' predictions of the future or consumer confidence. Blanchard interprets such consumer confidence as *animal spirits*.

3. Studies of the outcomes of sporting events suggest a relation between events that could be expected to affect confidence and thus economic behavior. College students estimate their own performance to be better following a win by their school's basketball team than following a loss (Hirt et al. 1992). Sales of lottery tickets rise in the days following the victory of a local team (Arkes et al. 1988). Furthermore these effects of sporting events on confidence have been shown to affect economic outcomes. One study of international soccer games in forty-two countries from 1973 to 2004 found that the average return over all days on investments in the countries' stock markets was 0.06% (or 15.6% a year). But the average return in the market of a given country on the day after a loss to another country was −0.13%, and the return on the day of a country's elimination from a tournament was −0.23% (Edmans et al. 2007).

4. Kahn (1931).

5. Hicks (1937).

6. Leven et al. (1934).

7. Carson (1975).

8. Commenting on Jan Tinbergen and his modeling efforts, Keynes (1940, p. 156) wrote: "That there is anyone I would trust with it at the present stage or that this brand of statistical alchemy is ripe to become a branch of science, I am not yet persuaded. But Newton, Boyle and Locke all played with alchemy. So let him continue."

9. We can test whether a confidence variable *causes* GDP using econometric methods pioneered by Clive Granger (1969) or Christopher Sims (1972). Matsusaka and Sbordone (1995) found that the Michigan Consumer Sentiment Index Granger-causes GDP in the United States; Berg and Bergström (1996) found that a measure of consumer confidence Granger-causes consumption in Sweden; and Utaka (2003) found that another measure of consumer confidence Granger-causes GDP in Japan. However, these tests involve only two

variables, confidence and GDP. Others have included confidence in a broader vector autoregressive (VAR) framework, with varying degrees of success. When many variables are included in a VAR, and with relatively few observations, results tend to be erratic. According to Bernanke et al. (2001, p. 388), "To conserve degrees of freedom, standard VARs rarely employ more than six to eight variables. This small number of variables is unlikely to span the information sets used by actual central banks, which are known to follow literally hundreds of data series, or by the financial market participants or other observers." These authors do not include confidence variables in their analysis. Other variables may be needed in the VAR to cleanse a mismeasured confidence index of errors, or to take account of other factors, such as monetary policy variables, which correlate with confidence but are separate from it. One approach has been to expand the VAR but to impose Bayesian priors on the coefficients to reduce the dimensionality problem, but here too the results are only as good as the priors. Leeper et al. (1996) are able to expand the list of included variables to eighteen, but they still do not include confidence measures among them. Inevitably, even if we did have good and comprehensive measures of confidence, when working with the macroeconomy there will be more data variables that we want to include than there are time-series observations, and the analysts' priors must begin to have a huge influence on the analysis. Our work here might be viewed as helping us to develop our Bayesian priors using a broad spectrum of information that is difficult to quantify.

10. Davis and Fagan (1997).

11. Fair (1994, pp. 303–11).

12. Blanchard (1993). A considerable literature has grown out of Blanchard's observation, concerning whether shocks to consumer confidence indices actually measure consumers' state of confidence, or whether they merely reflect consumers' predictions about the future. Ludvigson (2004) has provided a review of the literature. Barsky and Sims (2006) come to the conclusion that shocks to the consumer confidence index are, in fact, mainly informational.

## Chapter Two
## Fairness

1. Rees (1973 [1962]).

2. Rees (1993, pp. 243–44).

3. "Many colors" is probably a mistranslation. Many scholars believe it was in fact a tunic "with sleeves."

4. Kahneman et al. (1986a).

5. Lohr (1992).

6. Kahneman et al. (1986b, pp. S287–88).

7. Fehr and Gächter (2000).

8. Chen and Hauser (2005).

9. De Quervain et al. (2005).

10. E-mail communication from Ernest Fehr to George Akerlof, November 1, 2008. Fehr also pointed out that—since the dorsal striatum is activated in anticipation of both getting water, if one is thirsty, and getting revenge, if one is angry—people can literally be "thirsty for revenge."

11. Brown (1986).

12. Blau (1963).

13. Akerlof and Kranton (2000, 2002, 2005, 2008).

## CHAPTER THREE
## CORRUPTION AND BAD FAITH

1. Galbraith (1997 [1955], p. 133) records the cyclical nature of economic bad faith. He describes its growth during the boom ("the bezzle grew apace") and its discovery after the crash.

2. Much of the basis for this chapter comes from Akerlof's joint work with Paul Romer (Akerlof and Romer 1993).

3. Jacobs (1961).

4. Chernow (1998).

5. This argument comes from Akerlof and Romer (1993).

6. Welch and Byrne (2001, p. 129).

7. Wolk and Nikolai (1997, p. 11).

8. These were 1993 dollars (Akerlof and Romer 1993, p. 36).

9. Akerlof and Romer (1993).

10. According to the argument of Grossman and Hart (1980).

11. Kornbluth (1992, pp. 323–24).

12. Crystal (1991).

13. Sands (1991).

14. Standard & Poor's/Case-Shiller Home Price Index, http://www.metroarea.standardandpoors.com.

15. Eichenwald (2005).

16. While the Securities and Exchange Commission investigation into Enron's financial irregularities did not come until October 19, 2001, late in the recession (which ran from March to November 2001), suspicions of Enron had already been mounting and the company's stock had been falling sharply well before then. Enron is cited here as an example of the kind of financial irregularity that was part and parcel of the period surrounding the recession, including the weak recovery that lasted until 2002–03.

17. Case (2008).

18. Mason and Rosner (2007, p. 2).

19. Shiller (2008a).

20. Calomiris (2008, p. 19).

21. For an excellent example of this see Kashyap et al. (2008, p. 9). They note that at UBS those who took in the subprime mortgages were able to book very high profits—which would be counted toward their bonuses.

22. Goetzmann et al. (2003) and Lo (2008).

23. Little is known about the holdings of hedge funds because they are not required to disclose such information. It would be a good idea, from the standpoint of public judgment of systemic risk, to require them to do so. There was a brief period in 2006 in the United States when hedge fund managers were required to file form ADV with the Securities and Exchange Commission. This form discloses a great deal of information relevant to judging the operational risk of a fund, though it does not include direct information about the fund's portfolio. It has been argued that the more stringent disclosure requirement had some impact, though the impact was only marginal (see Brown et al. 2007). It would be better if the actual portfolio of a fund were disclosed.

24. Calomiris (2008).

25. Becker (1968).

26. Sah (1991).

27. In 1933 New York Governor Herbert H. Lehman stated: "Nothing, in my opinion, can now stop the movement for repeal which is sweeping all parts of the country. The fight against hypocrisy and racketeering and disrespect for the law is almost won, thanks to the force of public opinion, which can accomplish miracles if given the opportunity of becoming vocal" ("Formal Addresses of Lehman, Smith, Root and Wadsworth at Repeal Convention").

28. "Contract Bridge Favorite Game among Women."

## CHAPTER FOUR
## MONEY ILLUSION

1. And yet there are a number of biases that inhibit the public's acceptance of indexation (Shiller 1997b).

2. Fisher (1928, pp. 75–78). Our more modern calculation suggests that the increase in prices had been closer to twofold.

3. Ibid., pp. 3–18.

4. Keynes (1940b).

5. Phillips (1958).

6. Friedman (1968).

7. More precisely they will seek to increase the prices for their products relative to the prices charged by other firms.

8. See, for example, Gordon (1977, p. 265). If inflationary expectations are formed as a moving average of recent past inflation, estimates of Phillips curves should find that the coefficients on lagged inflation sum to one. Many estimates of Phillips curves fail to reject that this sum is equal to one. Given the importance of such findings, it is remarkable that their robustness to spec-

ifications of time period, data, and exact specification of the Phillips curve have never been subjected to tough tests—even though everything else about the Phillips curve, including the natural rate of unemployment itself, is considered to be estimated with great imprecision. Akerlof et al. (2000) provide a range of estimates for both wage and price equations with many different specifications. These estimates, particularly when made for periods of low inflation, show considerable variation in the sum of the coefficients on lagged inflation, dependent on the specification. Another bit of evidence that suggests such estimates will be sensitive to specification comes from the high standard errors on the natural rate itself (Staiger et al. 1997); it would be surprising that the sum of lagged coefficients could be estimated precisely if another component of the Phillips curve, the natural rate, could be estimated only with very low precision. Gordon's own estimates show very different values for this sum of coefficients. Of course, there is a theoretical reason why estimates of such a sum should not be robust. With rational expectations, rather than a simple mechanical theory of the formation of inflationary expectations, Sargent (1971) shows that there is no theoretical reason that they should sum to one.

9. There were high standard errors.

10. Before Friedman, Edmund Phelps (1968) had demonstrated the accelerationist view of the Phillips curve. In 2006 he was belatedly awarded the Nobel Prize in economics, mainly for this insight.

11. Tobin (1972b, p. 3).

12. Christofides and Peng (2004, Table 1, p. 38).

13. Ibid., note 19, p. 11.

14. The following studies have all found significant signs of nominal wage rigidity: Card and Hyslop (1997), Kahn (1997), Altonji and Devereux (1999), Bewley (1999), and Lebow et al. (1999) for the United States; Dwyer and Leong (2000) for Australia; Fortin (1996) for Canada; Bauer et al. (2003) and Knoppik and Beissinger (2003) for Germany; Kimura and Ueda (2001) and Kuroda and Yamamoto (2003a–c) for Japan; Castellanos et al. (2004) for Mexico; Cassino (1995) and Chapple (1996) for New Zealand; Agell and Lundborg (2003) for Sweden; Fehr and Goette (2004) for Switzerland; and Nickell and Quintini (2001) for the United Kingdom.

15. Carlton (1986).

16. Modigliani and Cohn (1979).

## CHAPTER FIVE
## STORIES

1. This line is frequently attributed to Edna St. Vincent Millay: "Life isn't one damn thing after another. It's the same damn thing again and again." However, she was reacting to much earlier uses of the line, whose true origins we have been unable to trace.

2. Schank and Abelson (1977, 1995).

3. Taleb (2001).
4. Sternberg (1998).
5. Harmon (2006).
6. Polti (1981 [1916]).
7. Tobias (1993, pp. iii–iv).
8. The role of politicians in spreading stories has been emphasized by Edward Glaeser (2002).
9. Finnel (2006).
10. Colburn (1984).
11. Finnel (2006).
12. Shiller (2000, 2005).
13. Shiller (2000, 2005) identified the biggest national stock price increases around the world in recent decades and undertook a media search for the stories in their respective national news media interpreting the increases. He found that journalists were especially creative in telling stories of why a new era was dawning for the economy of the particular country. Yet despite these stories, the stock market increases tended to be reversed later.
14. The classic mathematical model of epidemics is Bailey (1975).

## Chapter Six
## Why Do Economies Fall into Depression?

1. Shiller (2008b).
2. See for example "Must Cut Prices if They Would Work" or "Miners Seem Hopelessly Divided."
3. "Want Old Rate Restored."
4. Lebergott (1957).
5. Romer (1986).
6. Short-term interest rates reached levels in 1893 not seen since the panic of 1873 (Macaulay 1938, Table 10, pp. A142–60). It was not only high interest rates but also "the impossibility of borrowing at any rate" that caused failures. The absence of credit led to "the pricking of many balloons" ("Lending on Collateral" and "Unable to Weather the Gale").
7. Noyes (1909).
8. Steeples and Whitten (1998).
9. Faulkner (1959), Turner (1894), and Schumpeter (1939).
10. Clark (1895).
11. Steeples and Whitten (1998, p. 128).
12. "Embezzlements of Last Year."
13. Degler (1967).
14. Baum, who died in 1919, never stated that his book was a metaphor. But nu-

merous parallels in the book to the bimetallism conflict have been pointed out; see Littlefield (1964).

15. "Wilson Insistent."

16. "Reynolds Sees New Hope with Currency Law Changes" and "President Wilson Looks to Business Prosperity as He Signs Currency Measure."

17. Young (1928, pp. 973 and 976).

18. Searching for the phrase "overheated economy" on LexisNexis under "General News, Major Papers" produced 1,987 hits.

19. Searching the full text of the entire Working Paper series of the National Bureau of Economic Research, representing over ten thousand scholarly working papers, turned up no papers at all that used the phrase *overheated economy.*

20. Di Tella et al. (2000) show that international empirical measures of life satisfaction are negatively related to inflation as well as unemployment.

21. Shiller (2000, 2005).

22. Quoted in McDonald (1962, p. 278).

23. Smith (1925).

24. Alexander Dana Noyes, http://www.newsbios.com/newslum/noyes.htm.

25. Eichengreen and Sachs (1985) and Eichengreen (1992).

26. U.S. Bureau of Labor Statistics (2008).

27. O'Brien (1989).

28. "Applaud Idea of Lowering City Salaries."

29. O'Brien (1989).

30. "Notes Real Signs of Business Uplift."

31 Economic historians Harold Cole and Lee Ohanian (2000, 2004) have argued that by allowing corporations to effectively collude and secure the advantages of monopoly power, the Roosevelt administration worsened the Depression in the United States. According to Cole and Ohanian, even after the U.S. Supreme Court struck down NIRA's competition rules in 1935, the government effectively continued to support the rules by suspending antitrust action against corporations that acquiesced to union demands to raise wages.

32. According to the textbook Keynesian model, in the extreme case of a depression the aggregate demand curve is vertical. Given rigid nominal wages, the aggregate supply curve sets the level of prices so as to make the real wage consistent with this level of output.

33. Higgs (1997, p. 568).

34. Cantril (1951, p. 175). A May 1939 poll of U.S. business executives asked "Which of these two statements do you come closest to agreeing [with]? (1) The policies of the administration have so affected the confidence of businessmen that recovery has seriously been held back; (2) businessmen have been unjustly blaming the administration for their troubles." Of the respondents, 64.8% agreed with the first statement, 25.6% agreed with the second, and 9.6% said they did not know (p. 64).

35. "Callisthenes" (1931).
36. "Out of the Trough of Depression."
37. "Confidence Is Recovery Key, Sloan Asserts."
38. Youngman (1938).
39. Romer (1992).
40. The Japanese consumer price index, which stood at 111.4 in 1990, was at 122.2 in 1998, with actual deflation having occurred only during the period 1994–95. But then the period 1998–2005 saw continued, albeit mild, deflation. There was virtually no inflation in 2006–07. See *Economic Report of the President* (2008, Table B-108, p. 350).

## CHAPTER SEVEN
## WHY DO CENTRAL BANKERS HAVE POWER OVER THE ECONOMY (INSOFAR AS THEY DO)?

1. Federal Reserve (2008a).
2. http://www.federalreserve.gov/releases/h41/Current/. This number should only be used as an indicator of order of magnitude. In the current financial crisis it is changing constantly.
3. But despite the appeal of this story to theoreticians, it misses something fundamental to the mission of the central bank. Hyman Minsky (1982, p. 250) remarked that central bankers who think that this is the central story are putting on "money supply blinders."
4. Goldfeld (1976).
5. See Bernanke and Blinder (1988, 1992) for a discussion of the loanable funds theory.
6. The exact percentage varies depending on the size and type of a bank's liabilities; see Federal Reserve (2008b).
7. An account is given by Friedman and Schwartz (1963, pp. 156–68).
8. "An Elastic Currency and Bankers' Bank."
9. "Mr. Lodge on Finance."
10. "Aldrich Banking System."
11. "Still Danger of Financial Panic."
12. Morris and Shin (2004) and Brunnermeier (2009).
13. Sorkin (2008). Later, however, JPMorgan Chase agreed to pay $10 per share. The original overnight deal was deemed too hasty, and it was renegotiated (Thomas and Dash 2008).
14. Andrews (2008).
15. Bernanke (2008a).
16. Lowenstein (2001, pp. 39, 40, 118, 191, and 207).

POSTSCRIPT TO CHAPTER SEVEN
THE CURRENT FINANCIAL CRISIS: WHAT IS TO BE DONE?

1.  U.S. law, from the Employment Act of 1946, gives two main goals for government economic policy. As enunciated in U.S. Code, Title 15, Section 1021, the government "declares and establishes as a national goal the fulfillment of the right to full opportunities for useful paid employment at fair rates of compensation of all individuals able, willing, and seeking to work." And furthermore "The Congress further declares that inflation is a major national problem requiring improved government policies." (http://www.law.cornell.edu/uscode/15/1021.html). In times of crisis low inflation targets should not be difficult to achieve.

2.  GDP was about $7 trillion in 1994 (*Economic Report of the President* 2001, Table B-1, p. 274).

3.  Federal Reserve Table B16, Commercial Paper Outstanding (http://www.federalreserve.gov/DataDownload/Download.aspx?rel=CP&series=40f558ddc745a653699dbcdf7d6baef9&lastObs=24&from=&to=&filetype=csv&label=include&layout=seriescolumn&type=package).

4.  Seasonally adjusted, it was $1.21 trillion in July 2007. By October 2008 it had fallen to $725 billion.

5.  Many mortgages could of course be passed on to Fannie Mae and Freddie Mac.

6.  Greenlaw et al. (2008) and Morris and Shin (2008).

7.  The credit target might best be considered an intermediate target, since it is not an ultimate goal of the Fed, as is full employment, but is instead used as a means of hitting an ultimate target. The concept of an intermediate target for monetary policy has been much discussed; see for example Friedman (1990).

8.  Bernanke and Blinder (1988, p. 438).

9.  Bernanke et al. (2001).

10.  http://www.frbsf.org/news/speeches/2008/1014.html. The Fed has also opened up a special credit market facility for primary dealers, the Primary Credit Dealer Facility, and a similar facility to grant liquidity to money market mutual funds. And in two notable instances it has made loans to prevent the bankruptcy of major financial entities: Bear Stearns (as we saw in Chapter 7) and American International Group (AIG). All of these actions by the Fed can be considered use of the discount window, although in nontraditional ways.

11.  http://www.federalreserve.gov/newsevents/press/monetary/20081007d.htm and http://www.federalreserve.gov/newsevents/press/monetary/20081021b.htm.

12.  See the explanation given by the Federal Reserve at http://www.federalreserve.gov/newsevents/monetary20081125a1.pdf.

13.  U.S. Department of the Treasury (2008, p. 2).

14. http://en.wikipedia.org/wiki/Fannie_Mae.

15. An excellent survey of Sweden's resolution of its banking crisis during the 1990s has been given by Englund (1999). After the crisis was over, the banks returned to profitability (Figure 6, p. 90).

16. Morgenson (2008).

17. Benoit et al. (2008).

## Chapter Eight
## Why Are There People Who Cannot Find a Job?

1. Much of this chapter is based on Akerlof's joint work with Janet Yellen (Akerlof and Yellen 1990).

2. Early examples of the theory include Solow (1979), McDonald and Solow (1981), and Akerlof (1982). See also Yellen (1984).

3. Pratt et al. (1979).

4. Ibid., pp. 206–7.

5. Juhn et al. (1993).

6. These numbers may considerably overstate the ranges because they fail to take into account measurement error. The use of the March Current Population Survey (CPS) supplements of the CPS as the data source, taking wages as annual reported earnings divided by annual reported hours, gives considerable measurement error (see Lemieux 2006).

7. Groshen (1991).

8. This was the average variation explained, not controlling for occupation (see Groshen 1991, p. 874).

9. Dickens and Katz (1987) and Krueger and Summers (1988). (Summers was later secretary of the treasury and president of Harvard University, and he is now a leading adviser to President Obama. This study is a demonstration of the excellence of his work as an economist.) Note that these studies are for the United States during a period when unionization was quite weak; it is thus unlikely to be the major factor underlying such wage differentials. In contrast Dunlop's wage differentials may have been mainly the result of differentials in union power. The role of union power in wage setting during the Great Depression of the 1930s is discussed by Cole and Ohanian (2004).

10. For some data on the countercyclical behavior of quits see Akerlof et al. (1988).

11. Ibid., p. 532.

12. Shapiro and Stiglitz (1984) and also Stoft (1982), Foster and Wan (1984), and Bowles (1985).

13. Lazear and Moore (1984).

14. Akerlof and Kranton (2005, p. 22).

15. The complexity of the emotional relationship between employees and employers is described in Katz (1986), Blinder and Choi (1990), and Uchitelle (2006).The importance of reciprocity has been underscored in a number of experiments. McCabe et al. (2003) find that people are willing to give something to an anonymous and unseen stranger in an experimental trust game, in hopes that the stranger will make an enlightened reciprocal choice. Blinder and Choi find strong evidence in favor of morale considerations for paying high wages as well as mixed evidence in favor of efficiency wages as a device for maintaining worker discipline. Bewley (1999) concludes that morale is an important reason for failure to make wage cuts. Campbell and Kamlani (1997) report that morale is a major reason firms do not make money wage cuts, but so is concern over quits by the best workers. Fang and Moscarini (2002) argue that firms' concerns with morale encourage a policy of nondifferentiation and wage compression whereby pay is unrelated to performance.

16. Akerlof and Yellen (1990) and Levine (1991).

17. Theories of unemployment that emphasize the role of workers already employed by the firm are called insider-outsider theories. Initially developed by Assar Lindbeck and Dennis Snower (1988), the insider-outsider theory has been applied by Olivier Blanchard and Lawrence Summers (1987) to explain continued high European unemployment.

CHAPTER NINE
WHY IS THERE A TRADE-OFF BETWEEN INFLATION
AND UNEMPLOYMENT IN THE LONG RUN?

1. Much of this chapter is based on Akerlof's joint work with William Dickens and George Perry (Akerlof et al. 1996, 2000; Akerlof and Dickens 2007). See also Schultze (1959), Tobin (1972), and Palley (1994).

2. Samuelson (1997 [1948]).

3. Card and Hyslop (1997) and Kahn (1997).

4. Fortin (1995, 1996).

5. Bewley (1999). Bewley conducted 334 interviews. A few of these involved more than one interviewee.

6. Ibid., pp. 535–54.

7. Firms often level wages, paying the same wage to everyone with the same job description even if some workers are manifestly more productive than others. This would seem to defy economic logic. Why not reward the more productive employees? But many firms strictly adhere to a level-wage policy. They do not give higher pay to the more productive workers not only because of a sense that doing so would be unfair, but also because of a perceived "morale hazard": a potential loss of confidence among the lower-paid workers, dis-

rupting their self-esteem and thus their commitment to their employer (Fang and Moscarini 2002).

8.  Akerlof et al. (1996, p. 31).

9.  Such a value for wage truncation between zero and 2% is in rough agreement with calculations of wage truncation taken from the asymmetry of the wage-change distribution by Card and Hyslop (1997). They obtain lower values for truncation, but that is to be expected since they are also looking at higher levels of inflation, at which truncation would be much less.

10. This argument is made precisely, with the underlying equations shown, in both Akerlof et al. (1996, 2000) and Akerlof and Dickens (2007).

11. This figure is arrived at using Okun's law, which says that for every percentage point increase in unemployment there is a 2% decrease in output.

12. Shiller (1997a).

13. See Shafir et al. (1997) for a formal model of this effect.

14. A simple and natural way for people to form inflationary expectations is as a weighted average (more formally, as a distributed lag) of past inflation. In this case the sum of the weights on past inflation in Phillips curve estimations indicates the extent to which natural rate theory holds. If the sum of the coefficients is one, then as expected inflation increases, wages will rise by exactly the same amount. If the weights are less than one, then wages will increase by less than inflationary expectations. For an exception to this argument see Sargent (1971).

15. When Phillips curves are estimated respectively for periods of low and high inflation for the United States, the sum of the weights on past inflation is close to zero when inflation is low. The sum of the weights on past inflation is close to one when inflation is high. If inflationary expectations are a weighted average of recent past inflation, then with complete pass-through of inflationary expectations into wages we might expect the sum of these weights to be one; with no pass-through we might expect them to be zero (Akerlof et al. 2000; Brainard and Perry 2000). The difference between the high and the low inflation estimatates could also occur for econometric reasons.

16. The data thus do seem to show that wage changes are more dependent on lagged inflation when inflation is high than when it is low. But we should also warn the reader that it is hard to estimate Phillips curves. There could be systematic reasons why these estimates are in error. But these reasons for error are hard—indeed perhaps impossible—to probe. For example, lagged inflation might be a noisier proxy of inflationary expectations at low inflation than at high inflation.

17. Fortin (1996).

18. Ibid., p. 761.

19. Ip (1994).

20. Fortin (1996, p. 765).

21. Ip (1994).

CHAPTER TEN
WHY IS SAVING FOR THE FUTURE SO ARBITRARY?

1.  Venti and Wise (2000).

2.  F. H. Buckley and Margaret Brinig (1998) point out that a near tripling in personal bankruptcy filings between 1980 and 1992 did not correspond to times when bankruptcy law was made more lenient. They provide evidence that the rise in bankruptcy filings is attributable to changes in social norms, such as those having to do with social conservatism, aversion to breaking promises, and sense of personal shame.

3.  Shefrin and Thaler (1988). Evidence from data on individual U.S. households from the Consumer Expenditure Survey confirms that households consume more out of dividends than from capital gains (Baker et al. 2006).

4.  Thaler and Benartzi (2004). The saving rate increased from 4.4% to 8.8% (p. S174). This behavior is also explained in terms of prospect theory by Kahneman and Tversky (1979). According to prospect theory the framing of decision making is important, and people resist taking losses. In the context of Thaler and Benartzi's study, the employees do not want to take losses in their consumption.

5.  Gale et al. (2005).

6.  Madrian and Shea (2001).

7.  Lusardi and Mitchell (2005, p. 11).

8.  Ibid., p. 12.

9.  Many saving anomalies are summarized in Shiller (1982), Grossman et al. (1987), Campbell and Deaton (1989), and Deaton (1992). Hall and Mishkin (1982) explain some anomalies by dividing individuals into consumers who are borrowing-constrained and those without such a constraint. Shea (1995b) shows evidence that neither borrowing constraints nor "myopia" can fully explain the predictability of consumption; he proposes that preferences involving loss aversion must play a role in explaining the predictability of consumption. Shefrin and Thaler assembled some of the evidence of anomalies and produced a behavioral life-cycle model that incorporates some of the best features of the life-cycle model of Ando and Modigliani (1963) and adjusts it for known facts about human behavior (Thaler 1994). For a broader discussion of these issues see Thaler (1994).

10. Keynes (1973 [1936], p. 96).

11. Hall (1978) found some apparently striking evidence in favor of this maximizing model in showing that a time series of aggregate U.S. consumption was approximately a random walk. However, subsequent evidence has generated other interpretations (Blinder et al. 1985; Hall 1988). Carroll and Summers (1991) found evidence against the random-walk hypothesis in that individual consumption tends to track predictable life-cycle changes in income, though Carroll (2001) backtracked a bit on their conclusions. Shea (1995a) found evi-

dence that individual consumption changes can be forecast using data on future incomes implicit in union contracts.

12. Modigliani and Brumberg (1954) and Friedman (1957).

13. As reported in Angeletos et al. (2001, p. 47), quoting Bernheim (1995) and Farkas and Johnson (1997).

14. Engen et al. (1999, p. 97) reach the opposite conclusion. They compare the actual wealth of households with that derived from a calibrated optimization model. Their preferred calibration has a rate of time preference of 3%. Using data from the U.S. Health and Retirement Survey and a broad definition of wealth that includes all home equity, they find that 60.5% of households have more than the median optimal wealth in the calibrated model. But we would focus on an alternative result from their simulations. If we exclude home equity investment in spendable financial capital, and assume a zero rate of intertemporal time discount, only 29.9% of persons reach the preretirement age of 60 or 61 with more than the optimal median wealth for someone of their age (Table 5, p. 99). Like the authors, for both empirical and a priori reasons, we view a zero rate of discount as more correct. This conforms to people's stated preference for nondeclining consumption at a zero rate of interest, and it weights utility at different ages on a one-for-one basis. Our choice to exclude home equity capital assumes that retirees should not have to leave their homes for financial reasons, or to reverse-mortgage them, as they get older.

15. Communication from Gary Burtless, table titled "Fraction of Non-Earnings Income by Source, by Income Quintile for Population 65 and Older."

16. Aaron and Reischauer (1999, p. 174).

17. Not adjusting for purchasing power parity, GDP per capita in Luxembourg is 897 times that in Burundi (Central Intelligence Agency 2008).

18. There is in fact, as has long been known, a strong historical connection (in terms of correlation across countries) between national savings rates and national economic growth rates (see, for example, Modigliani 1970 and Carroll and Weil 1994).

19. See http://ask-us.cpf.gov.sg/?prof=mem.

20. Peebles (2002).

21. In standard growth accounting the contribution of savings to GDP growth would be the product of the "share of capital" (which is typically between $1/4$ and $1/3$) and the rate of growth of the capital stock. With a capital output ratio of 3 and a net savings rate of $1/3$ the capital stock will be growing at the rate of $1/9$. The contribution of savings to GDP growth will be between $1/36$ and $1/27$.

22. The information that follows comes from Andy Di Wu's personal interviews.

23. Feinberg (1986, p. 355).

24. Prelec and Simester (2001).

25. Laibson et al. (2000, p. 38) argue that people "appear to be of two minds" about their savings. They have separate mental accounts for retirement savings

(which they put in liquid assets) and credit card debt. This can help explain the widespread practice of running up a substantial credit card debt that has a higher interest rate than is earned on the retirement assets.

26. Barenstein (2002).

## Chapter Eleven
## Why Are Financial Prices and
## Corporate Investments So Volatile?

1.  Parts of this chapter are based on Shiller's joint work with John Y. Campbell, for example, Campbell and Shiller (1987, 1988).

2.  These computations use the Standard and Poor's Composite Stock Price Index divided by the Consumer Price Index for All Urban Consumers, as computed by the U.S. Bureau of Labor Statistics; see http://www .robertshiller.com.

3.  Paul A. Samuelson has said that the stock market is micro efficient and macro inefficient. We have found an element of truth in this statement (Jung and Shiller 2005).

4.  Shiller (2000, 2005).

5.  Shiller (1981) and Campbell and Shiller (1987).

6.  Terry A. Marsh and Robert C. Merton, commenting on papers by LeRoy and Porter (1981) and Shiller (1981), once tried to give "inspiring evidence" that stock prices are indeed a present value of optimally forecasted dividends (Marsh and Merton 1986). In fact they did nothing of the sort (Shiller 1986). The reasons given for thinking that any market inefficiencies will be "arbitraged away" by smart money have a number of limitations (Shleifer and Vishny 1997; Barberis and Thaler 2003).

7.  These ads are displayed and discussed in Mullainathan and Shleifer (2005).

8.  Allen et al. (2002).

9.  Higgins (2005).

10. Shiller (1984, 2002, 2005, pp. 56–81).

11. Campbell (2006).

12. Geanakoplos (2003) and Fostel and Geanakoplos (2008).

13. Greenlaw et al. (2008) and Morris and Shin (2008).

14. Shleifer and Vishny (1992).

15. A similar sort of feedback can occur at the household level, operating through household balance sheets much as it does through bank balance sheets (Mishkin 2007).

16. Borio (2003) and Bernanke (2008b).

17. Cusumano (1985).

18. Fukuzawa (1969 [1876]).

19. "Kaiser Argentine Plant Hit by Faulty Parts, Strikes, Delays."

20. Moffitt (1963).

21. Ikegami (2005).

22. Cusumano (1985).

23. There was a major strike in 1920 at the Yahata Steel Company, labor rioting at the Singer Sewing Machine Company in 1933, and a labor-union-led strike by geishas in 1937, but no discord as serious as that which had been seen in Argentina.

24. Alexander (2003).

25. "Kaiser Argentine Car Plant Hit by Faulty Parts, Strikes, Delays."

26. Econometric models are generally well described as feedback models involving only observable data, with all unobservables relegated to so-called error terms. While we believe these models to be often useful, they most certainly neglect some important structure that involves psychological variables that we cannot quantify.

27. http://research.stlouisfed.org/fred2/series/OILPRICE.

28. Akerlof's personal knowledge from working at the Council of Economic Advisers in 1973.

29. Meadows et al. (1972, p. 125).

30. De Long and Summers (1992), in a comparison of countries around the world, showed that those with higher levels of investment, particularly high equipment investment, have higher growth of income per capita. Hsieh and Klenow (2003, p. 1) additionally conclude that "one of the strongest relationships established in the empirical growth literature is the positive correlation between the rate of investment in physical capital and the level of output per worker."

31. Welch and Byrne (2001, pp. 93, 94, 107, and 171).

32. Truman Bewley (2002), relying on experiments by Daniel Ellsberg showing that people have uncertainty aversion, describes people's reaction to uncertainty as inertial, that is, they tend to stay with the status quo. Some macroeconomic models have been developed that model people as reacting to uncertainty through a decision process that minimizes the maximum loss, using a theory of uncertainty developed by Gilboa and Schmeidler (1989). Sims (2001) reviews this macroeconomic literature but argues that these models have generally construed uncertainty too narrowly, missing the forest of uncertainty while dealing only with a few trees. Caballero and Krishnamurthy (2006) argue that fundamental uncertainty creates difficult-to-manage fears about unspecified possible systemic economic breakdowns, and that these fears in turn cause businesspeople to react with an excessive demand for safety, thus triggering a financial crisis.

33. Welch and Byrne (2001, p. 172).

34. Brainard and Tobin (1968).

35. Asset values also affect the chances that firms will go bankrupt. Firms close to bankruptcy find it difficult, if not impossible, to borrow and thus commonly

forgo profitable investment opportunities after a change in asset values has an impact on their balance sheets.

36. Morck et al. (1990) have investigated Tobin's $q$ model using firm-level data, and Blanchard et al. (1993) have done so using ninety years of aggregate U.S. data. Both studies found a weak correlation between $q$ and investment. On the other hand, Baker et al. (2002) have shown some encouraging results, of a sort, for the model—results that are encouraging for a subset of firms. They argue that even if firms do not respect the valuations given their shares in the market, certain firms—those that are "equity constrained" and that therefore need to rely on equity financing for their investment needs—will respond in their investment behavior to their own stock price. They find strong evidence for an effect of Tobin's $q$ on investment for these firms. Their results support the notion that the observed weak correlation between Tobin's $q$ and the stock market is causal, and that variations in the stock market caused by purely speculative changes are indeed a part of the reason for macroeconomic fluctuations.

37. Blanchard et al. (1993) ran a horse race (in explaining investment) between a measure of $q$ constructed from estimates of expected future profits and a conventional measure based on stock market prices. The stock market measure was the clear loser—as it was again in a reenactment by Bond and Cummins (2000), who pitted stock market $q$ against a measure constructed from analysts' forecasts of future earnings.

## Chapter Twelve
## Why Do Real Estate Markets Go through Cycles?

1. Much of this chapter is based on Shiller's joint work with Karl Case, for example, Case and Shiller (1988, 2003). Allan Weiss, who led the development of the Case-Shiller home-price indices, has also been a formative influence.

2. Case (2008, p. 4).

3. Kelly and Tuccillo (2004, p. vii).

4. Those who answered incorrectly were consistently wrong on a number of variations of the problem, implying that they had an incorrect model of the behavior of moving objects.

5. McCloskey et al. (1980).

6. "Not a Boom but Growth."

7. Brown (1952). Further evidence on past views about real estate as an investment is given in Shiller (2008a).

8. Urban Land Price Index—Japan Residential—Six Largest Cities, Japan Real Estate Institute, http://www.reinet.or.jp, deflated by Japan CPI Nationwide General Ex Fresh Food—Core Ex Fresh Food.

9. Brunnermeier and Julliard (2006).

10. The value was arrived at using the U.S. Department of Agriculture Average Farm Real Estate Value series for the century from 1900 to 2000 (ending before most of the recent real estate boom) and deflating this series by means of the Consumer Price Index.

11. Shiller (2005). Updated U.S. home price data (Shiller 2008b) are at www .robertshiller.com.

12. King (1999).

13. Barrett (2008).

14. An excellent history of the growth of the subprime lending industry is offered in Gramlich (2007); see also Zandi (2008).

15. See the Standard & Poor's/Case-Shiller Tiered Home Price Indices, http:// www.metroarea.standardandpoors.com.


## CHAPTER THIRTEEN
## WHY IS THERE SPECIAL POVERTY AMONG MINORITIES?

1. The basis for this chapter is Akerlof's joint work with Rachel Kranton (Akerlof and Kranton 2000, 2008). It is also informed by Robert Akerlof (2008).

2. Hispanics have a similar but less extreme history of discrimination.

3. An eloquent statement of these problems is presented in Wilson (1987).

4. These are the estimates of Civil Rights Watch from the U.S. Census for 2000. See http://www.hrw.org/legacy/backgrounder/usa/race/pdf/table3.pdf.

5. http://www.hrw.org/reports/2000/usa/Table3.pdf.

6. This is an estimate based on incarceration rates in 1993.

7. U.S. Department of Justice (2008, Table 13, p. 9).

8. Wentura (2005, p. 217).

9. Geisel (1984).

10. The strength of sense of identity with a socioeconomic group, and the perception of the permanence of one's relationship with that group, appears to be an important factor in human happiness (Alesina et al. 2001).

11. Lamont (2000).

12. Friedman and Friedman (1980).

13. Liebow (1967).

14. This identity-based theory of disadvantage, proposed by Akerlof and Kranton, is consistent with a considerable body of evidence. For example, it captures the central findings of studies by authors such as Frazier (1957), Clark (1965), Du Bois (1965), Hannerz (1969), Rainwater (1970), Wilson (1987, 1996), and Anderson (1990). Benabou and Tirole (2000) describe how those who derive benefits from performance have incentives to manipulate others' self-confidence. The worker may recognize this manipulation and adopt a different identity, may self-deprecate, to lower expectations. Glaeser (2002) shows that the hatred that minority groups sometimes experience is largely the con-

sequence of deliberate instigation by elements that benefit from such hatred, and the supply of that hatred responds to economic conditions. A framework for thinking of equilibrium consequences of complex social interactions is provided by Brock and Durlauf (2003).

15. Holzer et al. (2004, Figure 2, p. 4). These figures refer to the noninstitutionalized population; inclusion of the incarcerated makes them yet higher.

16. Thernstrom and Thernstrom (1997).

17. Shipler (1997).

18. Glenn Loury (1995) has suggested that affirmative action may also have the opposite effect: it may exacerbate blacks' sense of exclusion and make them feel that they are viewed as not belonging even when they do achieve.

19. Ferguson (2000).

20. See Krueger and Whitmore (1999) on the effect of class size and Ferguson (1998) on the effect of teacher quality.

21. For example, take the case of Central Park East Secondary School (CPESS) in New York. In the school's neighborhood, more students go to jail than to college. Yet at CPESS there are almost no dropouts; it sends 90% of its graduates on to college, of whom 90% graduate (Fliegel 1993). The school's success is largely a result of its efforts to foster a sense of group identity among its students. See Akerlof and Kranton (2008) for more on CPESS and the importance of identity for the economics of education.

22. Delpit (1995).

23. In 2004 blacks made up 17% of all civilian federal employment (U.S. Census 2008, Table 486), and 25% of lower-level federal jobs (pay grades 1–6; see U.S. Office of Personnel Management 2004, Table 2). The fraction of blacks in total U.S. employment was 10.7% (*Economic Report of the President* 2008, Table B37, p. 271).

24. Levitt (1996) has demonstrated the short-run gains from incarceration.

## Chapter Fourteen
## Conclusion

1. *Economic Report of the President* (2002, Chart 1-1, p. 24).

2. The bill is known as the Economic and Growth Tax Relief and Recovery Act of 2001 (abbreviated as EGTRRA and pronounced *egg-terra*). There was a later further stimulatory tax cut, the Jobs and Growth Tax Relief and Reconciliation Act of 2003 (JGTRRA). The Congressional Budget Office estimated the ten-year (2001–11) impact of JGTRRA on federal revenues to be $1.3 trillion as legislated, and $1.7 trillion with adjustments taking account of reasonable sunset and alternative minimum tax revisions (Gale and Potter 2002, Table 2).

3. Federal Reserve Bank of New York, "Historical Changes of the Target Federal Funds and Discount Rates, 1971 to Present," http://www.newyorkfed.org/markets/statistics/dlyrates/fedrate.html. We should note that these rates are

especially low because of the definition of the series at the time. The reported series was changed in January 2003; after that the discount and federal funds rates were revised to "track the primary and secondary credit rates," which at the time of the break were considerably higher.

4. GDP growth had rebounded from a low of 0.7% in 2001 to 3.6% in 2004 (calculated from *Economic Report of the President* 2008, Table B-2, p. 226).

5. From 1991 to 2000, gross private domestic investment, which started the period at $829.1 billion, increased by 102.5%. Its subcomponent, equipment and software, which started at $345.9 billion, grew even more remarkably, by 165.6%. In comparison, over that period GDP had grown by only 38.3% (*Economic Report of the President* 2008, Table B-2, p. 226; level numbers are in 2000 chained dollars).

6. In levels, residential fixed investment started at $448.5 billion (again from *Economic Report of the President* 2008, Table B-2, p. 226, and again in 2000 chained dollars).

7. Standard & Poor's/Case-Shiller Home Price Index, http://www.metroarea.standardandpoors.com. CPI deflator from *Economic Report of the President* (2008, Table B-7, p. 234).

8. In Los Angeles prices rose 173%; in Miami they rose 181% (Case 2008, Table 2).

9. We have two estimates of the size of hedge funds. Andrew Lo (2008) claims that they have capital in excess of $1 trillion. Other sources put their capital as high as $2.68 trillion. See http://en.wikipedia.org/wiki/Hedge_fund for a discussion and also references. Surely these numbers are not well defined, since they depend on what is included under the rubric *hedge fund*. What matters is that the capital of hedge funds is large, and with their leverage they hold *very large* quantities of assets. Indeed this imprecise language describes the true position of hedge funds with much more precision than any specific number.

10. The possible exception is those booms and busts associated with war and peace.

11. This debate is covered marvelously by Howe (2007), who clearly sides with the Whigs and against the Jacksonians.

# References

Aaron, Henry J., and Robert D. Reischauer. 1999. *Setting National Priorities: The 2000 Election and Beyond*. Washington, D.C.: Brookings Institution Press.

Agell, Jonas, and Per Lundborg. 2003. "Survey Evidence on Wage Rigidity and Unemployment: Sweden in the 1990s." *Scandinavian Journal of Economics* 105(1): 15–29.

Akerlof, George A., 1982. "Labor Contracts as Partial Gift Exchange." *Quarterly Journal of Economics* 97(4):543–69.

Akerlof, George A., and William T. Dickens. 2007. "Unfinished Business in the Macroeconomics of Low Inflation: A Tribute to George and Bill by Bill and George." *Brookings Papers on Macroeconomics* 2:31–48.

Akerlof, George A., and Rachel E. Kranton. 2000. "Economics and Identity." *Quarterly Journal of Economics* 115(3):715–53.

———. 2002. "Identity and Schooling: Some Lessons for the Economics of Education." *Journal of Economic Literature* 40(4):1167–201.

———. 2005. "Identity and the Economics of Organizations." *Journal of Economic Perspectives* 19(1):9–32.

———. 2008. "Economics and Identity." Unpublished paper, University of California–Berkeley, and Duke University, July.

Akerlof, George A., and Paul M. Romer. 1993. "Looting: The Economic Underworld of Bankruptcy for Profit." *Brookings Papers on Economic Activity* 2:1–74.

Akerlof, George A., and Janet L. Yellen. 1990. "The Fair Wage-Effort Hypothesis and Unemployment." *Quarterly Journal of Economics* 105(2):255–83.

Akerlof, George A., Andrew K. Rose, and Janet L. Yellen. 1988. "Job Switching and Job Satisfaction in the U.S. Labor Market." *Brookings Papers on Economic Activity* 2:495–582.

Akerlof, George A., William T. Dickens, and George L. Perry. 1996. "The Macroeconomics of Low Inflation." *Brookings Papers on Economic Activity* 1:1–59.

———. 2000. "Near-Rational Wage and Price Setting and the Long-Run Phillips Curve." *Brookings Papers on Economic Activity* 1:1–44.

Akerlof, Robert J. 2008. "A Theory of Social Interactions." Unpublished paper, Department of Economics, Harvard University.

"Aldrich Banking System." 1911. *Washington Post*, February 18, p. 6.

Alesina, Alberto, Rafael di Tella, and Robert McCulloch. 2001. "Inequality and Happiness: Are Europeans and Americans Different?" National Bureau of Economic Research Working Paper 8198, April.

Alexander, Robert. 2003. *A History of Organized Labor in Argentina*. Westport, Conn.: Praeger.

Allen, Franklin, Stephen Morris, and Hyun Song Shin. 2002. "Beauty Contests, Bubbles, and Iterated Expectations in Asset Markets." Unpublished paper, Yale University, April.

REFERENCES

Altonji, Joseph G., and Paul J. Devereux. 1999. "The Extent and Consequences of Downward Nominal Wage Rigidity." National Bureau of Economic Research Working Paper 7236, July.

Anderson, Elijah. 1990. *Streetwise: Race, Class, and Change in an Urban Community*. Chicago: University of Chicago Press.

Ando, Albert, and Franco Modigliani. 1963. "The Life-Cycle Theory of Saving: Aggregate Implications and Tests." *American Economic Review* 53(1):55–84.

Andrews, Edmund L. 2008. "Fed Acts to Rescue Financial Markets." *New York Times*, March 17.

Angeletos, George-Marios, David I. Laibson, Andrea Repetto, Jeremy Tobacman, and Stephen Weinberg. 2001. "The Hyperbolic Consumption Model: Calibration, Simulation, and Empirical Evaluation." *Journal of Economic Perspectives* 15(3):47–68.

"Applaud Idea of Lowering City Salaries." 1932. *Hartford Courant*, February 19, p. 8.

Arkes, H., L. Herren, and A. Isen. 1988. "The Role of Potential Loss in the Influence of Affect on Risk-Taking Behavior." *Organizational Behavior and Human Decision Processes* 66:228–36.

"Attitude of Waiting." 1902. *Washington Post*, December 21, p. 22.

Bagehot, Walter. 1920 [1873]. *Lombard Street: A Description of the Money Market*. New York: Dutton.

Bailey, Norman J. 1975. *The Mathematical Theory of Infectious Diseases and Its Applications*. London: Griffin.

Baker, Malcolm, Jeremy C. Stein, and Jeffrey Wurgler. 2002. "When Does the Market Matter? Stock Prices and the Investment of Equity-Dependent Firms." National Bureau of Economic Research Working Paper 8750, January.

Baker, Malcolm, Stefan Nagel, and Jeffrey Wurgler. 2006. "The Effects of Dividends on Consumption." National Bureau of Economic Research Working Paper 12288, June.

Barberis, Nicholas, and Richard Thaler. 2003. "A Survey of Behavioral Finance." In George Constantinides, Milton Harris, and René Stulz, eds., *Handbook of the Economics of Finance*. New York: Elsevier Science, pp. 1053–128.

Barenstein, Matias Felix. 2002. "Credit Cards and Consumption: An Urge to Splurge?" Unpublished paper, University of California–Berkeley.

Barrett, Wayne. 2008. "Andrew Cuomo and Fannie and Freddie." *Village Voice*, August 5.

Barro, Robert J. 1979. "On the Determination of the Public Debt." *Journal of Political Economy* 87(5):940–71.

Barsky, Robert B., and Eric R. Sims. 2006. "Information Shocks, Animal Spirits, and the Meaning of Innovations in Consumer Confidence." Unpublished paper, University of Michigan, October 30.

Bauer, Thomas, Holger Bonin, and Uwe Sunde. 2003. "Real and Nominal Wage Rigidities and the Rate of Inflation: Evidence from German Microdata." Institute for the Study of Labor Discussion Paper 959.

Becker, Gary S. 1968. "Crime and Punishment: An Economic Approach." *Journal of Political Economy* 76:169–217.

Benabou, Roland. 2008. "Groupthink: Collective Delusions in Organizations and Markets." Unpublished paper, Princeton University.

Benabou, Roland, and Jean Tirole. 2000. "Self-Confidence and Social Interactions." National Bureau of Economic Research Working Paper 7585, March.

Benoit, Bernard, Ben Hall, Krishna Guha, Francesco Guerrera, and Henry Sender. 2008. "US Prepares $250bn Banks Push; Global Rebound; S&P 500 Soars 11.6 % as Markets Cheer Europe's $2,546bn Move." *Financial Times*, October 14, p. 1.

Berg, Lennart, and Reinhold Bergström. 1996. "Consumer Confidence and Consumption in Sweden." Unpublished paper, Department of Economics, Uppsala University.

Bernanke, Ben S. 2008a. "Developments in the Financial Markets." Testimony before the Committee on Banking, Housing, and Urban Affairs, U.S. Senate. April 3. http://www.federalreserve.gov/newsevents/testimony/bernanke2+0080403a .htm.

———. 2008b. "Reducing Systemic Risk." Speech at the Federal Reserve Bank of Kansas City Economic Symposium, "Maintaining Stability in a Changing Financial System," Jackson Hole, Wyoming, August 22. http://www .federalreserve.gov/newsevents/speech/bernanke20080822a.htm.

Bernanke, Ben S., and Alan Blinder. 1988. "Credit, Money, and Aggregate Demand." *American Economic Review* 78(2):435–39.

———. 1992. "The Federal Funds Rate and the Channels of Monetary Transmission." *American Economic Review* 82(4):901–21.

Bernanke, Ben S., Thomas Laubach, Frederic Mishkin, and Adam Posen. 2001. *Inflation Targeting: Lessons from the International Experience*. Princeton, N.J.: Princeton University Press.

Bernanke, Ben S., Jean Boivin, and Piotor Eliasz. 2005. "Measuring the Effects of Monetary Policy: A Factor-Augmented Vector Autoregressive (FAVAR) Approach." *Quarterly Journal of Economics* 120(1):387–422.

Bernheim, B. Douglas. 1995. "Do Households Appreciate Their Financial Vulnerabilities? An Analysis of Actions, Perceptions, and Public Policy." In *Tax Policy for Economic Growth in the 1990s*. Washington, D.C.: American Council for Capital Formation, pp. 1–30.

Bewley, Truman. 1999. *Why Wages Don't Fall during a Recession*. Cambridge, Mass.: Harvard University Press.

———. 2002. "Knightian Decision Theory. Part I." *Decisions in Economics and Finance* 25(2):79–110.

Billett, Matthew T., and Yiming Qian. 2005. "Are Overconfident Managers Born or Made? Evidence of Self-Attribution Bias from Frequent Acquirers." Unpublished paper, University of Iowa.

Blanchard, Olivier J. 1993. "Consumption and the Recession of 1990–1991." *American Economic Review* 83(2):270–74.

Blanchard, Olivier, and Nobuhiro Kiyotaki. 1987. "Monopolistic Competition and the Effects of Aggregate Demand." *American Economic Review* 77(4): 647–66.

Blanchard, Olivier, and Lawrence Summers. 1987. "Hysteresis in Unemployment." *European Economic Review* 31(1/2):288–95.

Blanchard, Olivier, Changyong Rhee, and Lawrence H. Summers. 1993. "The Stock Market, Profit, and Investment." *Quarterly Journal of Economics* 108(1):115–36.

Blau, Peter Michael. 1963. *The Dynamics of Bureaucracy; A Study of Interpersonal Relations in Two Government Agencies.* Chicago: University of Chicago Press.

Blinder, Alan S., and Don H. Choi. 1990. "A Shred of Evidence on Theories of Wage Stickiness." *Quarterly Journal of Economics* 105(4):1003–15.

Blinder, Alan S., Angus Deaton, Robert E. Hall, and R. Glenn Hubbard. 1985. "The Time Series Consumption Function Revisited." *Brookings Papers on Economic Activity* 2:465–511.

Bond, Stephen R., and Jason G. Cummins. 2000. "The Stock Market and Investment in the New Economy: Some Tangible Facts and Intangible Fictions." *Brookings Papers on Economic Activity* 1:61–108.

Borio, Claudio. 2003. "Towards a Macroprudential Framework for Financial Regulation." BIS Working Paper 128, Bank for International Settlements, February.

Bowles, Samuel. 1985. "The Production Process in a Competitive Economy: Walrasian, Neo-Hobbesian, and Marxian Models." *American Economic Review* 75(1):16–36.

Bracha, Anat, and Donald Brown. 2007. "Affective Decision Making: A Behavioral Theory of Choice." Cowles Foundation Discussion Paper 1633, November.

Brainard, William C., and George L. Perry. 2000. "Making Policy in a Changing World." In William Brainard and George Perry, eds., *Economic Events, Ideas, and Policies: The 1960s and After.* Washington, D.C.: Brookings Institution Press, pp. 43–82.

Brainard, William C., and James Tobin. 1968. "Pitfalls in Financial Model Building." *American Economic Review* 58(2):99–122.

Brock, William A., and Steven N. Durlauf. 2003. "Multinomial Choice and Social Interactions." Unpublished paper, University of Wisconsin–Madison, January 27.

Brown, Lucia. 1952. "Individualistic Interiors Mark Dozen Exhibit Homes." *Washington Post,* September 7, p. H3.

Brown, Roger. 1986. *Social Psychology,* 2nd ed. New York: Free Press.

Brown, Stephen, William Goetzmann, Bing Liang, and Christopher Schwarz. 2007. "Mandatory Disclosure and Operational Risk: Evidence from Hedge Fund Registration." Unpublished paper, New York University.

Brunnermeier, Markus K. 2009. "Deciphering the 2007–8 Liquidity and Credit Crunch." *Journal of Economic Perspectives,* forthcoming.

Brunnermeier, Markus K., and Christian Julliard. 2006. "Money Illusion and Housing Frenzies." National Bureau of Economic Research Working Paper 12810, December.

Buckley, F. H., and Margaret F. Brinig. 1998. "The Bankruptcy Puzzle." *Journal of Legal Studies* 27(1):187–207.

Burton, Robert. 1632. *The Anatomy of Melancholy.* Oxford: Henry Cripps.

Caballero, Ricardo, and Arvind Krishnamurthy. 2006. "Flight to Quality and Collective Risk Management." Unpublished paper, Massachusetts Institute of Technology.

"Callisthenes." 1931. "The Duty of Confidence." *The Times* (London), January 21, p. 12.

Calomiris, Charles W. 2008. "The Subprime Turmoil: What's Old, What's New and What's Next." Paper prepared for the Federal Reserve Bank of Kansas City Economic Symposium, "Maintaining Stability in a Changing Financial System," Jackson Hole, Wyoming, August 22.

Calvo, Guillermo A. 1983. "Staggered Prices in a Utility-Maximizing Framework." *Journal of Monetary Economics* 12(3):383–98.

Campbell, Carl M., III, and Kunal S. Kamlani. 1997. "The Reasons for Wage Rigidity: Evidence from a Survey of Firms." *Quarterly Journal of Economics* 112(3): 759–89.

Campbell, John Y. 2006. "Household Finance." *Journal of Finance* 61(4): 1553–604.

Campbell, John Y., and Angus Deaton. 1989. "Is Consumption Too Smooth?" *Review of Economic Studies* 56(3):357–73.

Campbell, John Y., and Robert J. Shiller. 1987. "Cointegration and Tests of Present Value Models." *Journal of Political Economy* 97(5):1062–88.

———. 1988. "Stock Prices, Earnings and Expected Dividends." *Journal of Finance* 43(3):661–76.

Cantril, Hadley. 1951. *Public Opinion 1935–46*. Princeton, N.J.: Princeton University Press.

Card, David, and Dean Hyslop. 1997. "Does Inflation 'Grease the Wheels' of the Labor Market?" In Christina D. Romer and David H. Romer, eds., *Reducing Inflation: Motivation and Strategy*. NBER Studies in Business Cycles, vol. 30. Chicago: University of Chicago Press, pp. 195–242.

Carlton, Dennis W. 1986. "The Rigidity of Prices." *American Economic Review* 76(4):637–58.

Carroll, Christopher D. 2001. "A Theory of the Consumption Function with and without Liquidity Constraints (Expanded Version)." National Bureau of Economic Research Working Paper 8387, July.

Carroll, Christopher D., and Lawrence H. Summers. 1991. "Consumption Growth Parallels Income Growth: Some New Evidence." In B. Douglas Bernheim and John Shoven, eds., *National Saving and Economic Performance*. Chicago: University of Chicago Press, pp. 305–43.

Carroll, Christopher D., and David N. Weil. 1994. "Saving and Growth: A Reinterpretation." *Carnegie-Rochester Conference Series on Public Policy* 40: 133–92.

Carson, Carol S. 1975. "The History of the United States National Income and Product Accounts: The Development of an Analytical Tool." *Review of Income and Wealth* 21(2):153–81.

Case, Karl E. 2008. "The Central Role of House Prices in the Current Financial Crisis: How Will the Market Clear?" Paper prepared for the Brookings Panel on Economic Activity, Washington, D.C., September 11.

Case, Karl E., and Robert J. Shiller. 1988. "The Behavior of Home Buyers in Boom and Post-Boom Markets." *New England Economic Review*, November, pp. 29–46.

## REFERENCES

———. 2003. "Is There a Bubble in the Housing Market?" *Brookings Papers on Economic Activity* 2:299–362.

Cassino, Vincenzo. 1995. "The Distribution of Wage and Price Changes in New Zealand." Bank of New Zealand Discussion Paper G95/6.

Castellanos, Sara G., Rodrigo García-Verdú, and David Kaplan. 2004. "Nominal Wage Rigidities in Mexico: Evidence from Social Security Records." National Bureau of Economic Research Working Paper 10383, March.

Central Intelligence Agency. 2008. *The World Factbook*. https://www.cia.gov/library/publications/the-world-factbook/.

Chapple, Simon. 1996. "Money Wage Rigidity in New Zealand." *Labour Market Bulletin* 2:23–50.

Chari, V. V., Patrick J. Kehoe, and Ellen R. McGrattan. 2008. "New Keynesian Models: Not Yet Useful for Policy Analysis." National Bureau of Economic Research Working Paper 14313, September.

Chen, Keith, and Marc Hauser. 2005. "Modeling Reciprocation and Cooperation in Primates: Evidence for a Punishing Strategy." *Journal of Theoretical Biology* 235:5–12.

Chernow, Ron. 1998. *Titan: The Life of John D. Rockefeller, Sr.* New York: Random House.

Christofides, Louis N., and Amy Chen Peng. 2004. "The Determinants of Major Provisions in Union Contracts: Duration, Indexation, and Non-Contingent Wage Adjustment." Unpublished paper, University of Cyprus.

Clark, John Bates. 1895. "The Gold Standard of Currency in the Light of Recent Theory." *Political Science Quarterly* 10(3):383–97.

Clark, Kenneth. 1965. *Dark Ghetto*. New York: Harper and Row.

Coibion, Olivier, and Yuriy Gorodnichenko. 2008. "What Can Survey Forecasts Tell Us about Informational Rigidities?" Unpublished paper, University of California–Berkeley.

Colburn, Forrest D. 1984. "Mexico's Financial Crisis." *Latin American Research Review* 19(2):220–24.

Cole, Harold L., and Lee E. Ohanian. 2000. "Re-examining the Contributions of Money and Banking Shocks to the U.S. Great Depression." *NBER Macroeconomics Annual* 15:183–227.

———. 2004. "New Deal Policies and the Persistence of the Great Depression: A General Equilibrium Analysis." *Journal of Political Economy* 112(4):779–816.

"Confidence Is Recovery Key, Sloan Asserts." 1938. *Chicago Daily Tribune*, January 1, p. 17.

"Contract Bridge Favorite Game among Women." 1941. *Washington Post*, March 5, p. 13.

Cooper, Russell, and Andrew John. 1988. "Coordinating Coordination Failures in Keynesian Models." *Quarterly Journal of Economics* 88(3):441–63.

Crystal, Graef S. 1991. *In Search of Excess: The Overcompensation of American Executives*. New York: W. W. Norton.

Cusumano, Michael A. 1985. *The Japanese Automobile Industry: Technology and Management at Nissan and Toyota*. Cambridge, Mass.: Harvard University Press.

Davis, E. Philip, and Gabriel Fagan. 1997. "Are Financial Spreads Useful Indicators of Future Inflation and Output Growth in EU Countries?" *Journal of Applied Econometrics* 12(6):701–14.

Deaton, Angus. 1992. *Understanding Consumption.* Oxford: Oxford University Press.

Degler, Carl N. 1967. *Age of Economic Revolution 1876–1900,* 2nd ed. Glenview, Ill.: Scott, Foresman.

De Long, J. Bradford, and Lawrence H. Summers. 1992. "Equipment Investment and Economic Growth: How Strong Is the Nexus?" *Brookings Papers on Economic Activity* 2:157–99.

Delpit, Lisa. 1995. *Other People's Children: Cultural Conflict in the Classroom.* New York: New Press.

De Quervain, Dominique J.-F., Urs Fischbacher, Valerie Treyer, Melanie Schellhammer, Ulrich Schnyder, Alfred Buck, and Ernst Fehr. 2005. "The Neural Basis of Altruistic Punishment." *Science* 305:1254–64.

Descartes, René. 1972 [1664]. *Traité de l'Homme.* Paris: La Gras. English translation: T. S. Hall, *Treatise of Man.* Cambridge, Mass.: Harvard University Press.

Dickens, William T., and Lawrence F. Katz. 1987. "Inter-industry Wage Differences and Industry Characteristics." In Kevin Lang and Jonathan S. Leonard, eds., *Unemployment and the Structure of Labor Markets.* New York: Blackwell, pp. 48–89.

Di Tella, Rafael, Robert J. McCulloch, and Andrew J. Oswald. 2000. "The Macroeconomics of Happiness." Unpublished paper, Harvard Business School.

Dougherty, Peter. 2002. *Who's Afraid of Adam Smith? How the Market Got Its Soul.* Hoboken, N.J.: Wiley.

Du Bois, W.E.B. 1965. *The Souls of Black Folk.* Greenwich, Conn.: Fawcett.

Dunlop, John T. "The Task of Contemporary Wage Theory." In John T. Dunlop, ed., *The Theory of Wage Determination.* New York: St. Martin's Press, pp. 3–27.

Dwyer, Jacqueline, and Kenneth Leong. 2000. "Nominal Wage Rigidity in Australia." Reserve Bank of Australia Discussion Paper 2000-08.

*Economic Report of the President.* Various issues. Washington, D.C.: U.S. Government Printing Office.

Edmans, Alex, Diego Garcia, and Øyvind Norli. 2007. "Sports Sentiment and Stock Returns." *Journal of Finance* 62(4):1967–98.

Eichengreen, Barry. 1992. *Golden Fetters: The Gold Standard and the Great Depression.* New York: Oxford University Press.

Eichengreen, Barry, and Jeffrey Sachs. 1985. "Exchange Rates and Economic Recovery in the 1930s." *Journal of Economic History* 45:925–46.

Eichenwald, Kurt. 2005. *A Conspiracy of Fools: A True Story.* New York: Broadway.

"An Elastic Currency and Bankers' Bank." 1913. *The Independent,* December 25, p. 565.

"Embezzlements of Last Year." 1895. *Chicago Daily Tribune,* January 1, p. 4.

Engen, Eric M., William G. Gale, and Cori E. Uccello. 1999. "The Adequacy of Household Saving." *Brookings Papers on Economic Activity* 2:65–187.

Englund, Peter. 1999. "The Swedish Banking Crisis: Roots and Consequences." *Oxford Review of Economic Policy* 15(3):80–97.

Fair, Ray C. 1994. *Testing Macroeconometric Models.* Cambridge, Mass.: Harvard University Press.

Fang, Hanming, and Giuseppe Moscarini. 2002. "Overconfidence, Morale, and Wage-Setting Policies." Paper presented at the National Bureau of Economic Research conference on "Macroeconomics and Individual Decision Making," November.

Farkas, Steve, and Jean Johnson. 1997. *Miles to Go: A Status Report on Americans' Plans for Retirement.* Washington, D.C.: Public Agenda.

Farmer, Roger E. 1999. *The Macroeconomics of Self-Fulfilling Prophecies,* 2nd ed. Cambridge, Mass.: MIT Press.

Faulkner, Harold Underwood. 1959. *Politics, Reform and Expansion, 1890–1900.* New York: Harper and Row.

Federal Reserve. 2008a. "Factors Affecting Reserve Balances." Statistical Release H.4.1, July 24.

———. 2008b. "Reserve Requirements." http://www.federalreserve.gov/monetary policy/reservereq.htm.

Fehr, Ernst, and Simon Gächter. 2000. "Cooperation and Punishment in Public Goods Experiments." *American Economic Review* 90(4):980–94.

Fehr, Ernst, and Lorenz Goette. 2004. "Robustness and Real Consequences of Nominal Wage Rigidity." *Journal of Monetary Economics* 52(4):779–804.

Feinberg, Richard. 1986. "Credit Cards as Spending Facilitating Stimuli: A Conditioning Interpretation." *Journal of Consumer Research* 13(3):348–56.

Ferguson, Ann Arnett. 2000. *Bad Boys: Public Schools in the Making of Black Masculinity.* Ann Arbor: University of Michigan Press.

Ferguson, Ronald F. 1998. "Can Schools Narrow the Test Score Gap?" In Christopher Jencks and Meredith Phillips, eds., *The Black-White Test Score Gap.* Washington, D.C.: Brookings Institution Press, pp. 318–74.

Festinger, Leon. 1954. "A Theory of Social Comparison Processes." *Human Relations* 7:114–40.

Finnel, Stephanie. 2006. "Once Upon a Time, We Were Prosperous: The Role of Storytelling in Making Mexicans Believe in Their Country's Capacity for Economic Greatness." Unpublished senior essay, Yale University.

Fischer, Stanley. 1977. "Long-Term Contracts, Rational Expectations, and the Optimal Money Supply Rule." *Journal of Political Economy* 85(1):191–205.

Fisher, Irving. 1928. *The Money Illusion.* New York: Adelphi.

Fliegel, Seymour. 1993. *Miracle in East Harlem: The Fight for Choice in Public Education.* New York: Random House.

"Formal Addresses of Lehman, Smith, Root and Wadsworth at Repeal Convention." 1933. *New York Times,* June 28, p. 16.

Fortin, Pierre. 1995. "Canadian Wage Settlement Data." Unpublished paper, Université de Québec à Montréal, April.

———. 1996. "The Great Canadian Slump." *Canadian Journal of Economics* 29(4):761–87.

Fostel, Ana, and John Geanakoplos. 2008. "Leverage Cycles and the Anxious Economy." *American Economic Review* 98(4):1211–44.

Foster, James E., and Henry Y. Wan Jr. 1984. "Involuntary Unemployment as a Principal-Agent Equilibrium." *American Economic Review* 74(2):476–84.

Frazier, Franklin. 1957. *The Black Bourgeoisie: The Rise of the New Middle Class in the United States.* New York: Free Press.

Friedman, Benjamin M. 1990. "Targets and Instruments for Monetary Policy." In Benjamin Friedman and Frank Hahn, eds., *Handbook of Monetary Economics.* New York: Elsevier Science, pp. 1185–230.

Friedman, Milton. 1957. *A Theory of the Consumption Function.* Princeton, N.J.: Princeton University Press.

———. 1968. "The Role of Monetary Policy." *American Economic Review* 58(1):1–17.

———. 1970. "A Theoretical Framework for Monetary Analysis." *Journal of Political Economy* 78(2):193–238.

Friedman, Milton, and Rose D. Friedman. 1980. *Free to Choose: A Personal Statement.* New York: Harcourt Brace Jovanovich.

Friedman, Milton, and Anna Jacobson Schwartz. 1963. *A Monetary History of the United States, 1867–1960.* Princeton, N.J.: Princeton University Press.

Fukuzawa, Yukichi. 1969. *An Encouragement of Learning,* 1876 edition translated by David A. Dilworth and Umeyo Hirano. Tokyo: Sophia University.

Galbraith, John K. 1997 [1955]. *The Great Crash: 1929.* New York: Houghton Mifflin.

Gale, William G., and Samara R. Potter. 2002. "An Economic Evaluation of the Economic Growth and Tax Reconciliation Act of 2002." Unpublished paper, Brookings Institution.

Gale, William G., J. Mark Iwry, and Peter R. Orszag. 2005. *The Automatic 401(k): A Simple Way to Strengthen Retirement Savings.* Washington, D.C.: Brookings Institution Press.

Geanakoplos, John. 2003. "Liquidity, Default, and Crashes: Endogenous Contracts in General Equilibrium." In Mathias Dewatripont, Lars Peter Hansen, and Steven J. Turnovsky, eds., *Advances in Economics and Econometrics: Theory and Applications, Eighth World Conference,* vol. 2. Cambridge: Cambridge University Press, pp. 170–205.

Geisel, Theodor Seuss (Dr. Seuss). 1958. *The Cat in the Hat Comes Back.* New York: Beginner Books.

———. 1984. *The Butter Battle Book.* New York: Random House.

Gilboa, Itzhak, and David Schmeidler. 1989. "Maximin Expected Utility with Non-Unique Priors." *Journal of Mathematical Economics* 18:141–53.

Glaeser, Edward L. 2002. "The Political Economy of Hatred." National Bureau of Economic Research Working Paper 9171, September.

———. 2005. "Should the Government Rebuild New Orleans, or Just Give Residents Checks?" *Economists' Voice* 2(4):article 4.

Goetzmann, William, Jonathan Ingersoll, and Stephen A. Ross. 2003. "High Water Marks and Hedge Fund Management Contracts." *Journal of Finance* 58:1685–718.

Goldfeld, Stephen. 1976. "The Case of the Missing Money." *Brookings Papers on Economic Activity* 3:683–730.

Gordon, Robert J. 1977. "Can the Inflation of the 1970s Be Explained?" *Brookings Papers on Economic Activity* 1:253–79.

Gosselin, Peter. 2005. "The New Deal: On Their Own in Battered New Orleans." *Los Angeles Times,* December 4, p. A-1.

Gramlich, Edward M. 2007. *Subprime Mortgages: America's Latest Boom and Bust.* Washington, D.C.: Urban Institute Press.

Granger, Clive. 1969. "Investigating Causal Relations by Econometric Models and Cross-Spectral Methods." *Econometrica* 37(3):424–38.

Greenlaw, David, Jan Hatzius, Anil K. Kashyap, and Hyun Song Shin. 2008. "Leveraged Losses: Lessons from the Mortgage Meltdown." Paper presented at the U.S. Monetary Policy Forum Conference, Chicago Graduate School of Business, February 29.

Groshen, Erica L. 1991. "Sources of Intra-Industry Wage Dispersion: How Much Do Employers Matter?" *Quarterly Journal of Economics* 106(3):869–84.

Grossman, Sanford J., and Oliver Hart. 1980. "Takeover Bids, the Free-Rider Problem, and the Theory of the Corporation." *Bell Journal of Economics* 11(1):41–64.

Grossman, Sanford J., Angelo Melino, and Robert J. Shiller. 1987. "Estimating the Continuous-Time Consumption-Based Asset-Pricing Model." *Journal of Business and Economic Statistics* 5(3):315–27.

Hall, Robert E. 1978. "Stochastic Implications of the Life Cycle–Permanent Income Hypothesis: Theory and Evidence." *Journal of Political Economy* 86(6): 971–88.

———. 1988. "Intertemporal Substitution in Consumption." *Journal of Political Economy* 96(2):339–57.

Hall, Robert E., and Frederic S. Mishkin. 1982. "The Sensitivity of Consumption to Transitory Income: Estimates from Panel Data on Households." *Econometrica* 50(2):461–82.

Haltiwanger, John, and Michael Waldman. 1989. "Limited Rationality and Strategic Complements: The Implications for Macroeconomics." *Quarterly Journal of Economics* 104:463–83.

Hannerz, Ulf. 1969. *Soulside: Inquiries into Ghetto Culture and Community.* New York: Columbia University Press.

Harmon, Amy. 2006. "DNA Gatherers Hit a Snag: The Tribes Don't Trust Them." *New York Times,* December 10, pp. A1, A38.

Harvey, Fred. 1929. "Stem 12,880,900 Share Run." *Chicago Daily Tribune,* October 25, p. 1.

Hicks, John R. 1937. "Mr. Keynes and the 'Classics': A Suggested Interpretation." *Econometrica* 5(1):147–59.

Higgins, Adrian. 2005. "Why the Red Delicious No Longer Is." *Washington Post,* August 5, p. A01.

Higgs, Robert. 1997. "Regime Uncertainty: Why the Great Depression Lasted So Long and Why Prosperity Resumed after the War." *Independent Review* 1(4):561–90.

Hirt, Edward R., Grant A. Erickson, Chris Kennedy, and Dolf Zillman. 1992. "Costs and Benefits of Allegiance: Changes in Fans' Self-Ascribed Competencies after Team Victory versus Defeat." *Journal of Personality and Social Psychology* 63:724–38.

Holzer, Harry J., Paul Offner, and Elaine Sorensen. 2004. "Declining Employment among Young Black Less-Educated Men: The Role of Incarceration and Child Support." Georgetown University, Institute for Research on Poverty, Discussion Paper 1281-04, May.

Howe, Donald W. 2007. *What Hath God Wrought: The Transformation of America, 1815–1848.* New York: Oxford University Press.

Hsieh, Chang-Tai, and Peter J. Klenow. 2003. "Relative Prices and Relative Prosperity." National Bureau of Economic Research Working Paper 9701, May.

Ikegami, Eiko, 2005. *Bonds of Civility: Aesthetic Networks and the Political Origins of Japanese Culture.* Cambridge, Mass.: Cambridge University Press.

Ip, Greg. 1994. "Routine No Longer Governs Crow's Life." *Financial Post* (Toronto), April 28, p. 15.

Jacobs, Jane. 1961. *The Death and Life of Great American Cities.* New York: Random House.

James, Henry. 1983 [1904]. *The Golden Bowl.* Oxford: Oxford University Press.

Juhn, Chinhui, Kevin M. Murphy, and Brooks Pierce. 1993. "Wage Inequality and the Rise in Returns to Skill." *Journal of Political Economy* 101(3):410–42.

Jung, Jeeman, and Robert J. Shiller. 2005. "Samuelson's Dictum and the Stock Market." *Economic Inquiry* 43(2):221–28.

Kahn, Richard F. 1931. "The Relation of Home Investment to Unemployment." *Economic Journal* 41(162):173–98.

Kahn, Shulamit. 1997. "Evidence of Nominal Wage Stickiness from Microdata." *American Economic Review* 87(5):993–1008.

Kahneman, Daniel, and Amos Tversky. 1979. "Prospect Theory: An Analysis of Decision under Risk." *Econometrica* 47(2):263–92.

———. 2000. *Choices, Values and Frames.* Cambridge, Mass.: Cambridge University Press.

Kahneman, Daniel, Jack Knetsch, and Richard H. Thaler. 1986a. "Fairness as a Constraint on Profit-Seeking: Entitlements in the Market." *American Economic Review* 76(4):728–41.

———. 1986b. "Fairness and the Assumptions of Economics." *Journal of Business* 59(4, part 2):S285–300.

"Kaiser Argentine Car Plant Hit by Faulty Parts, Strikes, Delays." 1958. *New York Times,* April 28, p. 33.

Kashyap, Anil K., Raghuram G. Rajan, and Jeremy C. Stein. 2008. "Rethinking Capital Regulation." Paper prepared for the Federal Reserve Bank of Kansas City Economic Symposium, "Maintaining Stability in a Changing Financial System," Jackson Hole, Wyoming, August 22.

Katona, George. 1960. *The Powerful Consumer: Psychological Studies of the American Economy.* New York: McGraw-Hill.

Katz, Lawrence F. 1986. "Efficiency Wage Theories: A Partial Evaluation." *NBER Macroeconomics Annual* 1:235–76.

Kelly, Tom, and John Tuccillo. 2004. *How a Second Home Can Be Your Best Investment.* New York: McGraw-Hill.

Keynes, John Maynard. 1940a. "On a Method of Statistical Business Cycle Research: A Comment." *Economic Journal* 50(197):154–56.

———. 1940b. *How to Pay for the War: A Radical Plan for the Chancellor of the Exchequer.* London: Macmillan.

———. 1973 [1936]. *The General Theory of Employment, Interest and Money.* New York: Macmillan.

Kimura, Takeshi, and Kazuo Ueda. 2001. "Downward Nominal Wage Rigidity in Japan." *Journal of the Japanese and International Economies* 15(1):50–67.

Kindelberger, Charles P. 1978. *Manias, Panics and Crashes: A History of Financial Crises.* New York: Basic.

King, Martin Luther, III. 1999. "Minority Housing Gap: Fannie Mae, Freddie Mac Fall Short." *Washington Times*, November 17, p. A17.

Kirchgaessner, Stephanie. 2008. "Bush Says Wall Street 'Got Drunk.'" *Financial Times*, July 23.

Klein, Lawrence R. 1977. *Project LINK.* Athens, Greece: Centre of Planning and Economic Research.

Knight, Frank H. 1921. *Risk, Uncertainty and Profit.* New York: Houghton Mifflin.

Knoppik, Christoph, and Thomas Beissinger. 2003. "How Rigid Are Nominal Wages? Evidence and Implications for Germany." *Scandinavian Journal of Economics* 105(4):619–41.

Kornbluth, Jesse. 1992. *Highly Confident: The Crime and Punishment of Michael Milken.* New York: William Morrow.

Krueger, Alan B., and Lawrence H. Summers, 1988. "Efficiency Wages and the Inter-Industry Wage Structure." *Econometrica* 56(2):259–93.

Krueger, Alan B., and Diane M. Whitmore. 1999. "The Effect of Attending a Small Class in the Early Grades on College-Test Taking and Middle School Test Results: Evidence from Project STAR." Unpublished paper, Industrial Relations Section, Princeton University, September.

Kuroda, Sachiko, and Isamu Yamamoto. 2003a. "Are Japanese Nominal Wages Downwardly Rigid? I. Examinations of Nominal Wage Change Distributions." *Monetary and Economic Studies* 21(2):1–29.

———. 2003b. "Are Japanese Nominal Wages Downwardly Rigid? II. Examinations Using a Friction Model." *Monetary and Economic Studies* 21(2):31–68.

———. 2003c. "The Impact of Downward Nominal Wage Rigidity on the Unemployment Rate: Quantitative Evidence from Japan." *Monetary and Economic Studies* 21(4):57–85.

Kydland, Finn E., and Edward C. Prescott. 1982. "Time to Build and Aggregate Fluctuations." *Econometrica* 50(6):1345–70.

Laibson, David I., Andrea Repetto, and Jeremy Tobacman. 2000. "A Debt Puzzle." National Bureau of Economic Research Working Paper 7879, September.

Lamont, Michele. 2000. *The Dignity of Working Men: Morality and the Boundaries of Race, Class, and Immigration.* Cambridge, Mass.: Harvard University Press.

Lauck, William Jett. 1897. *The Causes of the Panic of 1893.* New York: Houghton Mifflin.

Lazear, Edward P., and Robert L. Moore. 1984. "Incentives, Productivity, and Labor Contracts." *Quarterly Journal of Economics* 99(2):275–96.

Lebergott, Stanley. 1957. "Annual Estimates of Unemployment in the United States, 1900–1954." In *The Measurement and Behavior of Unemployment*, Conference of the Universities–National Bureau Committee for Economic Research, Princeton. Princeton, N.J.: Princeton University Press (for National Bureau of Economic Research), pp. 213–41.

Lebow, David E., Raven E. Saks, and Beth Anne Wilson. 1999. "Downward Nominal Wage Rigidity: Evidence from the Employment Cost Index." Board of Governors of the Federal Reserve System, Finance and Economics Discussion Series 99/31, July.

Leeper, Eric, Christopher Sims, and Tao Zha. 1996. "What Does Monetary Policy Do?" *Brookings Papers on Economic Activity* 2:1–63.

Lemieux, Thomas. 2006. "Increasing Residual Wage Inequality: Composition Effects, Noisy Data, or Rising Demand for Skill?" *American Economic Review* 96(3):461–98.

"Lending on Collateral," *New York Times*, June 13, 1893, p. 4.

LeRoy, Stephen, and Richard Porter. 1981. "Stock Price Volatility: A Test Based on Implied Variance Bounds." *Econometrica* 49:97–113.

Leven, Maurice, Harold G. Moulton, and Clark Warburton. 1934. *America's Capacity to Consume*. Washington, D.C.: Brookings Institution Press.

Levine, David I. 1991. "Cohesiveness, Productivity, and Wage Dispersion." *Journal of Economic Behavior and Organization* 15(2):237–55.

Levine, Madeline. 2006. *The Price of Privilege: How Parental Pressure and Material Advantage Are Creating a Generation of Unhappy and Disconnected Kids*. New York: HarperCollins.

Levitt, Steven D. 1996. "The Effect of Prison Population Size on Crime Rates: Evidence from Prison Overcrowding Litigation." *Quarterly Journal of Economics* 111(2):319–51.

Liebow, Elliot. 1967. *Tally's Corner: A Study of Negro Streetcorner Men*. Boston: Little, Brown.

Lindbeck, Assar, and Dennis J. Snower. 1988. *The Insider-Outsider Theory of Employment and Unemployment*. Cambridge, Mass.: MIT Press.

Littlefield, Henry. 1964. "The Wizard of Oz: Parable on Populism." *American Quarterly* 16:47–58.

Lo, Andrew W. 2008. *Hedge Funds: An Analytical Perspective*. Princeton, N.J.: Princeton University Press.

Lohr, Steve. 1992. "Lessons from a Hurricane: It Pays Not to Gouge." *New York Times*, September 22.

López Portillo, José. 1965. *Quetzalcóatl*. Mexico City: Librería de Manuel Porrua.

Loury, Glenn C. 1995. *One by One from the Inside Out*. New York: Free Press.

Lowenstein, Roger. 2001. *When Genius Failed: The Rise and Fall of Long-Term Capital Management*. New York: Random House.

Lucas, Robert E., Jr. 1972. "Expectations and the Neutrality of Money." *Journal of Economic Theory* 4(2):103–24.

Ludvigson, Sydney C. 2004. "Consumer Confidence and Consumer Spending." *Journal of Economic Perspectives* 18(2):29–50.

Lusardi, Annamaria, and Olivia S. Mitchell. 2005. "Financial Literacy and Planning: Implications for Retirement Well-being." De Nederlandsche Bank Working Paper 78, December.

Macaulay, Frederic. 1938. *Some Theoretical Problems Suggested by Movements in Interest Rates, Bond Yields and Stock Prices in the United States since 1856.* New York: National Bureau of Economic Research.

Madrian, Brigitte C., and Dennis F. Shea. 2001. "The Power of Suggestion: Inertia in 401(k) Participation and Savings Behavior." *Quarterly Journal of Economics* 116(4):1149–87.

Mankiw, N. Gregory. 1985. "Small Menu Costs and Large Business Cycles: A Macroeconomic Model." *Quarterly Journal of Economics* 110(2):529–38.

Mankiw, N. Gregory, and Ricardo Reis. 2002. "Sticky Information versus Sticky Prices: A Proposal to Replace the New Keynesian Phillips Curve." *Quarterly Journal of Economics* 117(4):1295–328.

Marsh, Terry A., and Robert C. Merton. 1986. "Dividend Variability and Variance Bound Tests for the Rationality of Stock Prices." *American Economic Review* 76(3):483–98.

Mason, Joseph R., and Josh Rosner. 2007. "How Resilient are Mortgage Backed Securities to Collateralized Debt Obligation Market Disruptions?" Unpublished paper, Hudson Institute.

Matsusaka, John G., and Argia M. Sbordone. 1995. "Consumer Confidence and Economic Fluctuations." *Economic Inquiry* 33(2):296–318.

McCabe, Kevin A., Mary Rigdon, and Vernon L. Smith. 2003. "Positive Reciprocity and Intentions in Trust Games." *Journal of Economic Behavior and Organization* 52(2):267–75.

McCloskey, Michael, Alfonso Caramazza, and Bert Green. 1980. "Curvilinear Motion in the Absence of External Forces: Naive Beliefs about the Motion of Objects." *Science* 210(4474):1139–41.

McDonald, Forrest. 1962. *Insull: The Rise and Fall of a Billionaire Utility Tycoon.* Washington, D.C.: Beard.

McDonald, Ian, and Robert M. Solow. 1981. "Wage Bargaining and Employment." *American Economic Review* 71(4):896–908.

Meadows, Donella H., Dennis L. Meadows, Jørgen Randers, and William W. Behrens III. 1972. *The Limits to Growth: A Report for the Club of Rome's Project on the Predicament of Mankind.* New York: Universe.

"Miners Seem Hopelessly Divided." 1894. *Chicago Daily Tribune,* February 10, p. 2.

Minsky, Hyman. 1982. *Can "It" Happen Again? Essays on Instability and Finance.* Armonk, N.Y.: M. E. Sharpe.

———. 1986. *Stabilizing an Unstable Economy.* New Haven, Conn.: Yale University Press.

Mishkin, Frederic S. 2007. "Housing and the Monetary Transmission Mechanism." National Bureau of Economic Research Working Paper 13518, October.

Modigliani, Franco. 1970. "The Life-Cycle Hypothesis of Saving and Inter-Country Differences in the Saving Ratio." In W. A. Eltis, M. F. G. Scott, and J. N. Wolfe, eds., *Induction, Growth and Trade: Essays in Honor of Sir Roy Harrod.* London: Clarendon Press.

Modigliani, Franco, and Richard Brumberg. 1954. "Utility Analysis and the Consumption Function: An Interpretation of Cross-Section Data." In Kenneth K. Kurihara, ed., *Post-Keynesian Economics.* New Brunswick, N.J.: Rutgers University Press, pp. 388–436.

Modigliani, Franco, and Richard A. Cohn. 1979. "Inflation, Rational Valuation and the Market." *Financial Analysts Journal* 35(2):24–44.

Moffitt, Donald A. 1963. "Industrial Paradox: Latin America Attracts Auto Making Facilities Despite Lag in Sales." *Wall Street Journal,* August 6, pp. 1, 16.

Morck, Randall, Andrei Shleifer, and Robert Vishny. 1990. "The Stock Market and Investment: Is the Market a Sideshow?" *Brookings Papers on Economic Activity* 2:157–215.

Morgenson, Gretchen. 2008. "Everyone Out of the Security Pool." *New York Times,* Sunday Business, November 16, p. BU-1.

Morris, Stephen A., and Hyun Song Shin. 2004. "Liquidity Black Holes." *Review of Finance* 8(1):1–18.

———. 2008. "Financial Regulation in a System Context." *Brookings Papers on Economic Activity* 2.

"Mr. Lodge on Finance." 1908. *New York Tribune,* March 13, p. 3.

Mullainathan, Sendhil, and Andrei Shleifer. 2005. "Persuasion in Finance." Unpublished paper, Harvard University.

"Must Cut Prices if They Would Work." 1894. *Chicago Daily Tribune,* January 11, p. 7.

Nakamoto, Michiyo, and David Wighton. 2007. "Bullish Citigroup Is 'Still Dancing' to the Beat of the Buy-out Boom." *Financial Times,* July 10.

Nickell, Stephen, and Glenda Quintini. 2001. "Nominal Wage Rigidity and the Rate of Inflation." London School of Economics Discussion Paper CEP DP 489.

"Not a Boom but Growth." 1887. *New York Times,* May 29, p. 9.

"Notes Real Signs of Business Uplift." 1932. *New York Times,* September 23, p. 2.

Noyes, Alexander Dana. 1909. *Forty Years of American Finance.* New York: G. P. Putnam.

O'Brien, Anthony Patrick. 1989. "A Behavioral Explanation for Nominal Wage Rigidity during the Great Depression." *Quarterly Journal of Economics* 104(4): 719–35.

"Out of the Trough of Depression: Lord Meston on New Trade Orientation." 1937. *The Times* (London), April 21, p. 18.

Palley, Thomas I. 1994. "Escalators and Elevators: A Phillips Curve for Keynesians." *Scandinavian Journal of Economics* 96:111–16.

Peebles, Gavin. 2002. "Saving and Investment in Singapore: Implications for the Economy in the Early 20th Century." In Koh Ai Tee, Lim Kim Lian, Hui Weng Tat, Bhanoji Rao, and Chng Meng Kng, eds., *Singapore Economy in the 21st Century: Issues and Strategies.* Singapore: McGraw-Hill, pp. 373–400.

Phelps, Edmund S. 1968. "Money-Wage Dynamics and Labor-Market Equilibrium." *Journal of Political Economy* 76(4):678–711.

Phelps, Edmund S., and John Taylor. 1977. "Stabilizing Powers of Monetary Policy under Rational Expectations." *Journal of Political Economy* 85(1):163–90.

Phillips, A. W. 1958. "The Relationship between Unemployment and the Rate of Change of Money Wages in the United Kingdom, 1861–1957." *Economica*, n.s., 25(100):283–99.

Polti, Georges. 1981 [1916]. *The Thirty-Six Dramatic Situations*. Boston: The Writer. First published as *Les trente-six situations dramatiques*.

Pratt, John W., David A. Wise, and Richard Zeckhauser. 1979. "Price Differences in Almost Competitive Markets." *Quarterly Journal of Economics* 93(2): 189–211.

Prelec, Drazen, and Duncan Simester. 2001. "Always Leave Home without It: A Further Investigation of the Credit-Card Effect on Willingness to Pay." *Marketing Letters* 12(1):5–12.

"President Wilson Looks to Business Prosperity as He Signs Currency Measure." 1913. *Christian Science Monitor*, December 24.

Rainwater, Lee. 1970. *Behind Ghetto Walls: Black Families in a Federal Slum*. Chicago: Aldine.

Rees, Albert. 1973 [1962]. *The Economics of Trade Unions*. Chicago: University of Chicago Press.

———. 1993. "The Role of Fairness in Wage Determination." *Journal of Labor Economics* 11(1):243–52.

"Reynolds Sees New Hope with Currency Law Changes." 1913. *Chicago Daily Tribune*, December 20, p. 13.

Romer, Christina. 1986. "Spurious Volatility in Historical Unemployment Data." *Journal of Political Economy* 94(1):1–37.

———. 1992. "What Ended the Great Depression?" *Journal of Economic History* 52(4):757–84.

Romer, David. 2006. *Advanced Macroeconomics*, 3rd ed. New York: McGraw-Hill/Irwin.

Sah, Raaj K. 1991. "Social Osmosis and Patterns of Crime." *Journal of Political Economy* 88(6):1272–95.

Samuelson, Paul A. 1997 [1948]. *Economics: An Introductory Analysis*, 1st ed. New York: McGraw-Hill (reprinted, with a new foreword).

Sands, David R. 1991. "GAO Chief Says Banks Must Win Confidence." *Washington Times*, March 8.

Santayana, George. 1955 [1923]. *Skepticism and Animal Faith*. New York: Dover.

Sargent, Thomas J. 1971. "A Note on the 'Accelerationist' Controversy." *Journal of Money Credit and Banking* 3(3):721–25.

Sargent, Thomas J., and Neil Wallace. 1975. "Rational Expectations, the Optimal Monetary Instrument, and the Optimal Money Supply Rule." *Journal of Political Economy* 83(2):241–54.

Schank, Roger C., and Robert P. Abelson. 1977. *Scripts, Plans, Goals and Understanding*. New York: Wiley.

————. 1995. "Knowledge and Memory: The Real Story." In Robert S. Wyer Jr., ed., *Knowledge and Memory: The Real Story.* Hillsdale, N.J.: Erlbaum, pp. 1–85.

Schultze, Charles L. 1959. "Recent Inflation in the United States." Study Paper 1, Joint Economic Committee, 86th Cong., 1st sess., September.

Schumpeter, Joseph A. 1939. *Business Cycles: A Theoretical, Historical, and Statistical Analysis of the Capitalist Process.* New York: McGraw-Hill.

Shafir, Eldar, Peter Diamond, and Amos Tversky. 1997. "Money Illusion." *Quarterly Journal of Economics* 112(2):341–74.

Shapiro, Carl, and Joseph E. Stiglitz. 1984. "Equilibrium Unemployment as a Worker Discipline Device." *American Economic Review* 74(3):433–44.

Shea, John. 1995a. "Union Contracts and the Life-Cycle/Permanent-Income Hypothesis." *American Economic Review* 85(1):186–200.

————. 1995b. "Myopia, Liquidity Constraints, and Aggregate Consumption: A Simple Test." *Journal of Money, Credit and Banking* 27(3):798–805.

Shefrin, Hersh, and Richard H. Thaler. 1988. "The Behavioral Life-Cycle Hypothesis." *Economic Inquiry* 24:609–43.

Shiller, Robert J. 1981. "Do Stock Prices Move Too Much to Be Justified by Subsequent Changes in Dividends?" *American Economic Review* 7(3):421–36.

————. 1982. "Consumption, Asset Markets and Macroeconomic Fluctuations." *Carnegie-Rochester Conference Series on Public Policy* 17:203–38.

————. 1984. "Stock Prices and Social Dynamics." *Brookings Papers on Economic Activity* 2:457–98.

————. 1986. "The Marsh-Merton Model of Managers' Smoothing of Dividends." *American Economic Review* 76(3):499–503.

————. 1989. *Market Volatility.* Cambridge, Mass.: MIT Press.

————. 1997a. "Why Do People Dislike Inflation?" In Christina D. Romer and David H. Romer, eds., *Reducing Inflation: Motivation and Strategy.* NBER Studies in Business Cycles, vol. 30. Chicago: University of Chicago Press, pp. 13–65.

————. 1997b. "Public Resistance to Indexation: A Puzzle." *Brookings Papers on Economic Activity* 1:159–211.

————. 2000. *Irrational Exuberance.* Princeton, N.J.: Princeton University Press.

————. 2002. "Bubbles, Human Judgment and Expert Opinion." *Financial Analysts Journal* 58(3):18–26.

————. 2005. *Irrational Exuberance,* 2nd ed. Princeton, N.J.: Princeton University Press.

————. 2008a. *The Subprime Solution: How Today's Global Financial Crisis Happened, and What to Do about It.* Princeton, N.J.: Princeton University Press.

————. 2008b. "Online Data: Stock Market Data." http://www.econ.yale.edu/~shiller/data.htm.

Shipler, David. 1997. *A Country of Strangers: Blacks and Whites in America.* New York: Knopf.

Shleifer, Andrei, and Robert W. Vishny. 1992. "Liquidation Values and Debt Capacity: A Market Equilibrium Approach." *Journal of Finance* 47(4):1343–66.

————. 1997. "The Limits of Arbitrage." *Journal of Finance* 52(1):33–55.

Sims, Christopher A. 1972. "Money, Income and Causality." *American Economic Review* 62:540–52.

————. 2001. "Pitfalls of a Minimax Approach to Model Uncertainty." *American Economic Review* 91(2):51–54.

Smith, Adam. 1776. *An Inquiry into the Nature and Causes of the Wealth of Nations.* London: Ward, Lock, Bowden & Co.

Smith, Edgar Lawrence. 1925. *Common Stocks as Long-Term Investments.* New York: Macmillan.

Solow, Robert. 1979. "Another Possible Source of Wage Rigidity." *Journal of Macroeconomics* 1(1):79–82.

Sorkin, Andrew Ross. 2008. "JP Morgan Pays $2 a Share for Bear Stearns." *New York Times,* March 17.

Soros, George. 2008. *The New Paradigm for Financial Markets: The Credit Crisis of 2008 and What It Means.* New York: Public Affairs.

Souleles, Nicholas S. 2001. "Consumer Sentiment: Its Rationality and Usefulness in Forecasting Expenditure—Evidence from the Michigan Micro Data." National Bureau of Economic Research Working Paper 8410, August.

————. 2004. "Expectations, Heterogeneous Forecast Errors, and Consumption: Micro Evidence from the Michigan Consumer Sentiment Surveys." *Journal of Money Credit and Banking* 36(1):39–72.

Staiger, Douglas, James H. Stock, and Mark W. Watson. 1997. "How Precise Are Estimates of the Natural Rate of Unemployment?" In Christina D. Romer and David H. Romer, eds., *Reducing Inflation: Motivation and Strategy.* NBER Studies in Business Cycles, vol. 30. Chicago: University of Chicago Press, pp. 195–242.

Steeples, Douglas, and David O. Whitten. 1998. *Democracy in Desperation: The Depression of 1893.* Contributions in Economic History, no. 199. Westport, Conn.: Greenwood Press.

Sternberg, Robert J. 1998. *Love Is a Story: A New Theory of Relationships.* New York: Oxford University Press.

Stoft, Steven. 1982. "Cheat-Threat Theory: An Explanation of Involuntary Unemployment." Unpublished paper, Boston University, May.

Taleb, Nassim Nicholas. 2001. *Fooled by Randomness: The Hidden Role of Chance in the Markets and in Life.* New York: Texere.

Taylor, John. 1979. "Staggered Wage Setting in a Macro Model." *American Economic Review* 69(2):108–13.

————. 1980. "Aggregate Dynamics and Staggered Contracts." *Journal of Political Economy* 88(1):1–23.

Thaler, Richard H. 1994. *Quasi-Rational Economics.* New York: Russell Sage Foundation.

Thaler, Richard H., and Shlomo Benartzi. 2004. "Save More Tomorrow: Using Behavioral Economics to Increase Employee Saving." *Journal of Political Economy* 112(1, pt. 2):S164–187.

Thernstrom, Stephan, and Abigail M. Thernstrom. 1997. *America in Black and White: One Nation, Indivisible.* New York: Simon and Schuster.

Thomas, Landon, Jr., and Eric Dash. 2008. "Seeking Fast Deal, JPMorgan Quintuples Bear Stearns Bid." *New York Times,* March 25.

Tobias, Ronald B. 1993. *20 Master Plots and How to Build Them.* Cincinnati: Writers' Digest.

Tobin, James. 1972a. "Friedman's Theoretical Framework." *Journal of Political Economy* 80(5):852–63.

———. 1972b. "Inflation and Unemployment." *American Economic Review* 62(1): 1–18.

Turner, Frederic Jackson. 1894. *The Significance of the Frontier in American History.* Madison: State Historical Society of Wisconsin.

Tversky, Amos, and Daniel Kahneman. 1974. "Judgment under Uncertainty: Heuristics and Biases." *Science* 185(4157):1124–31.

"A Twenty-Five Million Pool." 1907. *Wall Street Journal,* March 29, p. 6.

Uchitelle, Louis. 2006. *The Disposable American: Layoffs and Their Consequences.* New York: Knopf.

"Unable to Weather the Gale." 1893. *New York Times,* July 1, p. 9.

U.S. Bureau of Labor Statistics. 1951. *Union Wages and Hours: Motortruck Drivers and Helpers.* Bulletin 1052, July 1. Washington, D.C.

———. 2008. "Consumer Price Index: All Urban Consumers. Not Seasonally Adjusted." CUUR0000SA0. http://www.bls.gov/roi/fax/9150.pdf.

U.S. Census. 2008. *The 2008 Statistical Abstract.* http://www.census.gov/compendia/statab/index.html.

U.S. Department of Justice. 1996. "Correctional populations in the US 1996." http://www.ojp.usdoj.gov/bjs/pub/pdf/cpius965.pdf.html.

———. 2008. "Prison and Jail Inmates at Midyear 2006." http://www.ojp.usdoj.gov/bjs/pub/pdf/pjim06.pdf.

U.S. Department of the Treasury. 2008. "Statement by Secretary Henry M. Paulson on Treasury and Federal Housing Finance Agency Action to Protect Financial Markets and Taxpayers." September 7. http://www.treasury.gov/press/releases/hp1129.htm.

U.S. Office of Personnel Management. 2004. "Demographic Profile of the Federal Workforce." https://www2.opm.gov/feddata/demograp/demograp.asp#RNO Data.

Utaka, Atsuo. 2003. "Confidence and the Real Economy: The Japanese Case." *Applied Economics* 35(3):337–42.

Venti, Steven F., and David A. Wise. 2000. "Choice, Chance, and Wealth Dispersion at Retirement." National Bureau of Economic Research Working Paper 7521, February.

"Want Old Rate Restored." 1894. *Boston Daily,* February 10, p. 10.

Warsh, David. 2006. *Knowledge and the Wealth of Nations: A Story of Economic Discovery.* New York: W. W. Norton.

Weinstein, Neil, and William M. Klein. 1996. "Unrealistic Optimism: Present and Future." *Journal of Social and Clinical Psychology* 15:1–8.

Welch, Jack, with John A. Byrne. 2001. *Jack: Straight from the Gut.* New York: Warner.

Wentura, Dirk. 2005. "The Unknown Self: The Social Cognition Perspective." In Werner Greve, Klaus Rothermund, and Dirk Wentura, eds., *The Adaptive Self: Personal Continuity and Intentional Self-Development.* Cambridge, Mass.: Hogrefe and Huber, pp. 203–22.

Wilson, William J. 1987. *The Truly Disadvantaged.* Chicago: University of Chicago Press.

———. 1996. *When Work Disappears: The World of the New Urban Poor.* New York: Knopf.

"Wilson Insistent." 1913. *Washington Post,* June 15, p. 4.

Wolk, Carel, and Loren A. Nikolai. 1997. "Personality Types of Accounting Students and Faculty: Comparisons and Implications." *Journal of Accounting Education* 15(1):1–17.

Woodford, Michael. 2001. "Imperfect Common Knowledge and the Effects of Monetary Policy." National Bureau of Economic Research Working Paper 8673, December.

Yellen, Janet L. 1984. "Efficiency Wage Models of Unemployment." *American Economic Review Papers and Proceedings* 74(2):200–205.

Young, Roy A. 1928. "The Banker's Responsibilities." *Bankers' Magazine* 117(6): 973–76.

Youngman, Anna P. 1938. "Abrupt Industrial Slump Puzzles Business Experts." *Washington Post,* January 3, p. X22.

Zandi, Mark. 2008. *Financial Shock: A 360° Look at the Subprime Mortgage Implosion and How to Avoid the Next Financial Crisis.* Upper Saddle River, N.J.: Pearson Education.

Zeldes, Stephen P. 1989. "Consumption and Liquidity Constraints: An Empirical Investigation." *Journal of Political Economy* 97(2):305–46

# Index

open market operations, 75–79
options theory, 84
Organization of Petroleum Exporting
  Countries (OPEC), 140–41, 142
Orszag, Peter R., 191n5
Oswald, Andrew J., 185n20
out-of-wedlock births, 158
overheated economy, 64–67, 185n18,19

Pact of San José, 53–54
Palley, Thomas I., 189n1
panic of 1837, 171
panic of 1873, 61, 184n6
panic of 1884, 61
panic of 1893, 60–61
panic of 1907, 80, 81
Paulson, Henry, xxi, 96
Peebles, Gavin, 192n20
Peng, Amy Chen, 183n12,13
People's Bank of China, 126
Perón, Juan, 139–40
Perry, George L., 110, 183n8, 189n1,
  190n8,10,15
Phelps, Edmund, 183n10
Phillips, A. W., 43, 45, 182n5
Phillips curve, 43–46, 107–8, 110, 183n10,
  189–90n15, 190n16; flawed view of asserted,
  108; inflationary expectations and, 113,
  182–83n8; principles of, 43
Pierce, Brooks, 102, 187n5
poker, 40
political-economic stories, 53–54
Pol Pot, 26
Polti, Georges, 52, 184n6
Porter, Richard, 193n6
Posen, Adam, 180n9, 187n9
Potter, Samara R., 197n2
poverty in minorities, 6, 157–66, 174,
  196–97n1–24. See also minorities
Pratt, John W., 188n3,4
Prelec, Drazen, 128, 192n24
Prescott, Edward C., 178n6
present value theory, 152–53
price rigidity, 48
prices: depression of the 1890s and, 59–60;
  fairness and, 6, 21, 22; Great Depression
  and, 68; money illusion and, 43–46, 48;
  variation in, 100. See also financial prices
price-to-earnings-to-price feedback, 135
price-to-GDP-to-price feedback, 154
price-to-price feedback, 134–35, 154
Primary Credit Dealer Facility, 187n10
Princeton University, 19
prohibition (of alcohol), 39
Project Link, 16

Pullman Palace Car Company, 63
Purdue University, 128

Quetzalcóatl (López Portillo), 53–54
Quintini, Glenda, 183n14
quits, wages and, 103–4, 106

railroad strike of 1910 (Argentina), 139
Rainwater, Lee, 162, 196n14
Rajan, Raghuram G., 182n21
Randers, Jørgen, 194n29
randomness, 52
random-walk hypothesis, 103, 191n11
ratings of securities, 37, 91, 94, 170
rational expectations, xxiii, 5, 6, 168, 173,
  178n4; bimetallism debate and, 60; in
  classical economics, 2, 3; confidence and,
  12–13, 14; corruption and, 39; fairness and,
  21, 22; feedback and, 140; financial prices
  and, 131, 132, 133, 136; money illusion and,
  41, 42; real estate market and, 150, 153;
  saving and, 120, 122
Reagan, Ronald, xxv, 32, 36, 172, 175
real business cycle models, 178n6
real estate market, 4, 6, 135, 136, 149–56,
  169–70, 172, 174, 195–96n1–15; baby boom
  and, 152; confidence and, 11, 13, 149, 156;
  confidence multiplier in, 153–55; naïve or
  intuitive beliefs about, 150–53; S&L crisis
  and, 32, 33. See also mortgages; subprime
  mortgages
real interest rates, 62
real wages, 43–44, 68–70, 185n32
recessions, 29–37, 86; of 1980s, 141, 142; of
  1990–91, 17, 29, 30 33, 38, 109, 171; of
  2001, 29, 33–35, 38; of 2007–8 (see financial
  crisis of 2007–8)
Reconstruction, 175
rediscounting. See discount window
  (rediscounting)
Rees, Albert, 19–20, 180n1,2
regression analysis, 84
Reischauer, Robert D., 192n16
Renault, 137
rents, housing, 136
Repetto, Andrea, 192n13,25
Resolution Funding Corporation, 32
resolution proceedings, bank, 82, 175
Resolution Trust Corporation, 30, 32, 93
retirement planning, 117, 118, 119, 120, 121, 122,
  129–30
Rhee, Changyong, 195n36,37
Rigdon, Mary, 189n15
risk, 144
Risk, Uncertainty and Profit (Knight), 144